MONARCH

ILLUSTRATED GUIDE TO KNITTING

PAM DAWSON

MONARCH PRESS · NEW YORK

This volume first published 1977

Standard Book Number: 0-671-18769-4

Library of Congress Catalog Card Number: 76-29158

Published by
MONARCH PRESS
a division of Simon & Schuster, Inc.
a Gulf +Western Company
1230 Avenue of the Americas
New York, N.Y. 10020

Printed in Great Britain.

Knitting abbreviations

alt	alternate(ly)	**rem**	remain(ing)
approx	approximate(ly)	**rep**	repeat
beg	begin(ning)	**RS**	right side
cont	continu(e)	**sl**	slip
dec	decrease	**sl st**	slip stitch
foll	follow(ing)	**sp**	space(s)
g st	garter stitch, every row knit	**st(s)**	stitches
gr(s)	group(s)	**st st**	stockinette stitch, 1 row knit, 1 row purl
in	inch(es)	**tbl**	through back of loop
inc	increase	**tog**	together
K	knit	**WS**	wrong side
K-wise	knitwise, as if to knit	**yd(s)**	yard(s)
No.	number	**yo**	yarn over needle
psso	pass slipped stitch over	**ybk**	yarn back
patt	pattern	**yfwd**	yarn forward
P	purl	**yrn**	yarn round needle
P-wise	purlwise, as if to purl		

The list given above contains many of the most commonly used knitting abbreviations. However, some have been adapted to make them more explicit for the beginner, e.g. "yfwd" and "ybk" (yarn forward and yarn back) often abbreviated solely as "yo". Some knitting pattern companies do, however, have their own style of abbreviating knitting terms so, before starting any pattern, study their list of abbreviations carefully.
Some of the patterns in this book also contain specific instructions for that pattern alone. Where this occurs the abbreviation will be given in the pattern.

Photographers
Stuart Brown, John Carter, Roger Charity, Monty Coles, Richard Dunkley, Alan Duns, David Finch, Jeany, Chris Lewis, Sandra Lousada, Tony Page, Peter Pugh-Cook, John Ryan, John Swannell, Jean Claude Volpeliere.

Symbols

An asterisk, *, shown in a pattern row denotes that the stitches shown after this sign must be repeated from that point. Square brackets, [], denote instructions for larger sizes in the pattern. Round brackets, (), denote that this section of the pattern is to be worked for all sizes.
Gauge—this is the most important factor in successful knitting. Unless you obtain the gauge given for each design, you will not obtain satisfactory results.

Acknowledgements
Knitted apron (page 3) and Egyptian sock (page 3), courtesy of the Victoria and Albert Museum, London.

CONTENTS

AN INTRODUCTION TO KNITTING

In presenting this book my genuine hope is that I can communicate some of my enthusiasm for this most beautiful craft to the reader and whether you approach it as a complete beginner or knowledgeable knitter, arouse your interest in its almost limitless possibilities.

For the first half of this century, knitting was tagged with the fuddy-duddy image it used to have and suffered an undeserved decline in popularity. Today it has rightly taken its place as a unique and practical way of interpreting fashion but, even now, most knitters are still not aware of its tremendous scope. In no other field of fashion or craft, other than the allied craft of crochet, do you have such complete control not only over the shape of the ultimate design, but the texture and color of the fabric. In this craft, you as the knitter, combine both the skill of a weaver and the practical knowledge of a dressmaker – and all for the price of a pair of needles and a few balls of yarn. Of all the crafts and skills acquired by man – and I use the word 'man' advisedly, in that women's skill in this field is only recent in terms of history – knitting has proved to be one of the most fascinating and enduring. It has survived, sometimes through countless centuries without any record, either written or visual, and has developed and evolved by word of mouth from one generation to the next, as the ideal means of clothing the world's population.

The first steps in knitting are as simple as those required for basic cookery, but its ultimate variety is akin to the art of cordon bleu cooking, where nothing that individual taste, ability and imagination can devise is mpossible. The only manufactured materials required are a pair of needles and a ball of spun thread but, with sufficient knowledge and time to experiment, even these are comparatively easy to produce by hand. The simple talents needed to encompass its full range are a willing pair of hands, an eye for color and fabric, some simple mathematical skill and basic dressmaking knowledge. Armed with these attributes the world of knitting is your oyster and you can begin to design garments to suit your own individual shape and taste, without being tied to existing patterns.

The main purpose of this book is to take the technical knowledge it contains and apply this to the basic guide to designing, which is also explained. You can, of course, accept it as it stands and still acquire the necessary skill to become a proficient knitter, but taking the step from knitter to designer is a relatively small one and out of all proportion to the exciting and creative field it opens up for you. With the present necessity to conserve all natural resources and survive an unhealthy economic period, it is even more important to know how to make warm, wearable and fashionable garments for the minimum of outlay, both in costs and materials. Knitting is the most practical and satisfying solution to these problems and has the added bonus of extending your own latent creative talents and the therapeutic benefit of making something beautiful with your own hands.

Pam Dawson

HISTORY OF KNITTING

Knitting is an ancient craft, which developed in the deserts of Arabia among the nomadic tribes who lived there 3,000 years ago. It may even have been a familiar technique in pre-biblical times, for knitting of high quality, well advanced in both technique and design, was certainly being produced in Arabia 1,000 years before the birth of Christ. No one can date the birth of knitting exactly. It has grown up with civilization. The early knitters were the men of the tribes, and they were very skilled at their craft. These people kept straggling herds of sheep and goats, and there was no shortage of material. The women gathered wool from the animals and spun it into yarn for the men, who would sit for hours, tending the flocks and knitting. The articles they produced were simple scarves, robes and socks which could be worn with sandals.

Ancient knitting

Very few examples of really early knitting are still in existence, but a pair of red sandal socks, pre-Christian in origin, still survive. They are beautifully made, with expertly turned heels. It is interesting to note that stitches have been carefully divided for the big toe, so that the socks were comfortable to wear with sandals.

The socks were knitted in the round on a circular frame, probably made of thin wire. Pins were inserted all around the edge of the circle, and loops were made on the pins. When the wool was wound around the outside of the pins and the loops drawn over it, circular knitting of a rather loose gauge was produced.

A spectacular fragment

Twin needles, hooked at the ends rather like today's crochet hooks, were used to make another surviving fragment of Arabic knitting. This piece of work was discovered at Fustat, an ancient ruined city near Cairo, somewhere in Egypt, and it has been dated between the 7th and the 9th centuries. From beneath the sand and dust of centuries a fragile piece of knitted silk fabric was retrieved. Worked with exquisite care on a pair of fine wire needles, to an easily-checked gauge of 36 stitches to the inch, the fragment reveals an elaborate design in maroon and gold.

Between the years 1000 and 1200 little round knitted caps called Coptic caps were being made in Egypt. They were worn by monks and missionaries and it is possible that these men carried the knowledge of knitting with them out of Egypt. Craftsmen in Spain, then in Italy and France and eventually in England and the New World, were fascinated by this new kind of fabric weaving. Knowledge of the craft quickly spread, each nation adding its own ideas and patterns. By the Middle Ages knitting was a common craft all over Europe. Italy and France were the great medieval homes of fine knitting, and there the knitters soon formed themselves, under Church patronage, into organized guilds.

The Knitters' Guilds

The Knitters' Guild of Paris was a typical example. Young boys of intelligence and manual ability were carefully selected as apprentices. They were bound for six years, three of which were spent working with a master-knitter at home and three learning new techniques in a foreign country. At the end of this time the apprentice was required to demonstrate his skill to his elders. The test was prodigious. In only thirteen weeks the apprentice had to knit an elaborate carpet eight feet by twelve, with extremely intricate designs incorporating flowers, birds, foliage and animals in natural colors, using between twenty and thirty different colored wools; a beret, sometimes to be felted and blocked after knitting; a woolen shirt; and a pair of socks with Spanish clocks.

No apprentice was accepted who did not produce masterpieces in all these categories, and when he became a master-knitter he knew that shoddy or skimped work would result in heavy fines and even expulsion from the guild, which meant loss of livelihood. The only women admitted to these guilds were the widows of master-knitters. For the most part, the women still sat at home spinning the wool for the men to knit up.

Apart from the domestic and commercial work being produced in England, much exquisite decorative knitting was done in the seclusion of the monasteries and the nunneries. The religious influence on the knitting of the 16th and 17th centuries is very marked.

The hand knitting tradition continued to be strong in England until the Industrial Revolution in the 19th century, the age of mass production when interest in handcrafts declined.

Individuality still flourished, however, notably in Scotland and the Channel Islands, where traditional sweaters (called 'jumpers') and jerseys were made. The 'guernsey', produced on the Channel Island of Guernsey for centuries, took two forms. The everyday one, in plain stockinette stitch, was the one most often seen, but on special occasions the men wore guernseys in heavy cable and bobble patterns, each family or village having its own distinctive design. They were called 'bridal shirts' because a courting girl would start to knit one for her sweetheart's wedding day.

Knitting in America

The colonists were for the most part English and brought with them English ways. However, knitting and needlecrafts in America became more varied and more colorful as immigration began to add to the eclectic composition of the population. English ways were influenced by German, Scandinavian, Irish and southern European settlers. Today's American knitter therefore has a wide heritage of traditions influencing his work.

The word 'knitting' comes from an old English word meaning 'a knot', and basic techniques have altered little over the centuries. Interest in the craft has revived strongly now after its decline during the Victorian era. Machine knitting techniques have gained popularity, but most knitters still practice the craft using needles very little different from those used by the Arab pioneer knitters. Knitting or Knotting, the ancient craft is more popular now than it has ever been before.

Right: An English apron, knitted in multi-colored yarn in the early nineteenth century.
Below: A sandal sock knitted in wool. It is Egyptian in origin and dates from the fifth century AD. However, it is thought that knitting probably originated centuries before this, possibly as much as 1000 years before the birth of Christ.

BASIC SKILLS

THE FIRST STEPS

Knitting needles

Modern needles are usually made of lightweight coated metal or plastic and are available in a comprehensive range of sizes, both in diameter and length. For American needles, the gauge or diameter of the needle is given as a figure, such as No.11, No.10, No.9 and so on, and the lower the number the smaller the diameter of the needle. The length of the needle is also given and the choice of length will depend on the size and type of garment to be knitted. British needle sizes use the reverse of the American system and the lowest number is used to denote the largest needle.
For 'flat' knitting – that is, working back and forth on two needles in rows – needles are manufactured in pairs and each needle has a knob at one end to prevent the stitches from slipping off.
For 'circular' knitting – that is, working in rounds without a seam – needles are manufactured in sets of four and each needle is pointed at both ends. A flexible circular needle is also manufactured and the effect is the same as dividing the work between three needles and working with the fourth, but a larger number of stitches may be used.

Holding yarn and needles

Until the art of holding both the yarn and needles comfortably has been mastered, it is impossible to begin to knit. For a right handed person the yarn will be looped around the fingers of the right hand to achieve firm, even knitting. The needle which is used to work the stitches is held in the right hand and the left hand holds the needle with the stitches to be worked. The reverse of these positions would be adopted by a left handed person.
To hold the yarn correctly, loop the yarn from the ball across the palm of the right hand between the 4th and 3rd fingers, around the 4th finger and back between the 4th and 3rd fingers, over the 3rd finger, between the 3rd and 2nd fingers, under the 2nd finger then over the index finger, leaving the end of the ball of yarn free, in which a slip loop (see over) will be made to begin casting on.

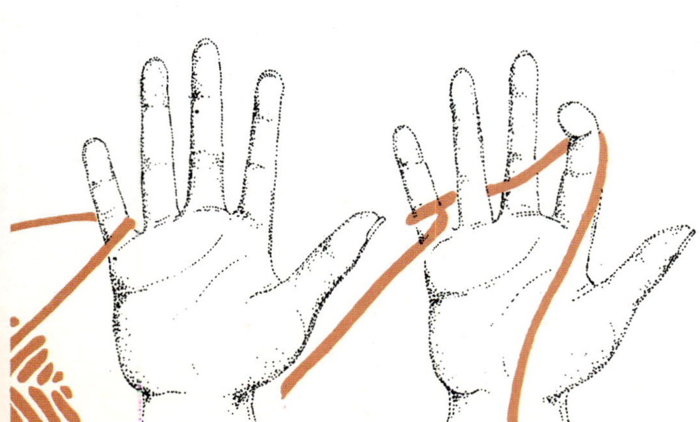

Casting on

This is the first step in hand knitting and it provides the first row of loops on the needle. Different methods of casting on produce different types of edges, each with its own appropriate use, and it is advisable to practice all these variations at some point or other.
The thumb method is an excellent way to begin most garments where an edge with some elasticity is required, such as the ribbing of a pullover, but the two needle method is necessary where extra stitches need to be made during the actual knitting of a garment, such as for buttonholes and pockets. Beginners should practice these two methods. The invisible method gives the appearance of a machine-made edge and is very flexible and neat. The circular method is required for knitting in rounds to produce seamless garments such as gloves and socks. Experienced knitters will find these methods of interest.

Two needle method of casting on

Make a slip loop (see over) in the end of the ball of yarn and put this loop on to the left hand needle. Holding the yarn in the right hand, insert the point of the right hand needle into the slip loop, wind the yarn under and over the point of the right hand needle and draw a new loop through the slip loop. Put the newly made stitch on to the left hand needle. Place the point of the right hand needle between the 2 loops on the left hand needle and wind the yarn under and over the point of the right hand needle again and draw through a new loop. Put the newly made stitch on to the left hand needle. Place the point of the right hand needle between the last 2 loops on the left hand needle and wind the yarn under and over the point of the right hand needle again and draw through a new loop. Put the newly made stitch on to the left hand needle. Continue in this manner until the required number of stitches are formed on the left hand needle. This method produces a firm edge and is also used as an intermediate stage in increasing.

Two needle method step 1

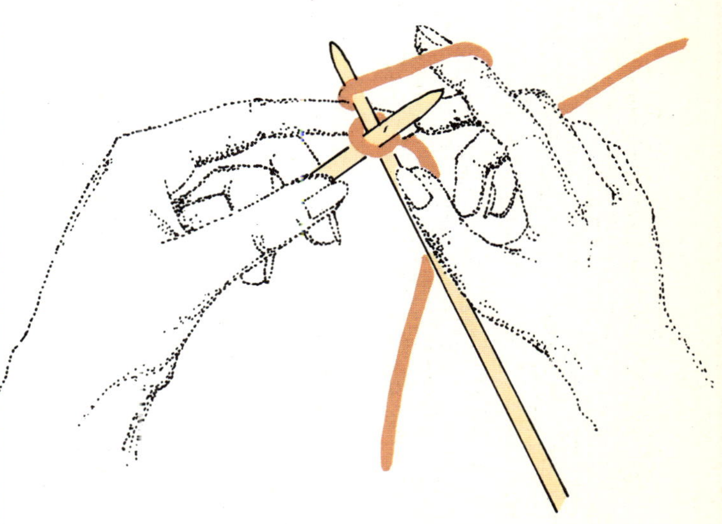

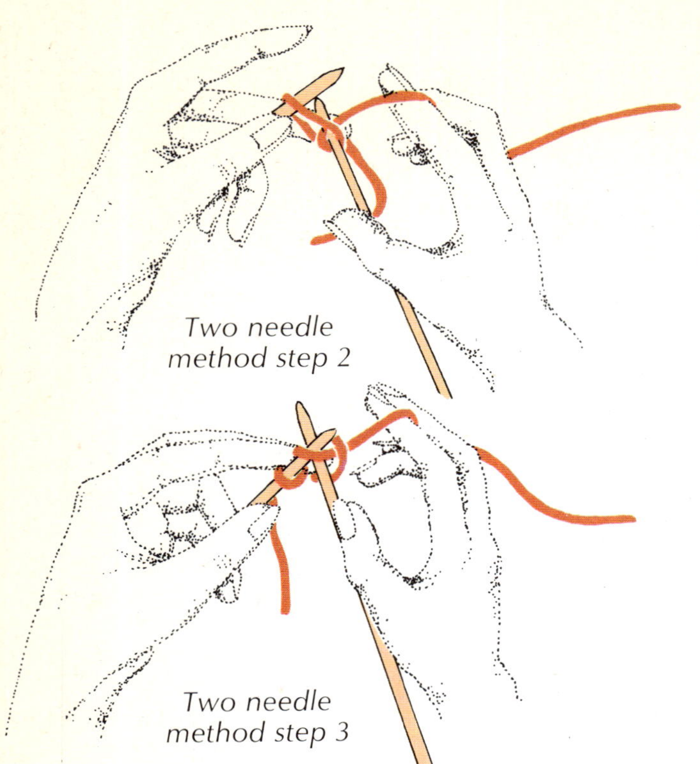

Two needle method step 2

Two needle method step 3

Thumb method of casting on using one needle

Make a slip loop in the ball of yarn about one yard from the end. This length will vary with the number of stitches to be cast on, but one yard will be sufficient for about one hundred stitches.

Put the slip loop on the needle, which should be held in the right hand. Working with the short length of yarn in the left hand, pass this between the index finger and thumb, around the thumb and hold it across the palm of the hand. Insert the point of the needle under the loop on the thumb and bring forward the long end of yarn from the ball. Wind the long end of yarn under and over the point of the needle and draw through a loop on the thumb, leaving the newly formed stitch on the needle. Tighten the stitch on the needle by pulling the short end of yarn, noting that the yarn is then wound around the left thumb ready for the next stitch.

Continue in this way until the required number of stitches are formed on the needle. This method produces a very durable elastic edge.

Thumb method step 1 – making a slip loop

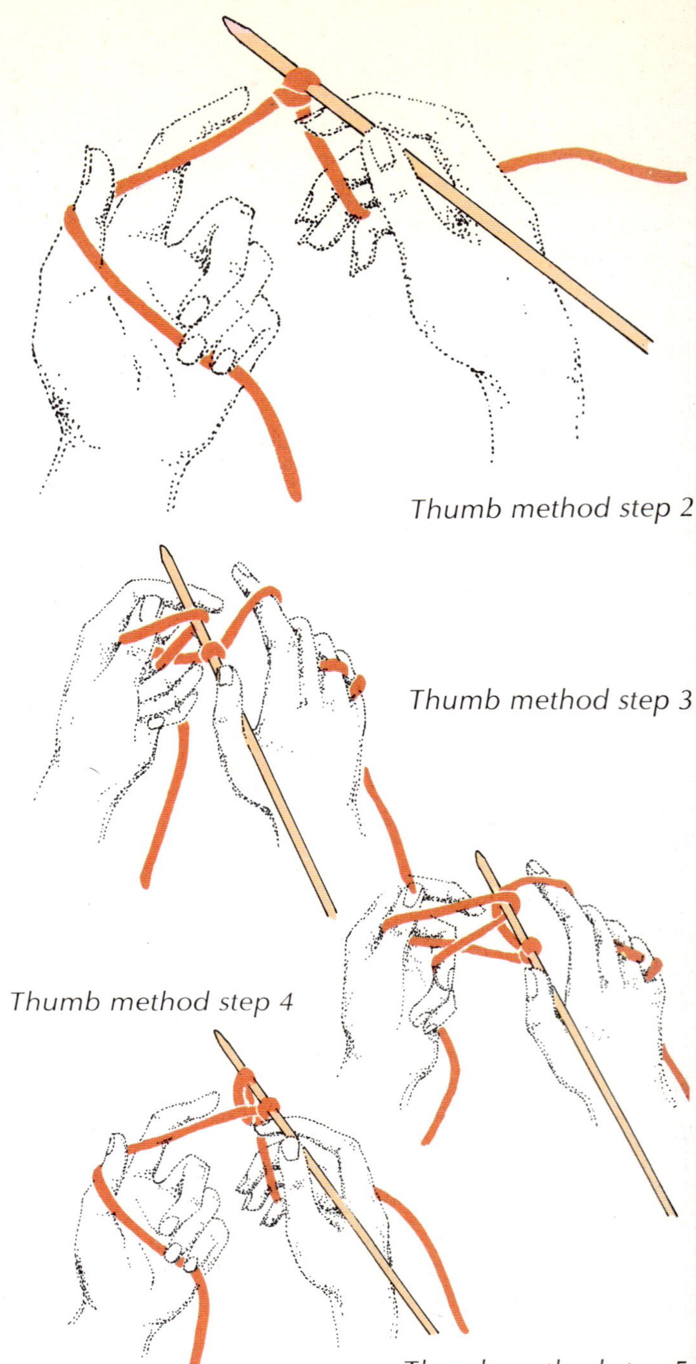

Thumb method step 2

Thumb method step 3

Thumb method step 4

Thumb method step 5

Invisible method of casting on

Using a length of yarn in a contrast color which is later removed, and the thumb method, cast on half the number of stitches required plus one extra. Using the correct yarn and two needles, begin the double fabric which forms the invisible method.

1st row Holding the yarn in the right hand and the needle with the cast on stitches in the left hand, insert the point of the right hand needle into the first stitch from front to back, wind the yarn under and over the point of the right hand needle and draw a loop through which is kept on the right hand needle – this is a knitted stitch and is called 'K1' –, *bring the yarn forward between the two needles and back over the top of the right hand needle to make a stitch on this row only – this is called 'yarn forward' or 'yfwd' –, K1, repeat from the point marked with a * to the end of the row.

2nd row K1, *yfwd and keep at front of work without taking it back over the right hand needle insert the point of the right hand needle into the front of the next stitch on the left hand needle from right to left, and lift it off the left hand needle onto the right hand needle without working it – this is a slipped stitch and is called 'sl 1' –, bring the yarn across in front of the sl 1 and back between the two needles again – this is called 'yarn back' or 'yb' –, K1, repeat from the point marked with a * to the end of the row.

3rd row Sl 1, *ybk, K1, yfwd, sl 1, repeat from the point marked with a * to the end of the row. Repeat the 2nd and 3rd rows once more. Now continue with the single ribbing which completes this method.

6th row K1, *bring the yarn forward between the two needles, insert the point of the right hand needle into the front of the next stitch on the left hand needle from right to left, wind the yarn over the top of the needle around to the front and draw through a loop which is kept on the right hand needle – this is a purled stitch and is called 'P1' –, put the yarn back between the two needles, K1, repeat from the point marked with a * to the end of the row.

7th row P1, *put the yarn back between the two needles, K1, bring the yarn forward between the two needles, P1, repeat from the point marked with a * to the end of the row.

Continue repeating the 6th and 7th rows until the rib is the required length, then pull out the contrast yarn used for casting on. This method gives the appearance of the ribbing running right around the edge with no visible cast on stitches.

Increasing on 1st row of invisible casting on

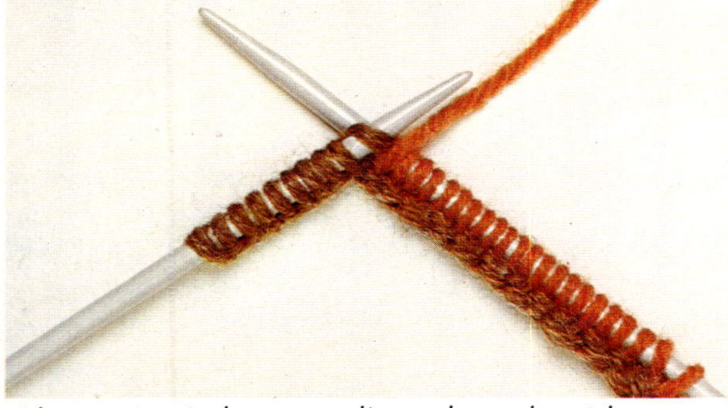

Alternate stitches are slipped on the 4th row

Contrast yarn is pulled out to give a ribbed edge

Circular method of casting on using four needles

When working with sets of four needles, one is used for making the stitches and the total number of stitches required is divided between the remaining three needles. Use the two needle method of casting on and either cast on the total number of stitches on to one needle and then divide them on to the 2nd and 3rd needles, or cast on the required number of stitches on to the first needle, then proceed to the 2nd and 3rd needles, taking care that the stitches do not become twisted. Form the three needles containing the stitches into a triangle shape and the fourth needle is then ready to knit the first stitch on the first needle. This method produces a circular fabric without seams.

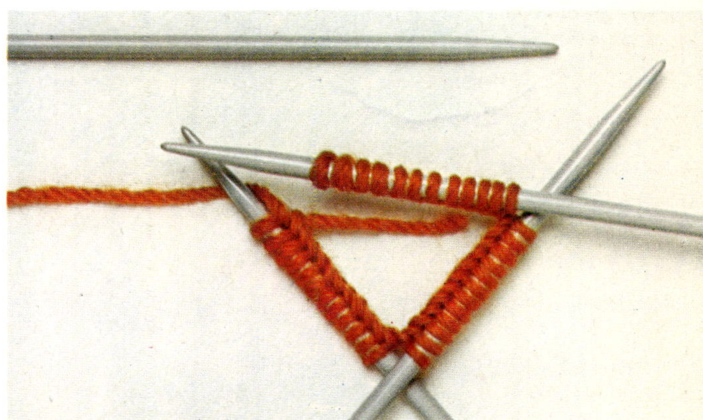

Starting to knit with 4 needles

Basic stitches

Once you have cast on your stitches and can hold the yarn and needles comfortably, you can begin to knit – it's as easy as that. All knitting stitches are based on just two methods – knitting and purling – and however complicated patterns may appear, they are all achieved by simple, or intricate, arrangements of these two methods to produce an almost infinite variety of fabrics and textures. Anything from the finest lace to the thickest carpet can be knitted. The advantages of knitted fabrics are almost too numerous to list and they have been used since time immemorial to achieve examples of exquisite beauty.

Tools of the trade
Before beginning to knit it would be useful to know that you have all the tools you will require on hand. Besides yarn and needles you should have:
A rigid metal or wooden ruler
Scissors
Blunt-ended sewing needles
Rustless steel pins required for blocking
Stitch holders to hold stitches not in use
Row gauge for counting rows
Knitting needle gauge to check needle sizes when not marked
Cloth or plastic bag in which to keep work clean
Iron and ironing surface with felt pad or blanket
Cotton cloths suitable for use when pressing

The basic stitches
To work knitted stitches: hold the needle with the cast on stitches in the left hand and the yarn and other needle in the right hand. Insert the point of the right hand needle through the first stitch on the left hand needle from the front to the back. Keeping the yarn at the back of the work pass it under and over the top of the right hand needle and draw this loop through the stitch on the left hand needle. Keep this newly made stitch on the right hand needle and allow the stitch on the left hand needle to slip off. Repeat this step into each stitch on the left hand needle until all the stitches are transferred to the right hand needle. You have now knitted one row. To work the next row, change the needle holding the stitches to your left hand so that the yarn is again in position at the beginning of the row and hold the yarn and free needle in your right hand.

To work purled stitches: hold the needle with the cast on stitches in your left hand and the yarn and other needle in the right hand. Insert the point of the right hand needle through the first stitch on the left hand needle from right to left. Keeping the yarn at the front of the work pass it over and around the top of the right hand needle and draw this loop through the stitch on the left hand needle. Keep this newly made stitch on the right hand needle and allow the stitch on the left hand needle to slip off. Repeat this step into each stitch on the left hand needle until all the stitches are transferred to the right hand needle. You have now purled one row. To work the next row, change the needle holding the stitches to your left hand so that the yarn is again in position at the beginning of the row and hold the yarn and free needle in your right hand.

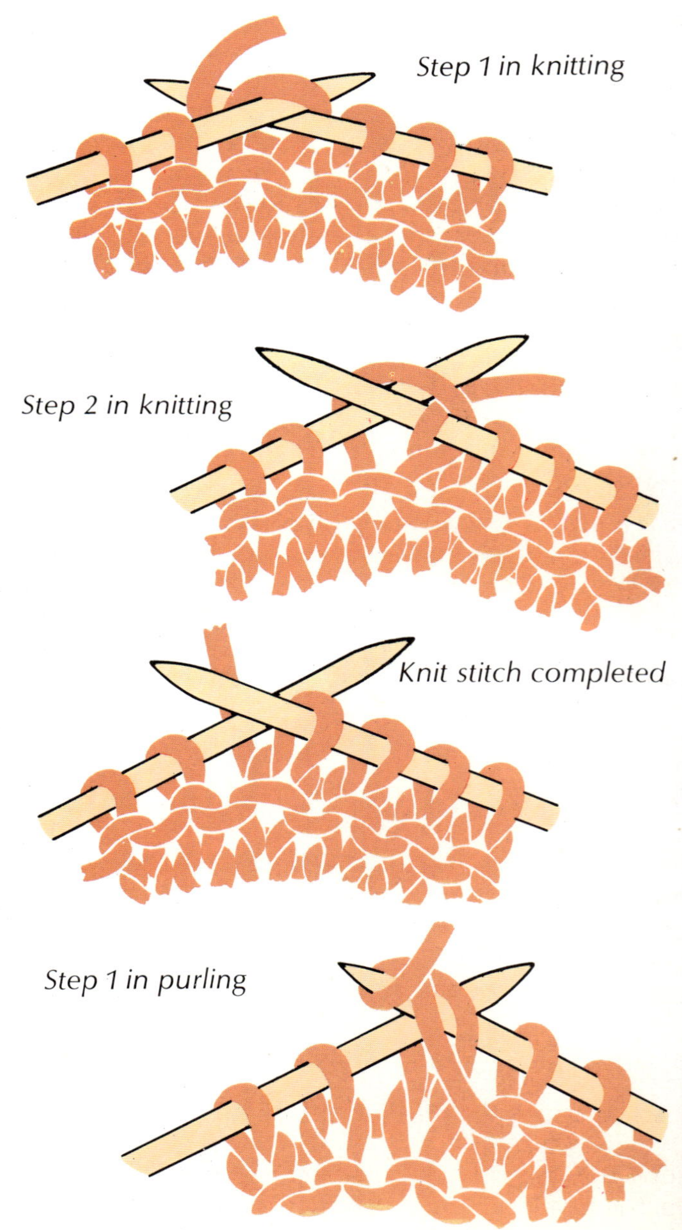
Step 1 in knitting
Step 2 in knitting
Knit stitch completed
Step 1 in purling

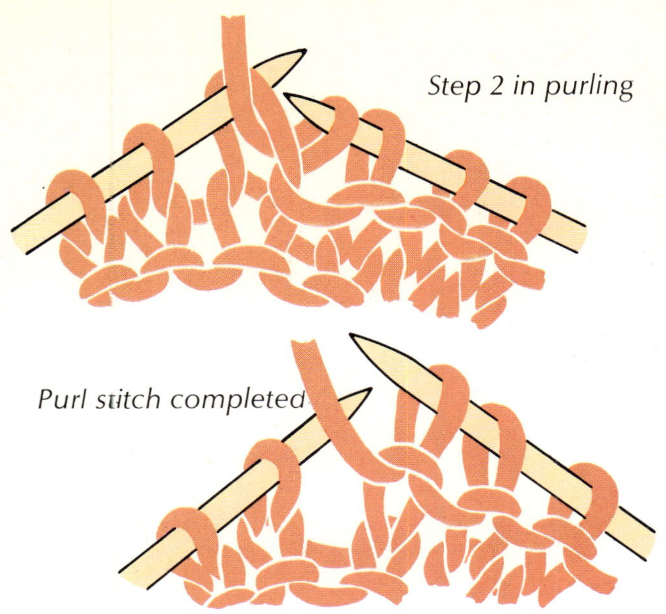

Garter stitch

This is the simplest of all knitted stitches and is formed by working every row in the same stitch, either knit or purl. If you purl every row, however, you will not produce as firm and even a fabric, and unless otherwise stated, wherever you see instructions referring to garter stitch, it is intended that every row should be knitted.

▲Purled garter stitch ▼Knitted garter stitch

Stockinette stitch

This is the smoothest of all knitted stitches and is worked by alternating one row of knitted stitches and one row of purled stitches. The smooth, knitted side of the fabric is usually called the right side of the work, but where a pattern uses the purl side of stockinette stitch as the fabric, it is referred to as reverse stockinette stitch.

Stockinette stitch

Single rib

This is one of the most useful of all knitted stitches and forms an elastic fabric, ideal for waistbands, cuffs and neckbands, since it always springs back into shape. It s formed by knitting the first stitch of the first row, bringing the yarn forward to the front of the work between the two needles, purling the next stitch, then taking the yarn back between the two needles, ready to knit the next stitch again, and continuing in this way until all the stitches are transferred to the right hand needle. On the next row, all the stitches that were knitted on the first row must be purled and all the stitches that were purled must be knitted. It is important to remember that the yarn must be brought forward after knitting a stitch so that it is in the correct position ready to purl the next stitch, and taken to the back again after purling a stitch so that it is in the correct position ready to knit the next stitch.

Single rib

Useful hints

Before beginning to knit any pattern, study the list of general abbreviations so that you become familiar with them.

Always wash your hands before starting to knit and keep them soft and cool.

A bag pinned over the finished work and moved up as it grows will help to keep your knitting clean.

Never leave your knitting in the middle of a row since you may change the tension of your work when picking it up again.

Never stick knitting needles through a ball of yarn as this can split the yarn.

When measuring knitting, place it on a flat surface and measure it in the center of the work, not at the edges.

Always join in a new ball of yarn at the beginning of a row, never in the center of a row with a knot.

Binding off

Binding off is the final stage in knitting and it securely finishes off any stitches that remain after all the shaping has been completed, or at the end of the work. It is also used as an intermediate step in decreasing, such as binding off the required number of stitches for an underarm or in the center of a row for neck shaping.
Where stitches need to be bound off at each end of a row it is customary to do this over two rows, by binding off the given number of stitches at the beginning of the first row then working to the end of the row, turning the work and binding off the same number of stitches at the beginning of the next row and then completing this row. If you bind off stitches at the beginning and end of the same row the yarn must then be broken off and rejoined to start the next row. This is necessary in some designs, but the pattern will always clearly state whether this needs to be done.
Care must be taken in binding off to keep the stitches smooth and even, in this way preventing the edge from becoming too tight or too loose and thus pulling the whole garment out of shape. In some patterns you will come across the phrase 'bind off loosely' and, in this case, it is advisable to use one size larger needle in the right hand and work the stitches with this needle, before binding them off.
The usual method of binding off produces a very firm, neat edge which is not always suitable for some designs such as the toe of a sock where, for example, this type of bound off edge would cause an uncomfortable ridge. In this case, the stitches can be woven together to give an almost invisible seam. Similarly, a ribbed neckband can be bound off by the invisible method to give a very elastic edge with the appearance of a machine-made garment.

Two needle method of binding off

To bind off on a knit row: knit the first two stitches in the regular way and leave them on the right hand needle then *with the point of the left hand needle lift the first stitch on the right hand needle over the top of the second stitch and off the needle, leaving one stitch on the right hand needle, knit the next stitch and leave it on the right hand needle, and repeat from the point marked with a * until the required number of stitches have been bound off and one stitch remains on the right hand needle. If this is at the end of the work, break off the yarn, draw it through the last stitch and pull it up tightly. If stitches have been bound off as a means of shaping, continue working to the end of the row noting that the stitch on the right hand needle will be counted as one of the remaining stitches.

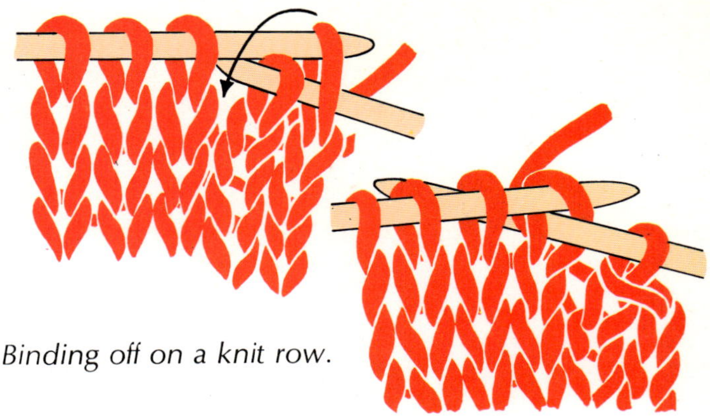

Binding off on a knit row.

To bind off on a purl row: work in exactly the same way but purl each stitch instead of knitting it.

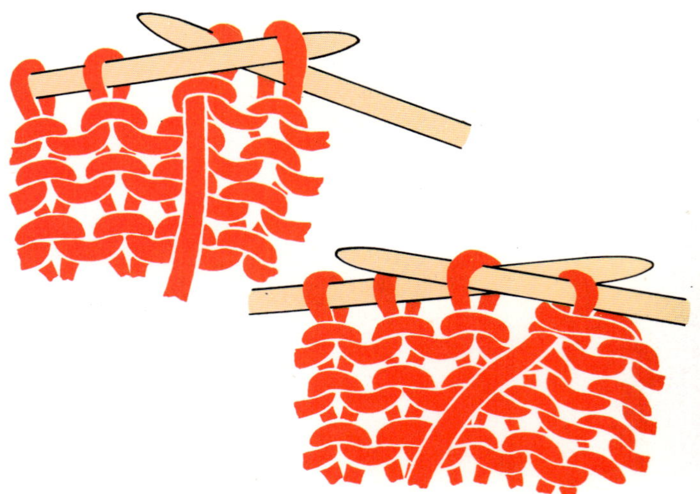

Circular method of binding off using 4 needles
Bind off the stitches on each needle as described for the two needle method of binding off.

Invisible method of binding off

These instructions are for binding off in single rib when an odd number of stitches has been used and the right side rows begin with K1. Work in ribbing until only two more rows are required to give the finished depth, ending with a wrong side row.

1st row K1, *yfwd, sl 1, ybk, K1, repeat from the point marked with a * to the end of the row.

2nd row Sl 1, *ybk, K1, yfwd, sl 1, repeat from the point marked with a * to the end of the row. Break off the yarn, leaving an end three times the length of the edge to be bound off and thread this into a blunt-ended sewing needle. Hold the sewing needle in the right hand and the stitches to be bound off in the left hand, working from right to left along the row.

1. Insert the sewing needle into the first knit stitch as if to purl it and draw the yarn through, then into the next purl stitch as if to knit it and draw the yarn through leaving both of the stitches on the left hand needle.

2. *Work two of the knit stitches then insert the sewing needle into the first knit stitch as if to knit it, draw the yarn through and slip this stitch off the left hand needle, pass the sewing needle in front of the next purl stitch and into the following knit stitch as if to purl it, and draw the yarn through.

3. Now work two of the purl stitches, then insert the sewing needle into the purl stitch at the end of the row as if to purl it, draw the yarn through and slip this stitch off the left hand needle, pass the sewing needle behind the next knit stitch and into the following purl stitch as if to knit it, draw the yarn through.

Repeat from the point marked with a * until all the stitches have been worked off. Fasten off the end of yarn.

Weaving stitches

To weave two stockinette stitch, or knitted, edges together, have the stitches on two needles, one behind the other, with the same number of stitches on each needle. Break off the yarn, leaving an end three times the length of the edge to be woven and thread this into a blunt-ended sewing needle. Have the wrong sides of each piece facing each other, with the knitting needle points facing to the right.

*Insert the sewing needle through the first stitch on the front needle as if to knit it, draw the yarn through and slip the stitch off the knitting needle, insert the sewing needle through the next stitch on the front needle as if to purl it, draw the yarn through and leave the stitch on the knitting needle, insert the sewing needle through the first stitch on the back needle as if to purl it, draw the yarn through and slip the stitch off the knitting needle, insert the sewing needle through the next stitch on the back needle as if to knit it, draw the yarn through and leave the stitch on the knitting needle, repeat from the point marked with a * until all the stitches have been worked off.

To weave two edges of purl fabric together, work in the same way for the stockinette stitch, reading knit for purl and purl for knit. It is possible, however, to weave purled edges by turning the work to the wrong side and weaving as for the stockinette stitch method, then turn the work to the right side when the weaving is completed.

To weave two garter stitch edges together, work in the same way as for the stockinette stitch method but, making certain that the last row knitted on the front needle leaves a ridge on the right side, or outside, of the work, and that the last row on the back needle leaves a ridge on the wrong side, or inside, of the work.

To weave two ribbed edges together, join each stockinette stitch or knit rib to each stockinette stitch or knit rib, using the stockinette stitch method, and each purl rib to each purl rib, using the purl method described above.

Variations

The ways of using a combination of simple knit and purl stitches to form interesting fabrics are numerous. The following patterns are simple to work and each one gives a different texture. Use knitting worsted yarn and No.5 needles to practice these stitches.

Reverse stockinette stitch
This variation of stockinette stitch uses the wrong side, or purl side, of the work to form the fabric.
Cast on any number of stitches.
1st row (right side) P to end.
2nd row K to end.
These 2 rows form the pattern.

Twisted stockinette stitch
This variation of simple stockinette stitch has a twisted effect added on every knitted row made by working into the back of every stitch.
Cast on any number of stitches.
1st row K into the back of each stitch to end.
2nd row P to end.
These 2 rows form the pattern.

Broken rib
Cast on a number of stitches divisible by 2+1.
1st row K1, *P1, K1, rep from * to end.
2nd row P1, *K1, P1, rep from * to end.
3rd row K to end.
4th row As 3rd
These 4 rows form the pattern.

Rice stitch
Cast on a number of stitches divisible by 2+1.
1st row K to end.
2nd row P1, *K1, P1, rep from * to end.
These 2 rows form the pattern.

Moss stitch
Cast on a number of stitches divisible by 2+1.
1st row K1, *P1, K1, rep from * to end.
This row forms the pattern.
Where an even number of stitches are cast on, moss stitch is worked as follows:
1st row *K1, P1, rep from * to end.
2nd row *P1, K1, rep from * to end.
These 2 rows form the pattern.

Irish moss stitch
Cast on a number of stitches divisible by 2+1.
1st row K1, *P1, K1, rep from * to end.
2nd row P1, *K1, P1, rep from * to end.
3rd row As 2nd.
4th row As 1st.
These 4 rows form the pattern.

Woven stitch
Cast on a number of stitches divisible by 2+1.
1st row K1, *yarn in front (yfwd), sl 1 as if to purl (P-wise), yarn back (ybk), K1, rep from * to end.
2nd row P to end.
3rd row K2, *yfwd, sl 1, P-wise, ybk, K1, rep from * to last st, K1.
4th row As 2nd.
These 4 rows form the pattern.

Honeycomb slip stitch
Cast on a number of stitches divisible by 2+1.
1st row P1, *sl 1 P-wise, P1, rep from * to end.
2nd row P to end.
3rd row P2, *sl 1 P-wise, P1, rep from * to last st, P1.
4th row As 2nd.
These 4 rows form the pattern.

Bright and easy knits
For each of these ideas you only need to know how to cast on, how to work the basic stitches and how to bind off!

Muffler
Materials
2 × 4 oz balls of any Knitting Worsted yarn
A pair of No.9 needles

To make
Cast on 60 stitches. Work in garter stitch until scarf measures 70in. Bind off.

Evening belt
Materials
3 × 20grm balls of any glitter yarn
A pair of No.4 needles
A 2in buckle

To make
Cast on 16 stitches. Work in single rib until belt measures desired length to go round waist plus approximately 8in. Bind off. Sew on buckle to one end.

Shoulder bag
Materials
1 × 4oz ball of Knitting Worsted yarn
A pair of No.5 needles

To make
Cast on 50 stitches. Work in stockette stitch until bag measures approximately 24in. Bind off. Fold bag in half with right sides facing and join side edges. Fold over 2in at top edge and sew down. Turn bag right side out. Embroider each side or sew on motifs. Cut remaining yarn into 60in lengths and braid together, knotting each end of braid. Stitch each end of braid along sides of bag, leaving center of braid free as shoulder strap.

GAUGE

Now that you have mastered the basic steps in knitting, the next step is to understand fully the significance of achieving the correct gauge. It is of such vital importance that it cannot be stressed too often and must not be overlooked, either by the beginner or by the more experienced knitter. It is the most important key to success and no amount of careful knitting will produce a perfect garment unless it is observed.

Gauge

Quite simply, the word 'gauge' means the number of rows and stitches to a given measurement, which has been achieved by the designer of the garment, using the yarn and needle size stated. As a beginner, it is vital to keep on practicing and trying to obtain the correct gauge given in a pattern. If it is impossible to hold the yarn and needles comfortably, without pulling the yarn too tight or leaving it too loose and at the same time obtain the correct gauge, then change the needle size. If there are too many stitches to the inch, try using one size larger needles; if there are too few stitches to the inch, try using one size smaller needles. Too many stitches means that the gauge is too tight and too few stitches means that the gauge is too loose and it is vital that your knitting is neither.

This advice applies not only to the beginner but to all knitters starting a new design. It is so often overlooked on the assumption that the knitter's gauge is 'average' and therefore accurate. The point to stress is that although all knitting patterns are carefully checked, the designer of a garment may have produced a tighter or looser gauge than average and all the measurements of the garment will have been based on calculations obtained from her gauge.

With this in mind, it will be readily appreciated that even a quarter of a stitch too many or too few can result in the measurements of the garment being completely inaccurate – through no fault of the designer. It doesn't matter how many times you have to change the needle size – what is important is to obtain the correct gauge given in a pattern, before beginning to knit it. Most instructions give the number of stitches in width, and some also, the number of rows in depth. If you need to choose between obtaining one and not the other, then the width gauge is the most important. Length can usually be adjusted by working more or less rows, as required, being sure to check first that the pattern is not based on an exact number of rows but is measured, rather, in inches.

How to check gauge

Before starting to knit any garment, always work a gauge sample at least 4in square, using the yarn, needle size and stitch quoted. Lay this sample on a flat surface and pin it down. Place a firm ruler over the knitting and mark out 4in in width. Count the number of stitches between the pins very carefully and make sure that you have the same number as given in the gauge. Pin out and count the number of rows in the same way. If there are too many stitches to the given gauge measurement then your gauge is too tight and you need to use needles one, or more sizes larger. If there are too few stitches, then your gauge is too loose and you need to use one size smaller needles.

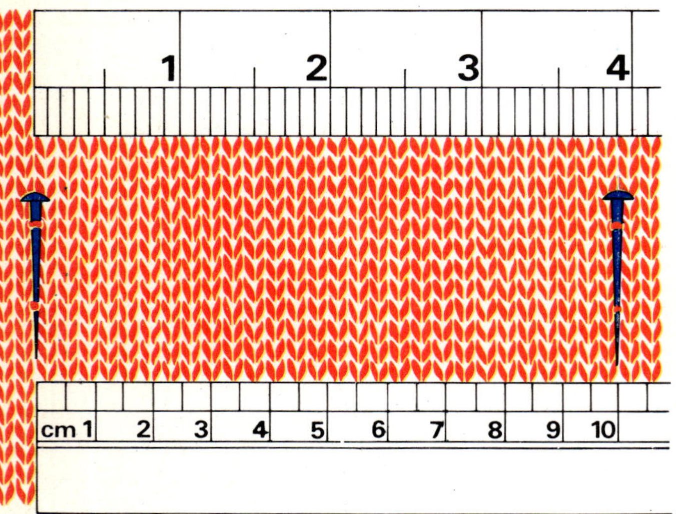

Here the gauge is correct

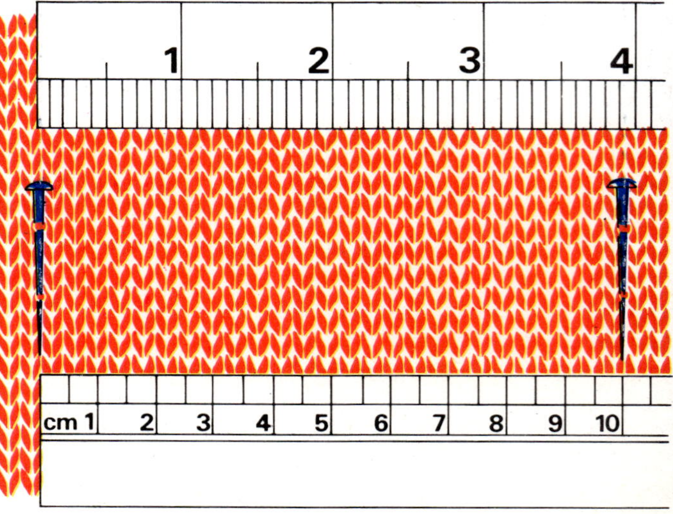

Here the gauge is too tight

A decorative pillow cover

An afghan, made from gauge samples, is a delightful mixture of colors, patterns and textures

Substituting yarns
Each design will have been worked out for the knitting yarn quoted and this is the yarn that should be used, if possible. If for any reason it is not possible to buy the correct yarn, then a substitute may be used but, in this case, it is even more vital to check your gauge before beginning the pattern.

To make an afghan or cushion cover
A few minutes spent in the preparation of a gauge sample need not be wasted. Similarly, samples of the stitches which interest you can be utilized. As each one is finished lay it aside, and when you have collected enough, they can be joined together to make a colorful and original afghan or pillow cover. The only requirement is that each sample must be worked to the same size – 4in square would be an ideal measurement. This way you can keep a lasting record of your progress as a knitter, which is interesting and will serve a useful purpose later.

Afghan
You will need a minimum of 120 squares. Join 10 squares together to form one row, and have a total of 12 rows. Bind all the edges with wool braid or work a blanket stitch around all the edges to finish them and give a professional look to your work.

Pillow cover
You will need 32 squares and a pillow form or foam chips for stuffing. Join 4 squares together to form one row, then 4 rows together to form one side of the pillow. Work the second side of the pillow in the same way. Place the right sides of each piece facing each other and join 3 sides together. Turn the cover right side out. Insert the pillow form or stuffing and join the remaining edge, inserting a zipper if you wish.

YARNS

Success in knitting designs is the result of combining two skills in one – those of a weaver and those of a dressmaker – as the fabric and the shape of the garment are produced at the same time. All knitters need to know something about the construction of the many colorful and interesting yarns which are now available. This knowledge, combined with the needle size to be used and the gauge obtained, will enable knitters to understand how the right fabric for any garment is achieved. To produce a durable, textured fabric, using variations of cable stitches, for example, you cannot select a fine baby yarn; similarly, a thick, bulky yarn would not be suitable for a lacy evening top.

Yarns and ply

'Yarn' is the word used to describe any spun thread, fine or thick, in natural fibers such as wool, cotton, linen, silk, angora or mohair, or in man-made fibers such as Acrilan, Orlon or Nylon. These fibers can be blended together, as with wool and Nylon or a Nylon mixture, to produce extra hard-wearing yarns which are not too thick.

The word 'ply' indicates a single spun thread of any thickness. Before this thread can be used it must be twisted together to make two or more plys to produce a specific yarn and this process is called 'doubling'. Because each single thread can be spun to any thickness, reference to the number of plys does not necessarily determine the thickness of the finished yarn. Some Shetland yarns, for instance, use only two ply very lightly twisted together to produce a yarn almost comparable to a knitting worsted quality although, generally speaking, the terms 2 ply, 3 ply, 4 ply and knitting worsted are used to describe yarns of specified thickness.

The following ply classification applies to the majority of hand knitting yarns, whether made from natural fibers, man-made fibers or a blend of both.

Baby yarns are usually made from the highest quality fibers and are available in 2 ply, 3 ply, 4 ply and knitting worsted weights.

Baby Quick-Knit yarns are generally equivalent to a 4 ply but as they are very softly twisted, they are light in weight.

2 ply, 3 ply and 4 ply yarns are available in numerous fibers and are usually produced by twisting two or more single spun threads together.

Knitting worsted yarns are usually made from four single spun threads twisted together to produce durable yarns.

Bulky and Quick-Knit yarns are extra-thick yarns which vary considerably in their construction. They are ideal for outer garments, and some makes are oiled to give a greater amount of warmth and increased protection.

Crepe yarns are rare. However, those that are available are usually in 4 ply qualities, sometimes called 'single crepe' and Knitting Worsted weights – called 'double crepe' – and are more tightly twisted than average yarns. They are used to produce a firm fabric which is particularly hard-wearing.

Weights and measures

Since there is no official standardization, yarns marketed by the various companies often vary in thickness and in yardage. As most yarns are sold by weight, rather than length, even the density of dye used to produce certain colors in each line can result in

more or less yarn in each ball, although the structure of the yarn is exactly the same. Although all knitting designs are carefully checked, it would be impossible to make up a separate garment for each color in the line of yarn quoted and you may sometimes find that you need one ball more or less than given in the instructions because of this difference in dye.

If it is impossible to obtain the correct yarn required in the instructions then another comparable yarn may be used, provided, of course, that it works up to the same gauge as that given in the pattern.

Equivalent yarns can knit up to the right gauge but the quantity of yarn involved will not necessarily be the same.

Always buy sufficient yarn at one time to insure that all the yarn used is from the same dye lot. Yarn from a different dye lot may vary slightly in color, although this variation may not be noticeable until you have started to knit with it.

Yarns and metrication

When purchasing yarn it is advisable to check the weight of each ball as they can now vary considerably due to the proposed introduction of the metric system. Metrication has been adopted in many countries, and others are in the process of changing over. Some American spinners have begun distribution of yarn measured in grams, but large stocks of yarns in ounces will take time to run out, so a confused situation may exist for some time.

Measurements and metrication

Many pattern companies are now giving both Imperial measurements and their metric equivalents. If working from a pattern like this, insure that you work with either one set of measurements or the other. Do not try to combine both sets as this will only lead to inaccuracies in design.

More simple knits

To illustrate how the same stitch worked in a different yarn can produce a variety of fabrics, try making the muffler given earlier in a mohair yarn, to give a lighter, softer version. Or use a yarn which combines a lurex thread to give a glitter effect to work an evening stole. The evening belt also given earlier could be worked equally well in a crisp cotton to make a useful summer accessory. The more you experiment, the more you will be delighted with the fabrics which can be produced.

Shawl

You will need 6oz of a baby or soft 3-ply yarn, and a pair of No.4 needles. You will also need 57in of narrow lace.

Cast on 288 stitches. Work in garter stitch until shawl measures 36in. Bind off loosely. Sew lace on all around the edges, gathering it slightly around the corners.

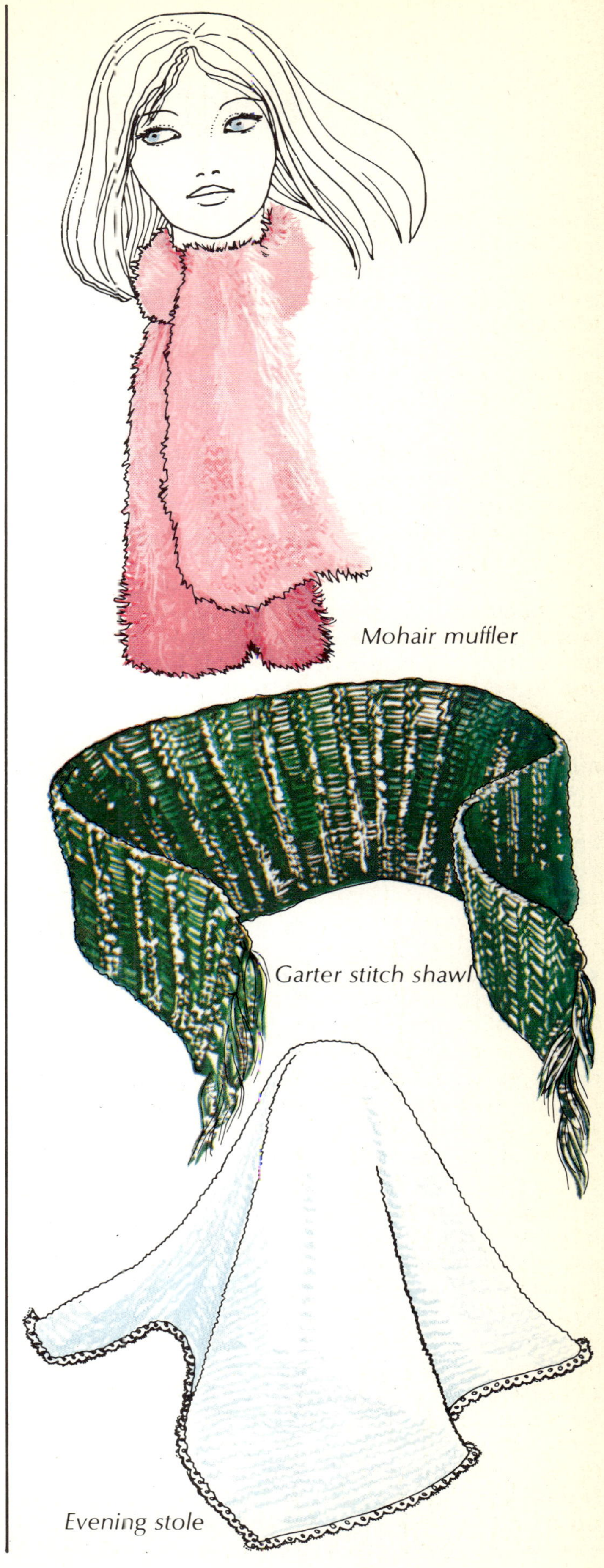

Mohair muffler

Garter stitch shawl

Evening stole

WORKING A PATTERN

A finished knitted garment should look just as attractive and fit just as well as in the illustration. A great deal of care is taken in designing knitting patterns to insure that this is possible. The secret lies in being completely objective about the design you choose, just as you would be when selecting ready-to-wear clothes. The range of knitting patterns which are available cater to every kind of garment in varying sizes. Where a design is only given in smaller sizes, such as a 32 or 34in bust, it is usually because the designer feels that it would not be suitable for a more generous figure. Similarly, if only one size is given it is probably because the pattern used for the design covers a large multiple of stitches and another whole repeat of the pattern, to give a larger size, would not be practical.

When you find a design which incorporates all the details you desire make sure you read through all the instructions before beginning to knit. Beginners and experts alike should pay particular attention to the finishing section – a deceptively simple shape may require a crochet edging to give it that couture look, or an unusual trimming effect such as a twisted cord belt.

Knitting patterns

Knitting publication styles vary considerably, but generally all instructions fall into three sections:

1 Materials required, gauge, finished sizes and abbreviations.

2 Working instructions for each section.

3 Finishing details, edges and trimmings.

Sizes

Check that the size range given in the instructions provides the size you need. If the skirt or sleeve lengths need altering to suit your requirements, read through the working instructions to see if the design allows for these changes. Some designs are based on an exact number of rows which cannot be altered. After the actual measurements of the design are given, take note that the instructions for the smallest size are given as the first set of figures and that the figures for any other sizes follow in order and are usually shown in brackets. Read through the instructions and underline all the figures which are applicable to the size you require, noting that where only one set of figures is given, it applies to all sizes.

Gauge

This section must not be overlooked as it is the vital key to success. Never begin any design without first making sure that you can obtain the correct gauge.

Materials

Each design will have been worked out for the knitting yarn which is quoted and this should be used, if possible. If for any reason it is impossible to obtain the specified yarn, you may select a substitute as long as you gain the correct gauge. But remember though that the quantity given will only apply to the original yarn and, if a substitute is used, you may need more or less yarn.

Abbreviations

All knitting patterns are abbreviated into a form of shorthand and every knitter soon comes to recognize the terms 'K2 tog' or 'sl 1, K1, psso' and their meanings. This book contains a complete list of general knitting abbreviations although the same terms may not be abbreviated in the same way by other publications and this can sometimes lead to confusion. It is therefore essential to read through any list of abbreviations before beginning a pattern to make sure you understand them. This is particularly important when they refer to increasing, as the terms, 'make 1' and 'increase 1' can mean two different things.

In this course, where a specific stitch or technique is given in a pattern, the working method is written out in full for the first time it is used in a row and its abbreviated form given at the end of the working instructions. From that point on, each time the same stitch or technique is used, its abbreviated term will be given.

Working instructions

Each section of a garment being worked will be given separately under an appropriate heading, such as, 'Back', 'Front', 'Sleeves' and so on. Each section should be worked in the correct order as it may be necessary to join parts of the garment together at a given point before you can proceed with the next step. When

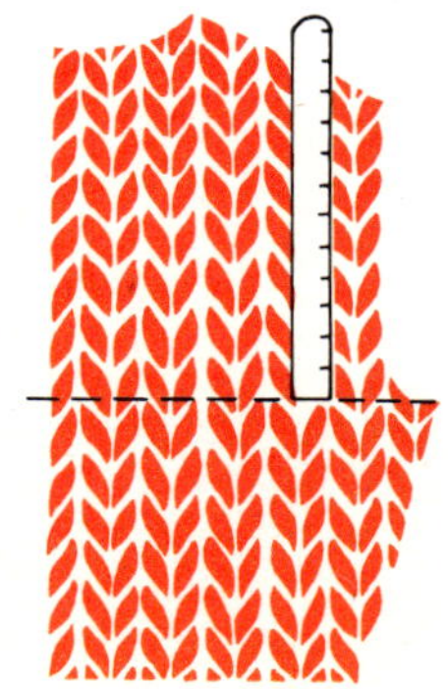

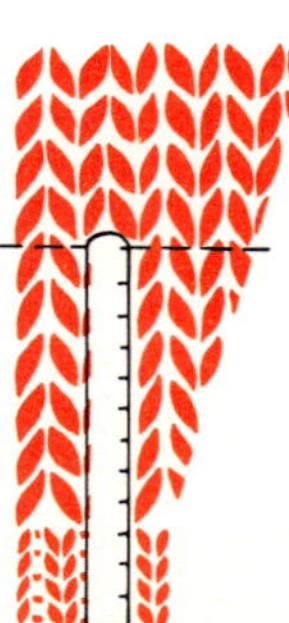

measuring knitting it is necessary to lay it on a flat surface and use a firm ruler. Never measure around a curve but, for example, on an armhole or sleeve, measure the depth in a straight line.

Where an asterisk, *, is used in a pattern row it means repeat from that point, as directed. This symbol is also used at the beginning of a section, sometimes as a double asterisk, **, or triple asterisk, ***, to denote a part which is to be repeated later on in the instructions.

When working in rows, always join in a new ball of yarn at the beginning of a row. You can easily gauge whether you have sufficient yarn for another row by spreading out your work and checking whether the remaining yarn will cover its width four times. Any odd pieces of yarn can always be used later for seaming.

If the yarn has to be joined in the middle of the work, which is necessary when working in rounds, then the ends of the old ball of yarn and the new ball should be spliced together. To do this, unravel the end of the new ball and cut away one or two strands from each end. Overlay the two ends from opposite directions and twist them together until they hold. The twisted ends should be of the same thickness as the original yarn. As the join will not be very strong, knit very carefully with the newly twisted yarn for a few rows. Then carefully trim away any odd ends with a pair of sharp scissors.

Never join in new yarn by means of a knot in the middle of your work, whether working in rows or rounds.

Finishing

Most knitters give a sigh of relief when they have bound off the very last stitch and look forward to wearing their new creation. If the finished garment is to be a success, however, the finishing of the separate pieces must be looked upon as an exercise in dressmaking. Details are always given in the instructions as to the order in which the sections are to be assembled, together with any final instructions for edgings or trimmings. Blocking instructions will also be given in this section and if a substitute yarn has been used, it is essential to check whether or not it requires blocking.

Mistakes!

These can happen – a dropped stitch, an interruption, a pattern row which has been misread and then needs ripping – but don't attempt to pull the stitches off the needle until you have tried other ways of rectifying the error.

To pick up a dropped stitch on a knit row: Insert a crochet hook into the dropped stitch from the front to the back, put the hook under the thread which lies between the two stitches above the dropped stitch and draw this thread through the dropped stitch. Continue in this way until the dropped stitch is level with the last row worked and transfer the stitch to the left hand needle. Then continue knitting in the usual way.

To pick up a dropped stitch on a purl row: Insert a crochet hook into the dropped stitch from the back to the front, put the hook over the thread which lies between the two stitches above the dropped stitch and draw this thread through the dropped stitch. Slip the stitch onto a spare needle and remove the hook, ready to insert it into the dropped stitch from the back to the front again. Continue in this way until the dropped stitch is level with the last row worked and transfer the stitch to the left hand needle. Then continue purling in the usual way.

To rip back stitches on a knit row: Insert the left hand needle from the front to the back into the stitch below the next stitch on the right hand needle, then withdraw the right hand needle from the stitch above and pull the yarn with the right hand to unravel this stitch, keeping the yarn at the back of the work. Continue in this way until the required number of stitches have been ripped.

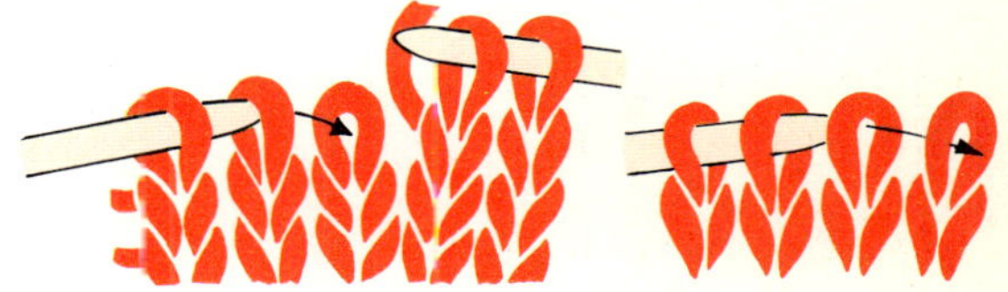

To rip back stitches on a purl row: Insert the left hand needle from the front to the back into the stitch below the next stitch on the right hand needle, then withdraw the right hand needle from the stitch above and pull the yarn with the right hand to unravel this stitch, keeping the yarn at the front of the work. Continue in this way until the required number of stitches have been ripped.

A BETTER FINISH

Shaping stitches

Knitting may be perfectly straight, as in a scarf, or intricately shaped as in a tailored jacket. Shaping is achieved by means of increasing the number of stitches in a row to make the work wider, or decreasing the stitches in a row to make the work narrower. This is usually done by making two stitches out of one, or by working two stitches together to make one stitch at a given point in the pattern. Sometimes the shaping forms an integral part of the design and decorative methods of increasing and decreasing are used to highlight the shaping, such as fully-fashioned seams on a raglan pullover.

By means of an eyelet hole method of increasing stitches, carrying the yarn over or around the needle in a given sequence and compensating for these new stitches later on in the row, beautiful lace patterns are produced.

How to increase

The simplest way is to make an extra stitch at the beginning or end of the row, but a pattern will always give exact details where more intricate shaping is required, such as for skirt darts.

To make a stitch at the beginning of a row, knit or purl the first stitch in the usual way but do not slip it off the left hand needle. Instead, place the point of the right hand needle into the back of the same stitch and purl or knit into the stitch again. One stitch has been increased.

To make a stitch at the end of a row, work until two stitches remain on the left hand needle, increase in the next stitch and work the last stitch in the usual way. One stitch has been increased.

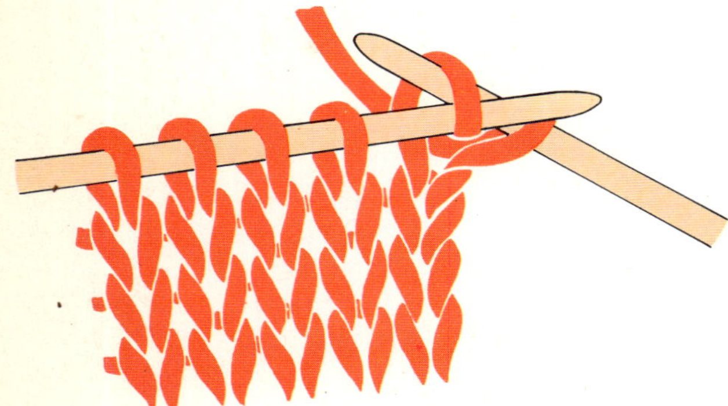

Invisible increasing

Insert the right hand needle into the front of the stitch on the row below the next stitch on the left hand needle and knit a new stitch in the usual way, then knit the next stitch on the left hand needle. One stitch has been increased.

If the increase is on a purl row, insert the right hand needle in the same way and purl a stitch in the usual way, then purl the next stitch on the left hand needle.

Increasing between stitches

With the right hand needle pick up the yarn which lies between the stitch just worked and the next stitch on the left hand needle and place this loop on the left hand needle. Knit into the back of this loop so that the new stitch is twisted and does not leave a hole in the work. Place the new stitch on the right hand needle. One stitch has been increased.

If the increase is on a purl row, pick up the yarn between the stitches in the same way and purl into it from the back, then place the new stitch on the right hand needle.

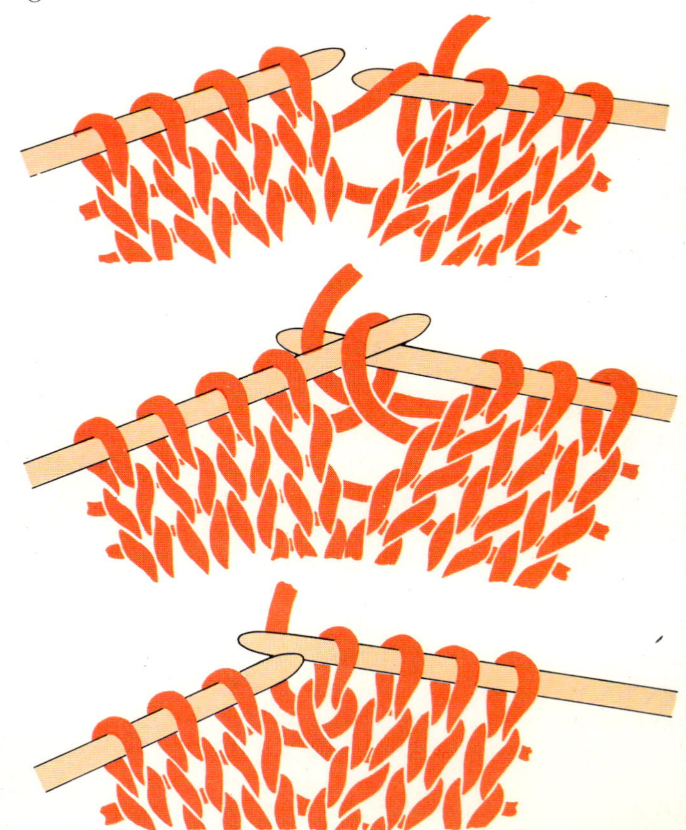

Decorative increasing

To make a stitch between two knit stitches, bring the yarn forward between the needles then back over the top of the right hand needle, ready to knit the next stitch. This is called 'yarn in front' or 'yarn forward' the abbreviation is 'yfwd' or 'yo'. To make a stitch between a purl and a knit stitch, the yarn is already at the front of the work and is carried over the top of the right hand needle ready to knit the next stitch. This is called 'yarn over needle' and the abbreviation is 'yon' or 'yo'.

To make a stitch between two purl stitches, take the yarn over the top of the right hand needle and around between the two needles to the front again ready to purl the next stitch. This is called 'yarn round needle' and the abbreviation is 'yrn' or 'yo'.

To make a stitch between a knit and a purl stitch, bring the yarn forward between the two needles, over the top of the right hand needle then around between the two needles to the front again ready to purl the next stitch. The abbreviation is 'yrn' or 'yo'.

How to decrease

The way to make a simple decrease is by working two stitches together, either at the ends of the row or at any given point. To do this on a knit row, insert the point of the right hand needle through two stitches instead of one and knit them both together in the usual way thus losing one stitch. This is called 'knit 2 together' or 'K2 tog'.

On a purl row, purl the two stitches together. This stitch will slant to the left and the abbreviation is 'P2 tog'.

▲ *Decreasing on a knit row* ▼ *Decreasing on a purl row*

Decreasing by means of a slipped stitch

This method is most commonly used where the decreases are worked in pairs, one slanting to the left and one slanting to the right, as on a raglan sleeve. Slip the stitch to be decreased from the left hand needle on to the right hand needle without working it, then knit the next stitch on the left hand needle. With the point of the left hand needle lift the slipped stitch over the knit stitch and off the needle. This stitch will slant to the left and the abbreviation is 'sl 1, K1, psso'.

On a purl row, purl the two stitches together through the back of the stitches. This stitch will slant to the right and the abbreviation is 'P2 tog through back loop' (tbl).

Decorative decreasing

The decorative use of decreasing can be accentuated by twisting the stitches around the decreased stitches to give them greater emphasis. This example shows a decrease which has been twisted and lies in the opposite direction to the line of the seam. The decrease is worked at the end of the knit row for the left hand side and at the end of a purl row for the right hand side.

Knit to the last six stitches, pass the right hand needle behind the first stitch on the left hand needle and knit the next two stitches together through the back of the stitches, then knit the first skipped stitch and slip both stitches off the left hand needle and knit the last three stitches in the usual way.

On a purl row, purl to the last six stitches, pass the right hand needle across the front of the first stitch on the left hand needle and purl the next two stitches together, then purl the first skipped stitch, slip both stitches off the left hand needle and purl the last three stitches in the usual way.

Decorative decreasing on knit and purl rows

More about shaping

Even the most basic stockinette stitch sweater needs careful shaping at the underarm, back and front neck and shoulders, sleeves and top of the sleeves, if it is to fit together correctly. The correct proportions for all these measurements will have been taken into account in every knitting design and the instructions will clearly state where and when the shaping is to be worked.

Where so many knitters find difficulty is in the accurate measuring of each section, so that when a garment is assembled it all fits together without stretching or easing one piece to fit another. The easiest way to overcome this problem is to use a row counter to insure that the back and front of a garment have exactly the same number of rows before beginning any shaping, and that both sleeves match. Many professional knitters prefer to knit both sleeves at the same time, using two separate balls of yarn, to make sure that the shaping for each sleeve is worked on the same row. Another useful tip is to make a note of the number of rows which have been worked for any section, such as the ribbing on the waist of a sweater, before beginning any pattern rows, so that when you are ready to do the next piece you do not even have to measure the length but can work to the same number of rows.

Whichever method you adopt, it is essential to know how to take accurate measurements if you are to achieve satisfactory results.

Taking measurements

Before taking any measurements it is necessary to lay the section of knitting on a flat surface. If you are sitting comfortably in a chair, it is tempting to try to measure it across your knees, or on the arm of the chair, but this will not give an accurate figure.

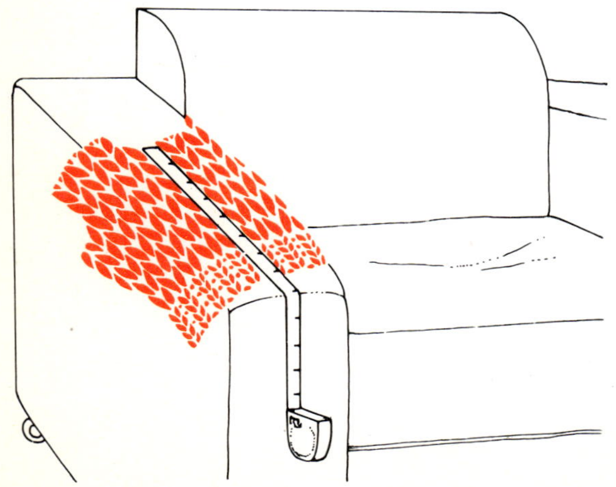

Always measure with a firm ruler and not a tape measure and never be tempted to stretch the section to the required length to avoid working a few extra rows before the next step.

Never measure around a curve but always on the straight of the fabric – a curved measurement is obviously greater and will result in an incorrect depth on armholes or sleeve seams. When measuring an armhole, sleeve or side edge of a section which has been shaped, place the ruler on the fabric in a straight line from the beginning of the section to the point you have reached.

Measurement and gauge

It cannot be stressed too often that every design you knit has been calculated on the gauge achieved by the designer of the garment and based on the correct proportions for each size. The normal ratio of a 2in difference between the bust and hip measurements will have been taken into account, also an allowance of 1in or 2in for movement, or what is known as tolerance. The width gauge, or number of stitches to a given measurement, is vital if you are to obtain an accurate fit. The length gauge, or number of rows to a given measurement, is not so important and can be adjusted where a pattern is not given over an exact number of rows and provided you remember that it is even more essential to measure each section accurately. The designer may have achieved more rows to the inch than you are obtaining and her shaping on the sleeves, for instance, will have been calculated to insure that this is completed well before the point has been reached to shape the cap of the sleeve. Where she is increasing on every 6th row in order to complete the shaping within a certain measurement, you may be working to a looser row gauge and will need to increase on every 5th row, in order to end up with the correct number of stitches within the same length. Similarly, if you are working to a tighter row gauge, you may need to adjust the shaping and work it on every 7th row, otherwise all the shaping may well be completed before reaching the elbow level and the whole sleeve will be out of shape.

Shaping in rows

Details of casting on or binding off stitches to achieve the correct shape, such as for the underarm, neck or shoulders, will be given in a pattern in detail.

When shaping is required on both side edges of a section, the pattern may simply say, 'decrease one stitch at each end of the next knitted row' and will leave the knitter to adopt whichever method she prefers. In this case, if you use the slip one, knit one, pass slipped stitch over method at the beginning of the row, producing a decreased stitch which slants to the left when the fabric is facing you, use the knit two together method at the end of the row to make a stitch which slants to the right.

In increasing on a row, whether it is at each end to increase two stitches, or across the row to increase a greater number of stitches, when working twice into a stitch the last stitch made is the increased stitch. If you increase in the first stitch at the beginning of a row, the new stitch will lie inside the first knitted stitch. At the end of the row you should increase in the next to last stitch, so that the increased stitch again lies inside the last stitch, which is then knitted in the usual way. Sometimes a pattern will tell you to increase a given number of stitches across a row, without giving exact instructions. To do this you must first work out the exact position for each increased stitch. As an example, if a pattern has begun with 80 stitches and at a given point you are required to increase 8 stitches evenly across a row, the accurate way to achieve this would be to increase in the 5th stitch and then in every following 10th stitch 7 times more, and then knit the last 5 stitches. In this way, each new stitch would be evenly spaced across the row.

Shaping in rounds

The same principles apply, if you are working in rows or in rounds. A skirt may be worked from the hem to waist in rounds and will need to be shaped by means of decreasing, to lose the extra width at the hem. As an example, if you are working a pattern in wide panels of stockinette stitch and narrow panels of reverse stockinette stitch, the shaping needs to be worked on the stockinette stitch panels to eventually bring them down to the same width as the reverse stockinette stitch panels. The pattern may simply say, 'decrease one stitch at each end of every stockinette stitch panel' and you should use the slip one, knit one, pass slipped stitch over method at the beginning of each panel and the knit two together method at the end of each panel. In this way, each decreased stitch lies in the same direction as the line of the stockinette stitch panels.

Using the same example, when increasing in rounds remember that if you increase in the first stitch of each panel you must increase in the next to the last stitch and not in the last stitch.

Binding off and forming edges

Each piece of knitted fabric has edges which are formed as the work progresses and these must be suitable for the fabric produced. Every section of flat knitting has a cast on edge, the right and left hand side edges and the bound off edge. Round knitting has only a cast on and bound off edge.
Various methods of casting on and binding off have already been given but the following methods are less popular. The ways of forming side edges are also important, as an edge which is too tight or too loose will pull the garment out of shape and present difficulties in finishing.

Double casting on
Two needles are required for this method, which are both held together in the right hand. Make a slip loop in the ball of yarn as for the thumb method and place this on both needles. Take both ends of the yarn, that is, the end of the yarn from the slip loop and the end from the ball and hold them together in the palm of the left hand, putting the slip loop end around the thumb and the ball end around the forefinger. Using both needles put them up under the first loop on the thumb and over and down through the loop on the forefinger, then through the thumb loop. Release the thumb loop and tighten the stitch on the needles with an upward movement of the right hand, without releasing either end of the yarn held in the palm of the hand. Continue in this way until the required number of stitches are formed on the needles, then withdraw the second needle, transfer the needle holding the stitches to the left hand and have the second needle in the right hand, ready to knit. This forms a very strong yet elastic edge.

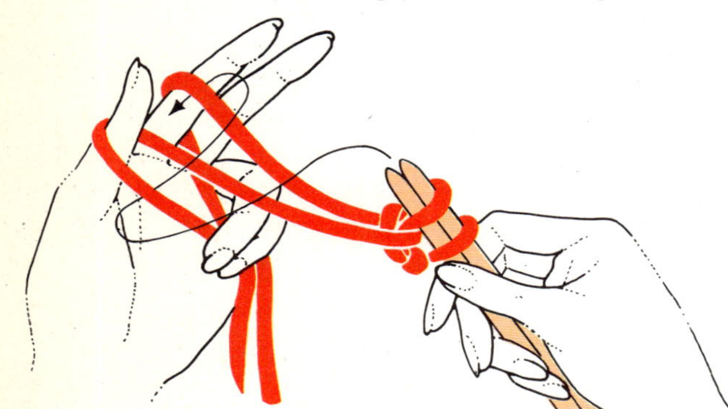

Picot casting on
Two needles are required for this method, one held in each hand. Make a slip loop and place this on the left hand needle, then cast on one stitch by the two needle method. Using these two loops make a strip long enough for the number of stitches required by placing the yarn over the needle, then slipping the first stitch on the left hand needle as if to purl, knitting the second stitch on the left hand needle and lifting the slipped stitch over the knitted stitch and dropping it off the right hand needle. Turn and repeat this row until the required number of picot loops have been formed by the yarn forward. Pick up these picot loops along one edge with a needle and then continue knitting in the usual way. The other side of the picot edge forms a dainty edge ideal for baby garments.

Suspended binding off
Knit the first two stitches in the usual way, then lift the first stitch over the second stitch but instead of allowing it to drop off the right hand needle, retain it on the point of the left hand needle. Pass the right hand needle in front of the held stitch and knit the next stitch on the left hand needle in the usual way, slipping the stitch and the held stitch off the left hand needle together, leaving two stitches on the right hand needle. Continue in this way until all stitches are bound off. This method avoids any tendency to bind off too tightly.

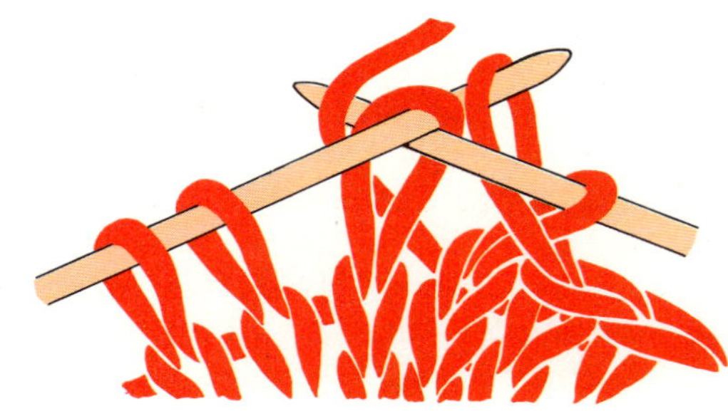

Shaped binding off
Preparation for this method must be made before the final binding off by turning the last few rows of knitting without completing them to form a shaped angle, then binding off all the stitches at one time on the final row. This is an ideal way of working shoulder shaping as it does not produce the stepped effect of normal binding off and makes seaming very much easier. For example, on a right back shoulder edge when the point

has been reached for the shoulder shaping, instead of binding off the required number of stitches at the beginning of the next knit row, on the previous purl row work to within this number of stitches then turn the work, slip the first stitch on the left hand needle and knit to the end of the row. Repeat in this manner the required number of times, then purl across all the stitches. Bind them off on the next knit row in the usual way. Reverse this for a left back shoulder edge by beginning the shaping on a knit row.

Three steps of shaped binding off

Side edges

Where side edges are to be joined together in finishing, they need to be firm to allow for a good edge for seaming. When both edges must show, as in a scarf, they need to be neat without pulling the sides out of shape.

To work an edge for seaming: Slip the first stitch purlwise and knit the last stitch on every row, when working in stockinette stitch. On garter stitch, bring the yarn to the front of the work, slip the first stitch on every row purlwise, then put the yarn to the back and knit to the end in the usual way.

To work an open edge: When working in stockinette stitch, slip the first and last stitch on every knit row to form a chain effect, then purl each stitch on the following row in the usual way.

Slipped stitches

Stitches which are slipped from one needle to the other without being worked are used in various ways – as edge stitches, as a means of decreasing and to form part of a pattern. When a slip stitch forms part of a decrease on a knit row, the stitch must be slipped knitwise, otherwise it will become twisted. On a purl row, the stitch must be slipped purlwise, when decreasing. In working a pattern, however, where the slip stitch is not part of a decrease it must be slipped purlwise on a knit row to prevent it from becoming twisted when it is purled in the following row.

To slip stitch knitwise on a knit row: Hold the yarn behind the work as if to knit the next stitch, insert the point of the right hand needle into the next stitch from front to back as if to knit it and slip it on to the right hand needle without working it.

To slip stitch purlwise on a knit row: Hold the yarn behind the work as if to knit the next stitch, insert the point of the right hand needle into the next stitch from back to front as if to purl it and slip it on to the right hand needle without working it.

To slip stitch purlwise on a purl row: Hold the yarn at the front of the work as if to purl the next stitch, insert the point of the right hand needle into the next stitch from back to front as if to purl it and slip it on to the right hand needle without working it.

FINISHING TOUCHES
Buttonholes

Details for working buttonholes will always be given in the instructions for a garment but unless they are neatly finished they can spoil the appearance of the garment. Various methods may be used, largely depending on the size of the button desired and the overall width of the buttonhole band or border. The buttonholes can be horizontal, vertical or, on a baby garment where a small button is required, simply worked by means of an eyelet hole.

Simple eyelet buttonholes
If the buttonhole is being incorporated in the main fabric, or the buttonhole band, work the front of the garment until the position for the first buttonhole is reached, ending with a wrong side row. On the next row work the first few stitches in the row to the position for the buttonhole, then pass the yarn forward, over or around the needle, depending on the stitch being worked, to make an eyelet hole, work the next two stitches on the left hand needle together to compensate for the made stitch, then work in pattern to the end of the row. On the next row, work across all the stitches in pattern, counting the new stitch as one stitch. Continue in this manner for as many buttonholes as are needed.

Horizontal buttonholes
These can either be worked as part of the main fabric or on a separate buttonhole band.
Buttonholes worked as part of the main fabric: In this case provision will already have been made for a turned under hem and buttonholes will have to be made in the hem and in the main fabric, to form a double buttonhole, which is then finished with a buttonhole stitch on completion. Work until the position for the buttonhole is reached, ending at the center front edge. On the next row work a few stitches across the hem, bind off the number of stitches required for the buttonhole by the two needle method, then continue across the remainder of the hem. Work the same number of stitches on the main fabric as were worked on the hem, then bind off the same number of buttonhole stitches and work in pattern to the end of the row. On the next row you

need to replace the same number of stitches as were bound off for each buttonhole on the previous row but need to avoid spoiling the buttonhole with a loose loop of yarn at one end, which would be the result of merely casting on the same number of stitches. To avoid this, work to the last stitch before the bound off stitches and increase in this last stitch by working into the front and back of it, then cast on one stitch less than was bound off on the previous row. Continue in this manner for as many buttonholes as are needed. If a turned under hem is not being worked in one with the main fabric, then only a single buttonhole is required.

Buttonholes worked in a separate border: Where only a single buttonhole is required work the band until the position for the buttonhole is reached, ending at the center front edge. On the next row work a few stitches until the position for the buttonhole is reached, bind off the required number of stitches for the buttonhole and work in pattern to the end of the row. On the next row, cast on the number of stitches needed to complete the buttonhole in the same way as when working buttonholes as part of the main fabric. Continue in this manner for as many buttonholes as are needed.

Vertical buttonholes

This method of working buttonholes is ideal when only a narrow band is required and they can be worked in one with the main fabric. The working instructions are the same for a separate band or when incorporated in the main fabric, remembering to make provision for a double buttonhole if a turned under hem is being worked with the main fabric. Work until the position for the buttonhole is reached, ending at the center front edge. On the next row

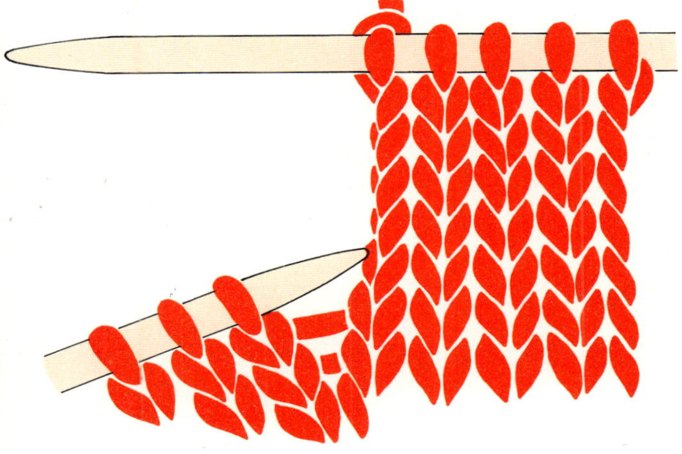

work across a few stitches to the buttonhole opening, then turn the work at this point and continue across these stitches only for the required number of rows to fit the size of the button, ending at the buttonhole opening edge. Break off the yarn and leave these stitches for the time being. Rejoin the yarn to the remaining stitches and work the same number of rows over these stitches, ending at the side edge away from the buttonhole opening. On the next row work across all the stitches to close the buttonhole. Continue in this manner for the number of buttonholes needed.

Finishing buttonholes

All buttonholes need to be finished and reinforced when they are completed. This can either be done by working around them in buttonhole stitch, using the same yarn or a matching silk thread, or by means of a ribbon facing.

Buttonhole stitch: Work along both sides of the buttonhole opening in buttonhole stitch for a horizontal or vertical buttonhole, finishing each end with three straight stitches. Be careful not to take too many stitches around the buttonhole, so that the edges become stretched, or too few stitches, which would make the hole smaller than you intended. Eyelet buttonholes need to be finished with several evenly spaced buttonhole stitches around the hole, keeping the loops lying towards the center.

Ribbon facing: The ribbon should be straight grained and wide enough to cover the buttonholes with an extra $\frac{1}{2}$in on either side and at each end of the band. Take care not to stretch the fabric when measuring the ribbon length and cut the buttonhole and button band facings together so that they match. Fold in the hems on the ribbon and pin in place on the wrong side of the knitting, easing the fabric evenly and checking that the buttonholes are correctly spaced. Pin the ribbon on each side of every buttonhole to hold it in place. Slip stitch neatly around the edges of the ribbon, then cut through the buttonholes in the ribbon making sure that they are exactly the same size as the knitted buttonholes. Work around the knitting and ribbon with buttonhole stitch to finish the edges.

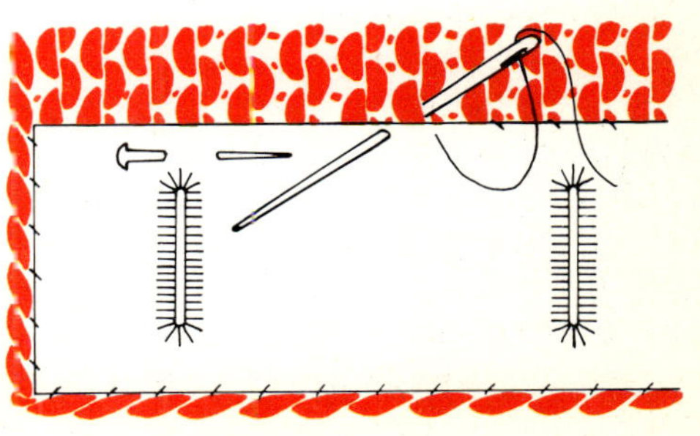

Hems and waistbands

Neat hems and waistbands are very important, particularly on babies' and children's garments where any unnecessary bulk produces an unattractive and uncomfortable edge.

Hems on skirts and dresses may be worked as part of the main fabric, then turned in and slip stitched into place when the garment is completed, or they may be knitted in to avoid seaming. Waistbands should be neatly ribbed and either folded in half to form a casing for the elastic, or the elastic may be directly applied to the wrong side of the fabric by means of a casing, or herringbone stitch.

Turned under stockinette stitch hem

Using one size smaller needles than for the main fabric, cast on the required number of stitches. Beginning with a knitted row work an odd number of rows in stockinette stitch, then change to the correct needle size. On the next row, instead of purling to the end, knit into the back of each stitch to form a ridge which marks the hemline. Beginning with a knitted row again, work one row less in stockinette stitch than was worked for the hem, thus ending with a purl row to complete the hem. **. When the garment is completed and the side seams have been joined, turn the hem to the wrong side of the work at the hemline and slip stitch in place.

Knitted in hem in stockinette stitch

Work as for the turned under hem to **. Before continuing with the pattern, use an extra needle and pick up the loops from the cast on edge from left to right, so that the needle point is facing the same way as the main needle. Hold this needle behind the stitches already on the left hand needle and knit to the end of the row, working one stitch from the left hand needle together with one stitch from the extra needle. When the garment is completed join the side seams, working through the double fabric of the hem.

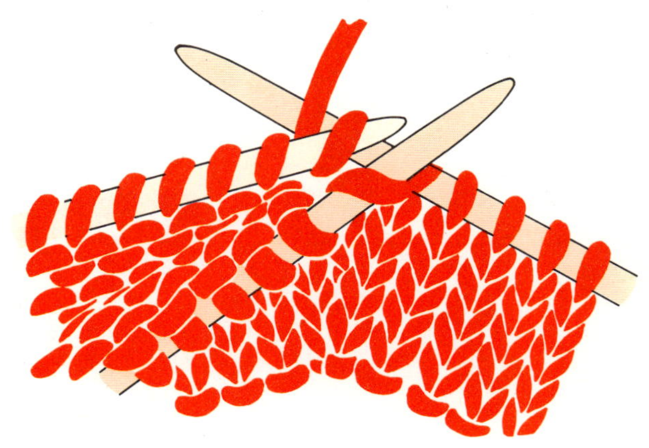

Picot hem

Using one size smaller needles than used for the main fabric cast on an odd number of stitches. Beginning with a knitted row work an even number of rows in stockinette stitch. Change to the correct needle size. **Next row** (eyelet hole row) *K2 tog, yfwd, rep from * to last st, K1.

Beginning with a purl row work one row more in stockinette stitch than was worked for the hem, thus ending with a purl row to complete the hem. When the garment is completed and the side seams have been joined, turn the hem to the wrong side at the eyelet hole row and slip stitch in place.

Ribbed waistband for elastic

Using one size smaller needles than those used for the main fabric, work in K1, P1 rib for twice the width of the elastic to be used, plus a few extra rows. If 1in elastic is being used, work 2in plus 2 extra rows, then bind off in rib. When the garment is completed and the side seams have been joined, turn in the waistband to the wrong side and slip stitch in place, leaving an opening at one side to thread the elastic through. Insert the elastic and sew ends securely, then seam the opening.

Casing stitch waistband

When the garment is completed, join the side seams. Cut the elastic to the necessary length, allowing 1in extra for an overlap, and join the two ends to form a circle.

Using rustless steel pins mark on the waistband and elastic into equal sections. Pin the elastic into place on the wrong side of the fabric. Thread a blunt ended sewing needle with matching yarn and secure to the side seam of the waistband. Hold the waistband and elastic, slightly stretched, over the fingers of the left hand then sew through the elastic and lightly through the top of the waistband from right to left. Sew through the elastic again and lightly through the fabric below the elastic from right to left about 2 stitches along to the right. Return to the top edge again about 2 stitches along to the right, and sew lightly through the fabric from right to left. Continue in this manner around the waistband until the elastic is secured, being very careful to distribute the knitting evenly, then fasten off.

Working casing stitch

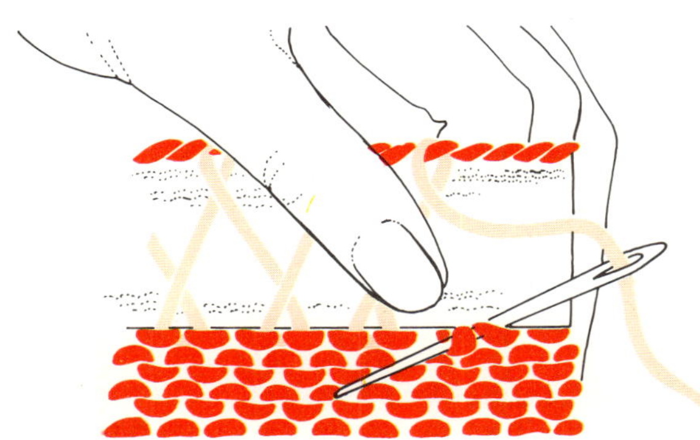

Baby's pants

Size

Directions are to fit 20in hips. Changes for 22 and 24in hips are in brackets [].
Length at side, 7[8:9]in

Gauge

30sts and 40 rows to 4in in stockinette stitch (st st) worked on No.2 needles

Materials

2[2:3] × 1$\frac{3}{4}$oz balls Bucilla Perlette
One pair No.2 needles
One pair No.1 needles
Waist length of 1in wide elastic
Leg lengths of $\frac{1}{2}$in wide elastic

Pants left side

Using No.2 needles cast on 93[99:105]sts. Beg with a K row and work 2 rows st st.

Shape crotch

Cont in st st, bind off 3 sts for back edge at beg of next and foll alt row then dec one st at same edge on every foll 4th row 4 times in all, *at the same time* binding off 2 sts for front edge on foll alt row and dec one st at same edge on every alt row 8 times in all. 73[79:85]sts. Cont without shaping until work measures 6[7:8]in from beg, ending with a P row.

Shape back

Next row K to last 24 sts, turn.
Next row Sl 1, P to end.
Next row K to last 32 sts, turn.
Next row Sl 1, P to end.
Cont working 8 sts less in this way on next and every alt row 4[5:6] times more. Change to No.1 needles.

Waistband

Next row K1, *P1, K1, rep from * to end.
Next row P1, *K1, P1, rep from * to end.
Rep last 2 rows 4 times more. Bind off in rib.

Pants right side

Work as for left side, reversing all shaping.

Leg bands

Using No.1 needles and with RS of work facing, K 93[99:105]sts around leg. Work 1in K1, P1 rib as for waistband.
Bind off in ribbing.

Finishing

Block each piece under a dry cloth with a cool iron. Join front, back and leg seams. Sew elastic inside waistband, using casing st. Fold leg bands in half to WS and sl st down. Thread elastic through leg bands and secure ends. Block seams.

Pockets

Pockets are always a practical addition, particularly on men's and children's garments. They can be easily added to any chosen design, and inserted horizontally or vertically as part of the main fabric, or applied as patch pockets when the garment is finished. In each case a certain amount of planning is required to work out the exact positioning for each pocket before beginning the garment. It must also be remembered that they will use extra yarn, so to be safe, buy an extra ball.

If you have, for example, a favorite cardigan pattern for a man but would like to add inserted horizontal pockets above the waistband, first check the given length to the underarm and work out the depth of pocket desired. About 4in by 4in would be a reasonable size and this should be calculated to allow the pocket lining to come above any ribbed waistband or inside any front edges. The same measurements apply to a patch pocket.

For an inserted vertical pocket the same calculations must be made to insure that the opening is correctly positioned and that the pocket lining has sufficient room to lie flat inside any front edges.

Patch pockets are the simplest to work and easy to apply, see later. They can be used as breast pockets on an otherwise plain sweater, applied to the sleeves above elbow level on a teenage jacket, or on the skirt of a dress at hip level. A straight turned down, buttoned flap can be added, or a plain square pocket can be given a highly individual touch if it is worked in a contrasting stitch or finished with embroidery.

Inserted horizontal pockets

First check the number of stitches you need to make the size of pocket desired – on a gauge of 6 stitches to 1in, a 4in pocket would need 24 stitches. Cast on this number of stitches and make the inside pocket flap first, working in stockinette stitch until it is the desired depth, ending with a wrong side row, then leave these stitches on a holder. Now work the main fabric of the garment until the desired depth for the pocket has been reached, ending with the right side of the work facing you. On the next row work until the position for the pocket opening is reached, slip the required number of stitches for the pocket top on to a holder, then with the right side of the pocket lining stitches facing the wrong side of the main fabric, work across the pocket lining stitches, then work to the end of the row across the main fabric. Complete the section as given in the instructions. With the right side of the work facing, rejoin the yarn to the pocket top stitches on the holder and work $\frac{1}{2}$in to 1in in rib or garter stitch to complete the pocket.

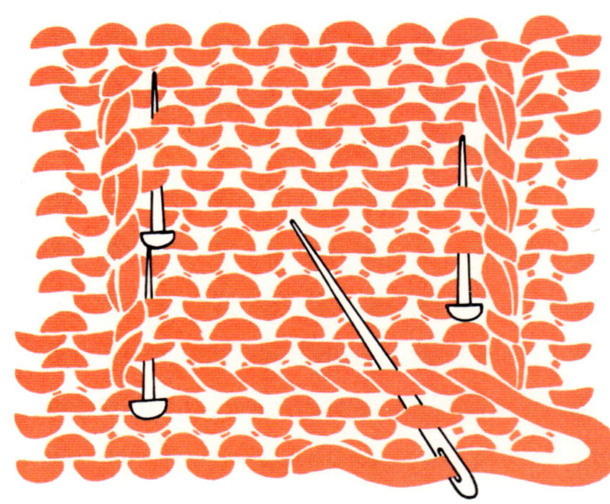

To finish the pocket, stitch the lining in place on the wrong side and slip stitch the side edges of the pocket top to the main fabric.

Inserted vertical pockets

First check the number of rows you need to make the size of pocket desired – if a gauge of 8 rows to 1in is given, a 4in pocket will require 32 stitches. Cast on this number of stitches and make the inside pocket flap first, working in stockinette stitch until it is the required depth, then place these stitches on a holder. Work the main fabric of the garment now until the required position for the pocket opening has been reached, ending with the right side of the work facing you. On the next row work until the position for the pocket opening is reached, turn at this point and work the required number of rows on this piece only, ending with a wrong side row. Break off the yarn.

Return to where the work was divided, rejoin the yarn to the remaining stitches, and work the same number of rows on this piece, ending with a wrong side row. Break off the yarn. Return to the first piece, rejoin

the yarn and work across all the stitches to close the pocket opening, then complete the piece according to the instructions. With the right side of the work facing you, rejoin the yarn along the edge of the first pocket piece worked on the right front of a garment, or along the second pocket piece worked on the left front of a garment, and pick up the required number of stitches.

Work $\frac{1}{2}$ inch to 1 inch ribbing or garter stitch to complete the pocket opening. With the right side of the pocket flap against the wrong side of the main fabric, join the flap to the other edge of the pocket opening and sew around the other 3 edges. Finish the pocket opening by slip stitching the edges to the main fabric.

Patch pocket

Check the number of stitches and rows required to give the correct size for the pocket. If using a patterned stitch, such as cable, make sure that the pattern will work out exactly over the number of stitches and adjust them accordingly – it is better to have a slightly smaller or larger pocket than an incorrect pattern repeat. Cast on the stitches and work the number of rows to give the desired depth, then bind off. With the wrong side of the patch pocket facing the right side of the main fabric, sew around the three sides of the pocket.

Patch pocket with flap

Work as for the patch pocket until the desired depth has been reached but do not bind off. Unless a completely reversible stitch, such as ribbing or garter stitch, has been used for the pocket, the pattern must now be reversed so that when the flap is turned down, the right side of the fabric will be showing. To do this if you have ended with a wrong side row, simply work another wrong side row for the first row of the flap, then continue in pattern for the desired depth of the flap and bind off. Similarly, if you have ended with a right side row, work another right side row and complete in the same way. Sew the pocket on as for patch pockets, then turn the flap over to the right side and trim with one button at each end, if desired.

Patch pockets with cable trim on a slipover and patch pockets with flaps on a basic pullover.

Neckbands and collars

Neckbands and collars

The neck opening on any garment, where the necessary shaping to give a good fit has been worked as part of the main fabric, will require finishing, either by means of a neckband or a collar. The most usual method of working a neckband on a round-necked pullover is to pick up the required number of stitches around the neck opening and work a few rows, or rounds, in single or double rib. This forms a neat edge with sufficient elasticity to hold its shape when it is pulled on or off over the head and to spring back into place when it has been stretched in this way.

Collars may be added to a pullover or cardigan, either by picking up stitches around the neck edge or by making a separate piece which is then sewn around the neck edge to complete the garment. When you are working either a neckband or collar on which the stitches must be picked up (see below), insure that stitches are picked up neatly and evenly round the opening.

Neckbands

To complete a round neck on a pullover, provision for an opening must be made if the neckband is to be worked on two needles. If a back or front neck opening has not been worked as part of the main fabric, only one shoulder seam should be joined, leaving the other seam open until the neckband has been completed. When a round neckband is worked on 4 needles no opening is needed and the stitches are simply picked up and worked in rounds to the desired depth. When working a ribbed neckband the depth can quite easily be adjusted to suit personal taste, to form either a round, crew or turtleneck. If a turtleneck is desired, however, it must be remembered that this will take extra yarn and you must therefore make provision for this when you are purchasing the yarn.

To complete a square neck on a pullover or cardigan, each corner must be mitered to continue the square shape and allow the neckband to lie flat. The best way to do this is to pick up the required number of stitches and mark each corner stitch with colored thread. Keep these marked stitches as knitted stitches on the right side of the work, whether working in rows or rounds, and decrease one stitch on either side of each marked stitch on every row or round, making sure that the decreased stitches slant towards the corner stitch. As an example, when working in rows of garter stitch with the right side of the work facing, work to within 2 stitches of the corner stitch, sl 1, K1, psso, K corner st, K2 tog, then K to within 2 stitches of the next corner. On the following row, the decreased stitches will be worked in the same way but the corner stitch must be purled.

Collars

Collars come in all styles and sizes but, to fit correctly around the neck, they must be carefully shaped. They can be worked in 2 pieces to form a divided collar, where a sweater has a center back neck opening, or in one piece to complete a pullover or a cardigan. Where the fabric used for the collar is reversible, such as garter stitch or ribbing, the stitches should be picked up around the neck in the usual way with the right side of the work facing. Where a fabric such as stockinette stitch is used for a collar, however, the stitches must be picked up with the wrong side of the work facing, to insure that the correct side of the fabric is shown when the collar is turned down.

Pullover with ribbed neckband or shirt collar

Sizes

Directions are to fit 34in bust. Changes for 36 and 38in bust are in brackets [].

Length to shoulder, 23[23½:24]in

Sleeve seam, 17[17½:18]in

Gauge

30sts and 38 rows to 4in in stockinette st (st st) worked on No.2 needles

Materials

12[13:14] × 1oz balls of any 3-ply fingering yarn plus 1 extra ball if collar is desired

One pair No.2 needles

One pair No.1 needles

5 buttons

Back

Using No 1 needles cast on 134[142:150] sts. Work 2in K1, P1 rib. Change to No.2 needles. Beg with a P row cont in reverse st st until work measures 16in from beg, ending with a K row.

Shape armholes

Bind off 5[6:7] sts at beg of next 2 rows. Dec one st at each end of next and every alt row until 102[108:114] sts rem. Cont without shaping until armholes measure 7[7½:8]in from beg, ending with a K row.

Shape shoulders

Bind off at beg of next and every row 12[12:13] sts twice, 12[13:13] sts twice and 12[13:14] sts twice. Place rem 30[32:34] sts on holder.

Front

Work as for back until front measures 15½in from beg, ending with a P row.

Divide for front opening

Next row K62[66:70] sts, bind off 10 sts, K to end.

Complete this side first. Cont in reverse st st until work measures same as back to underarm, ending at armhole edge.

Shape armhole

Bind off 5[6:7] sts at beg of next row. Dec one st at armhole edge on every alt row until 46[49:52] sts rem. Cont without shaping until armhole measures 5½in from beg, ending at center front edge.

Shape neck
Bind off 3[4:5] sts at beg of next row. Dec one st at neck edge on every alt row until 36[38:40] sts rem. Cont without shaping until armhole measures same as back to shoulder, ending at armhole edge.

Shape shoulder
Bind off at beg of next and every alt row 12[12:13] sts once, 12[13:13] sts once and 12[13:14] sts once.

With RS of work facing, rejoin yarn to rem sts and complete to correspond to first side, reversing shaping.

Sleeves
Using No.1 needles cast on 64[68:72] sts. Work 3in K1, P1 rib. Change to No.2 needles. Beg with a P row, cont in reverse st st, inc one st at each end of 7th and every foll 8th row, until there are 96[100:104] sts. Cont without shaping until sleeve measures 17[17½:18]in from beg, ending with a K row.

Shape top
Bind off 5[6:7] sts at beg of next 2 rows. Dec one st at each end of next and every alt row until 60 sts rem, ending with a K row. Bind off 4 sts at beg of next 10 rows. Bind off rem 20 sts.

Button band
Using No.1 needles cast on 12 sts. Beg 1st row with P1, work in P1, K1 rib until band fits up left front edge to beg of neck shaping, when slightly stretched. Place sts on holder. Mark position for 4 buttons with 5th to be worked in neckband.

Buttonhole band
Work as for button band, beg 1st row with K1 and making buttonholes as markers are reached, as foll:

Next row (buttonhole row) Rib 5, bind off 2, rib 5.

Next row Rib to end, casting on 2 sts above those bound off on previous row.

Ribbed neckband
Join shoulder seams. Sew on button and buttonhole bands, making sure that next row will beg and end with K1. Using No.1 needles and with RS of work facing, rib across buttonhole band, K 28[30:32] sts up right side of neck, K across back neck sts inc 5 sts evenly spaced across these sts and K 28[30:32] sts down left front neck, then rib across button band. 115[119:123] sts. Work 9 rows K1, P1 rib, making buttonhole as before on 5th and 6th rows. **. Bind off.

Collar
Work as for neckband to **.

Next row Bind off 6 sts, rib 5 sts and place on holder, rib to last 11 sts, rib 5 sts and leave on holder, bind off 6 sts. Break off yarn.

Change to No.2 needles. Using 2 strands of yarn, work 15 more rows rib, inc one st at each end of every row. Dec one st at each end of next 6 rows. Bind off 3 sts at beg of next 6 rows. Bind off rem sts.

Edging
Using No.1 needles and one strand of yarn, rejoin yarn to WS of first set of 5 sts. Work in rib until edging fits around outer edge of collar to center back. Bind off. Work other side in same way. Sew edging around collar, joining at center back.

Finishing
Block. Join side and sleeve seams. Set in sleeves. Sew on buttons.

FINAL FINISHING

BLOCKING AND SEAMS

The finishing of a garment requires as much care and skill as the actual knitting of each part of it. The technical knowledge which has been involved in producing an interesting fabric and the correct shape and proportions of the garment will be of no avail if the pieces are hurriedly assembled, or if scant attention is paid to the specific instructions for handling the yarn used. Some yarns do not require blocking and, in fact, they lose their character if they are blocked and the texture of certain stitches, such as Aran patterns, can be completely ruined by over-blocking. Read the instructions carefully before starting any finishing and if you have not used the yarn specified, check whether or not the substitute requires blocking by referring to the instructions given on the label.

Handling yarns

Each yarn, whether it is made from natural fibers, man-made fibers, or various blends of both, requires a different method of handling in finishing.

Most yarn labels will state the proper care for the yarn you are using. The following list gives a guide to the correct method of handling various qualities but, with so many new and exciting yarns becoming available, it is even more essential to check the specific requirements of each yarn.

Pure wool This quality should be blocked under a damp cloth with a warm iron.

Blends of wool and nylon fibers If the wool content is greater than the nylon content, such as 60% wool and 40% nylon, the yarn should be blocked lightly under a damp cloth with a warm iron.

Blends of wool and acrylic fibers Do not block.

Nylon Block under a dry cloth with a cool iron.

Acrylic fibers Do not block.

Cotton Block under a damp cloth with a fairly hot iron.

Mohair Block very lightly under a damp cloth with a warm iron.

Blends of mohair and acrylic fibers Do not block.

Glitter yarns Do not block, unless otherwise clearly stated on the label.

Angora Using a very damp cloth with a warm iron, steam press by holding the iron over the cloth to make steam but do not apply any pressure.

Embossed stitches Heavy cables, Aran patterns and any fabric with a raised texture should be steam pressed. This will give finish to the fabric without flattening the pattern.

Warning! If in doubt, do not block.

Blocking

As so many yarns now available do not require blocking, it is not always necessary to block out each piece to the correct size and shape. If blocking is required, however, place each piece right side down on an ironing pad and pin it evenly around the edges to the pad.

Always use rustless tailor's pins and never stretch the knitting, for if you do the pins will tend to make a fluted edge.

Take care to see that the stitches and rows run in straight lines and that the fabric is not pulled out of shape. Once the pieces are pinned into place, check with a firm ruler to see that the width and length are the same as those given in the instructions.

	HOT	WARM	COOL	DO NOT IRON
IRONING				
DRY CLEAN			F	
	Usual dry cleaning	Normally dry cleanable in most solvents. If dry cleaned, inform cleaner of composition of yarn	Drycleanable in some solvents It is important that the cleaner is informed of the composition of the yarn if dry-cleaning is to be undertaken	DO NOT DRY CLEAN

Use a clean cloth and place it over the piece to be blocked, then place the iron down on top of the cloth and lift it up again, without moving it over the surface of the cloth as you would if you were actually ironing. Each area should be blocked evenly but not too heavily before lifting the iron to go on to the next area.
Ribbed or garter stitch edges on any piece should never be blocked otherwise they will lose their elasticity.

Seams
The choice of a seaming method will largely depend on the type of garment being assembled. A baby's vest needs invisible seams without any hard edges and the flat seam method is normally used to join any ribbed edges where a neat, flat edge is required. Use a blunt ended needle and the yarn from which the garment is made for joining pieces together. If the yarn is not suitable for sewing purposes, as with mohair, use a finer quality such as 3 ply in the same color.

Invisible seam
Fasten the sewing yarn to one side of the pieces to be joined. With the right sides of both the pieces facing you, pass the needle across to the other side of the work, pick up one stitch and draw the yarn through. Pass the needle across the back to the first side of the work, pick up one stitch and draw the yarn through. Continue working in this way, making rungs across from one piece to the other and pulling each stitch up tightly so that it is not seen on the right side of the work when the seam is completed.

Back stitch seam
Place the right sides of each piece to be joined together and work along the wrong side of the fabric about one stitch in from the edge. Keep checking the other side of the seam to make sure that you are working in a straight line. Begin by securing the sewing yarn, making two or three small running stitches one on top of the other, then * with the needle at the back of the work move along to the left and bring the needle through to the front of the work the width of one stitch from the end of the last stitch, and draw the yarn through, take the needle back across the front of the work at the end of the last stitch and draw the yarn through. Continue in this way repeating from * until the seam is completed, taking care to pull each sewing stitch firmly through the knitting without stretching the pieces or drawing up the seaming stitches too tightly.

Flat seam
Place the right sides of each piece to be joined together and place your forefinger between the two pieces. Fasten the sewing yarn to one side of the pieces to be joined, then pass the needle through the edge stitch on the underside piece directly across from the corresponding stitch on the upper side piece and draw the yarn through. Turn the needle and work back through the next stitch on the upper side piece again drawing the yarn through. Continue in this way until the seam is completed.

Slip stitch seam
This is used for turning hems and facings to the wrong side of the work. Turn the hem or facing so that the wrong side of the main fabric is toward you. Fasten the sewing yarn at a seam, then insert the needle and lightly pick up one stitch from the main fabric and draw the yarn through. Move along to the left the width of one stitch, insert the needle into the edge stitch of the hem or facing and pick up one stitch, then draw the yarn through. Move along to the left the width of one stitch and continue in this way until the seam is completed.

MORE ABOUT FINISHING

More about finishing! As we have already explained in the previous chapter, the care and attention to detail required in finishing are as essential as in knitting the pieces themselves. The correct seaming method, the correct handling and blocking of yarns, the correct method of finishing hems, applying pockets, completing edgings – all these techniques mean the difference between a handmade garment and a couture design. Here are more tricks of the trade which will enable you to give all your garments the finish and flair of a ready-to-wear design.

Sewn on bands
Where bands are worked separately and are not incorporated into the working instructions for the main sections, such as button and buttonhole bands, use a flat seam to apply the bands. Each band should be slightly less than the finished length of the main fabric and should be slightly stretched and pinned into position before seaming.

Sewn on pockets
Use a slip stitch seam to apply the pocket, taking care to keep the line of the pocket and main fabric straight. A useful tip is to use a fine knitting needle, pointed at both ends, to pick up every alternate stitch along the line of the main fabric, then catch one stitch from the edge of the pocket and one stitch from the needle alternately. Make sure that the lower edge of the pocket lies in a straight line across a row of the main fabric.

Applying the pocket

Shoulder seams
Use a firm back stitch seam, taking the stitches across the steps of shaping in a straight line. On heavy outer garments, such as sports jackets, or any garment where extra strength is needed, reinforce these seams with ribbon or tape.

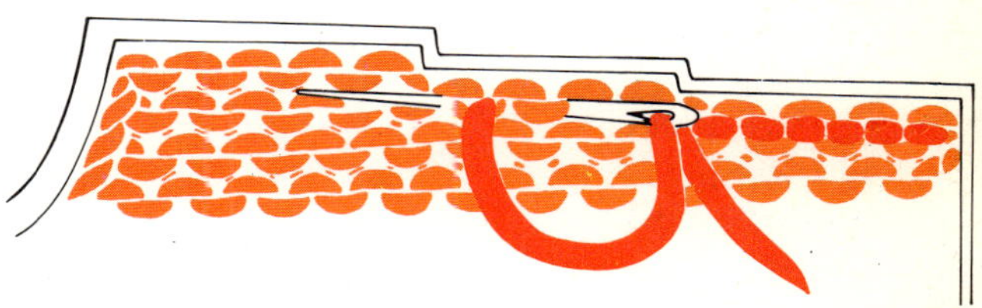

Set-in sleeves
Mark the center top of the sleeve cap and pin this to the shoulder seam, then pin the bound off underarm stitches to the underarm stitches of the body. Use a back stitch seam, working in a smooth line around the curve of the armhole and taking care not to pull the stitches too tightly.

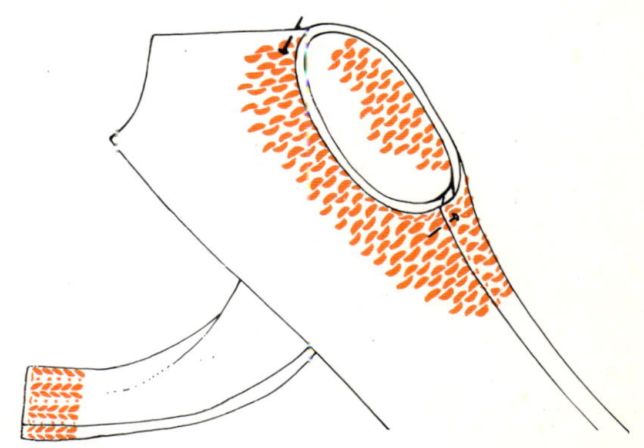

Side and sleeve seams
Use a back stitch seam and join in one piece, working extra stitches across the underarm seam to secure it firmly.

Sewing in a zipper
Pin the zipper into the desired opening, taking care not to stretch the knitting. With the right side of the work facing, sew in the zipper using a back stitch seam and keeping as close to the edge of the knitting as possible. On something like a back neck opening or skirt side seam, work in a straight line down the zipper from top to bottom, then work extra stitches across the end of the zipper to secure it and continue up the other side of the zipper.
When inserting an open-ended zipper, keep the fastener closed and insert it as for an opening from top to lower edge, anchoring it securely at the end. Break off the yarn and work along the other side in the same way. This insures that both sides match and that one side is not pulled out of shape, making it difficult to operate the zipper smoothly.

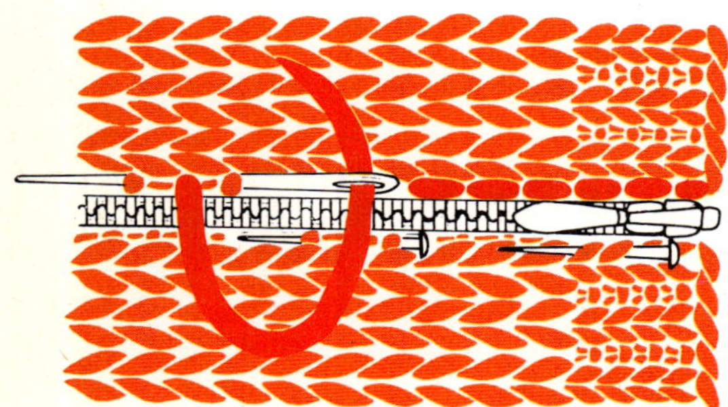

Picking up stitches
You will frequently have to pick up and knit stitches, such as around a neckline or along a front edge or pocket top as a means of finishing an edge. This is usually worked with the right side of the garment facing you. The instructions will always state clearly where stitches are required to be picked up with the wrong side facing you, such as would be needed for a stockinette stitch collar, where the turned down collar fabric must match the main fabric. You can either pick up these stitches directly onto a knitting needle, or use a crochet hook to pick up the stitches and then transfer them to a knitting needle.

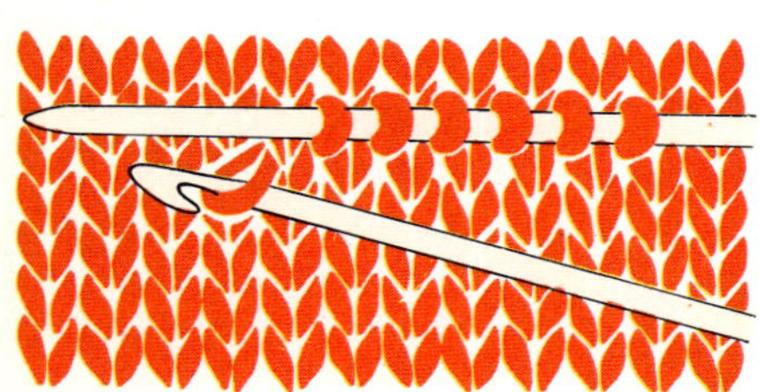

Picking up stitches across the line of main fabric

Picking up stitches across the line of main fabric: Have the right side of the fabric facing you and hold the yarn at the back of the work. Use a crochet hook and put this through the work from the right side to the wrong side and pick up a loop of yarn from the back. Bring this loop through to the right side and transfer the stitch to a knitting needle. Continue in this way until the required number of stitches have been picked up.
Picking up stitches around a curved edge: This could apply to a neckband or armhole band. Place the yarn at the back of the work, with the right side of the fabric facing you. Put a knitting needle through from the front to the back of the fabric and pick up a loop of yarn. Bring this loop through to the right side of the work and leave the stitch on the needle. If a crochet hook is used, pick up the loop in the same way with the hook, then transfer the stitch to a knitting needle. Continue in this way until the required number of stitches have been picked up.
An easy way to insure that stitches are picked up evenly is to mark the main section of fabric with pins at regular intervals of about 2in and pick up the same number of stitches between each pin. As a guide, make sure that, where you are picking up stitches across stitches, you pick up one loop for each stitch; and across rows, approximately one stitch for every two rows.

Picking up front bands: Count the number of rows on the main fabric, then check this against the number of stitches to be picked up and make sure that you knit them up evenly. Mark sections as for picking up stitches around a curved edge and pick up the same number of stitches between each pin. Unless otherwise stated in the instructions, always work the button band first so that you can mark the exact position for each button and then work the appropriate buttonhole on the buttonhole band as these markers are reached.

CARE FOR KNITWEAR

The correct after-care of all knitted garments is extremely important if they are to retain their original texture and shape. Many of the yarns available today are machine-washable and the label will clearly indicate where this is applicable. If you are in any doubt at all, however, always hand wash rather than risk ruining the garment. Similarly, check the label to see whether the yarn can be dry cleaned.

Care in washing

Whether you are machine washing or hand washing a garment, it is essential that the minimum amount of handling occurs when the fabric is wet. Before washing, turn the garment inside out. Never lift the garment by the shoulders, thus allowing the weight of the water to pull the design out of shape. Squeeze out any excess moisture very gently but never wring the garment. Always support the whole weight with both hands.

Always rinse two or three times, making sure that all soap or detergent deposits have been thoroughly removed, using a fabric conditioner if desired. Once the garment has been rinsed, gently lift it onto a draining board, again supporting the weight while you prepare a drying area.

Care in drying

Very few yarns react well to contact with direct heat or sunlight and the garment should always be allowed to dry out naturally. You also run the risk of pulling the whole garment out of shape if you pin it to a line while it is still wet, however carefully. The best possible way of drying any garment, whatever the composition of the yarn used, is on a flat surface – a kitchen table top is ideal.

First place 3 or 4 old newspapers over the surface which is to be used for drying. Spread them out well beyond the full extent of the garment. Cover the newspapers completely with one or two clean towels which are color-fast – a white garment placed on a red towel which is not completely color-fast could result in some unsightly pink patches!

Gently place the garment on the center of the towel. Spread it into its original size and shape and gently pat it flat on the towel, smoothing out any creases formed during washing.

Leave the garment until all the excess moisture has been absorbed by the towels and newspapers. Then – and only then – can it be carefully lifted and placed on a clothes line for a final airing, pinning the garment at the underarms only. Knitted garments should never be hung from the shoulders.

Care in blocking

If the garment has been smoothed out well and allowed to dry in place it should not need blocking. If it does need it, however, check the instructions given on the label, then refer to earlier chapter on handling details.

Care in wear

However careful you are, a garment may become snagged or the yarn may 'pill' into little balls of fluff. It is a simple matter to remedy these faults before the damage has gone too far.

To prevent the risk of snagging, do not put on a garment while you are wearing any jewelry which could catch the yarn and pull a thread. Should you discover a snag in a garment, however, never cut it off or you will risk having the fabric unravel. Using a blunt ended sewing needle, push the snagged end of yarn through to the wrong side of the fabric and gently tighten the yarn until the stitch is the correct size, then knot the end of yarn and leave it on the wrong side.

Where pilling occurs in the yarn, gently pull these

little balls of fluff off, taking care not to snag the yarn. If the pilling is excessive, the fabric should be gently brushed over with a clothes brush to remove the fluff.

Make do and mend

Hand knitting need never be wasted, even if the original garment has outgrown its use. Open the seams of the garment, taking great care not to cut the fabric, and unravel each section, winding the yarn into hanks by passing it around the backs of two chairs. To remove any crinkles from the yarn, either hand wash each hank and hang out to dry, or hold it taut in front of the spout of a gently steaming kettle, moving it back and forth through the steam until the kinks have disappeared. Some spots may wear thin with use, particularly on knitted children's garments. These can easily be reinforced by means of Swiss darning. It doesn't matter if you cannot match the original yarn – a contrasting color darned into a motif will give an interesting new lease of life to the design.

Elbows which are worn through can easily be covered with a patch of leather or suede applied to the right side of the fabric. To disguise the fact that these are patches and add new interest to the garment, make leather patch pockets to match.

KNITTING IN ROUNDS

BASIC TECHNIQUES

Knitting in rounds, as opposed to knitting in rows to produce flat knitting, literally means producing a seamless, tubular piece of fabric. This method may be worked on sets of needles, usually 4, which are pointed at both ends and manufactured in varying lengths and the length of needle used will be determined by

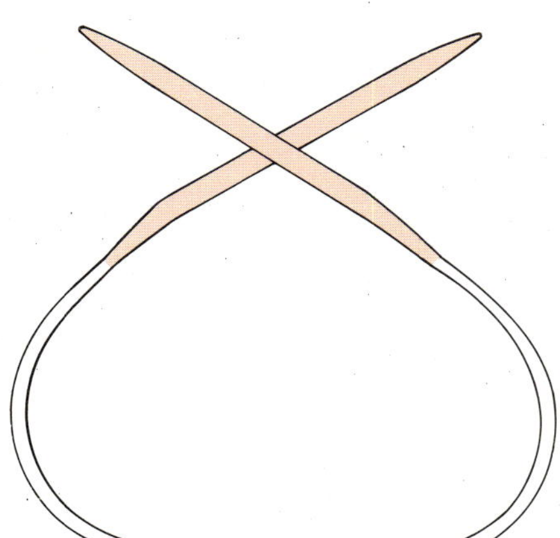

the total number of stitches required.
Circular needles are also available. They are made of two rigid, shaped needle sections pointed at one end, with the other end of each section being joined into one continuous length by a light-weight, flexible strip of nylon. Before using circular needles the twist which the nylon strip may develop through packing may be removed by immersing it in fairly warm water and then drawing it between the fingers until it lies in a gradual curve. These are also manufactured in varying lengths – 16, 24, 29 and 36 inches long. The more stitches you have the longer circular needle you will require. The advantage of circular needles over sets of needles is that they may also be used as an ordinary pair of needles for working in rows.
As knitting in rounds dispenses with seaming, it is the

GAUGE Stitches to 1 inch	LENGTHS OF CIRCULAR NEEDLES AVAILABLE AND MINIMUM NUMBER OF STITCHES REQUIRED						
	16″	20″	24″	27″	30″	36″	42″
5	80	100	120	135	150	180	210
5½	88	110	132	148	165	198	230
6	96	120	144	162	180	216	250
6½	104	130	156	175	195	234	270
7	112	140	168	189	210	252	294
7½	120	150	180	202	225	270	315
8	128	160	192	216	240	288	336
8½	136	170	204	220	255	306	357
9	144	180	216	243	270	324	378

ideal way of making socks and stockings, gloves and mittens hats, skirts and even sweaters. The minimum of seaming on a sweater is possible simply by working the body in one piece to a point where the work can be divided and then continuing in rows.

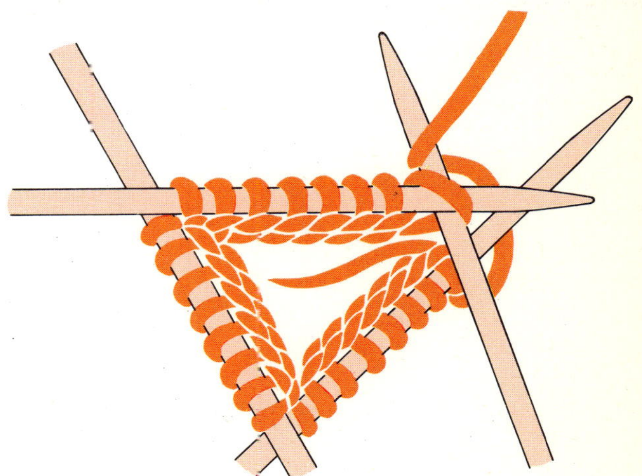

Casting on
Details of casting on with more than two needles have already been given earlier. The total number of stitches required can either be cast on to one needle and then divided between three of the needles, leaving the fourth needle to knit with, or can be cast on to each of the three needles separately.
When casting on with a circular needle, simply use each shaped section as a pair of needles, having one section in the left hand and one in the right.
Whether using sets of needles or a circular needle, the important point to remember is that the cast on stitches must not become twisted before you join them into a round.

Knitting in rounds
Once you have cast on the required number of stitches using sets of needles, form them into a circle by putting the spare needle into the first stitch on the left hand needle and knit this stitch in the usual way. Continue to knit all the stitches on the first needle. Once this is free, use it to knit the stitches on the second needle, then use the second needle to knit the stitches on the third needle. Always pull the yarn tightly across to the first stitch of each needle to avoid a loose stitch.
With a circular needle, simply continue knitting each stitch until you come to the beginning of the round again.

As it is easy to lose track of where each round of knitting begins, mark the beginning of the round with a knotted loop of contrast yarn on the needle before the first stitch of every round and slip this loop from the left hand needle to the right hand needle without knitting it.

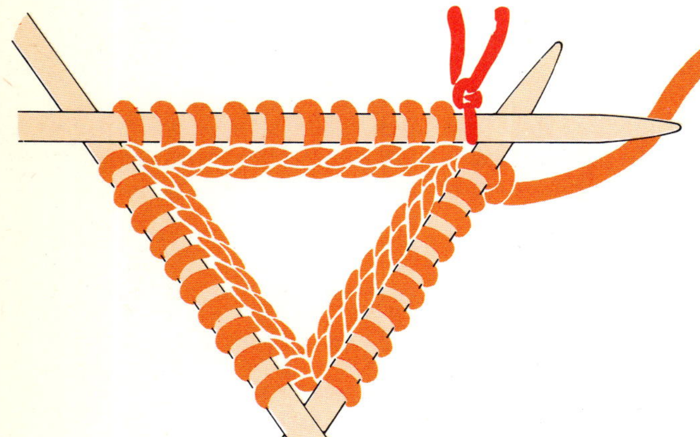

Stockinette stitch in rounds
Since the right side of the fabric is always facing the knitter and the work is not turned at the end of each row as in flat knitting, stockinette stitch (st st) in rounds is produced by knitting every round. This has a great advantage when working complicated, multi-colored patterns.

Garter stitch in rounds
Because the work is not turned, to produce garter stitch in rounds the first round must be knitted and the second round purled, in order to form the ridged effect.

Ribbing in rounds
Here again, the right side of the fabric is facing so each knit stitch must be knitted on every round and each purl stitch purled on every round. When working in rounds of ribbing, remember that if you begin a round with one or more knitted stitches, you must end with one or more purled stitches to complete the round exactly.

Socks without heel shaping
This practical way of producing socks without heel shaping must be worked on sets of needles.

Size
Round top of sock, 8in
Length to toe, 23in, adjustable

Gauge
32 sts and 36 rows to 4in in patt worked on No.1 needles

Materials
5 × 1oz balls of Bucilla 3-ply Fingering Yarn
Set of 4 No.1 double pointed needles

Socks
Using set of 4 No.1 needles cast on 80 sts, 26 each on 1st and 2nd needles and 28 on 3rd needle. Mark beginning of round with colored thread.
1st round *K1, P1, rep from * to end.
Rep 1st round for single ribbing until work measures 4in from beg. Commence patt.
1st patt round *K3, P2, rep from * to end.
Rep 1st patt round 3 times more.
5th patt round P1, *K3, P2, rep from * to last 4 sts, K3, P1.
Rep 5th patt round 3 times more.
9th patt round *P2, K3, rep from * to end.
Rep 9th patt round 3 times more.
13th patt round K1, *P2, K3, rep from * to last 4 sts, P2, K2.
Rep 13th patt round 3 times more.
17th patt round K2, *P2, K3, rep from * to last 3 sts, P2, K1.
Rep 17th patt round 3 times more. These 20 rounds form patt. Cont in patt until piece measures $20\frac{1}{2}$in from beg, or desired length less $2\frac{1}{2}$in. Cont in st st, K each round.
Shape toe
1st round *K8 sts, K2 tog, rep from * to end.
Work 2 rounds st st without shaping.
4th round *K7 sts, K2 tog, rep from * to end.
Work 2 rounds st st without shaping.
7th round *K6 sts, K2 tog, rep from * to end.
Work 2 rounds st st without shaping.
10th round *K5 sts, K2 tog, rep from * to end.
Work 2 rounds st st without shaping.
13th round *K4 sts, K2 tog, rep from * to end.
Work 2 rounds st st without shaping.
16th round *K3 sts, K2 tog, rep from * to end.
Work 2 rounds st st without shaping.
19th round *K2 sts, K2 tog, rep from * to end.
Work 2 rounds st st without shaping.
22nd round *K1 st, K2 tog, rep from * to end.
23rd round *K2 tog, rep from * to end.
Break off yarn, thread through rem sts, draw up and fasten off securely.

DOUBLE FABRICS

A double stockinette stitch fabric can quite easily be produced by working in rounds and using this tube of material as a double sided fabric. Alternatively, double fabric can also be worked in rows on two needles by the simple means of a slipped stitch. This method is most effective when two different yarns, giving the same gauge, are used for each side of the material. The ideas shown here will enable you to practice both these methods to make a warm scarf or a glamorous evening hood.

Scarf

We have made our scarf in stockinette stitch, knitting every round, in wide stripes. You can just as easily work narrow stripes in more than two colors or a simple, all-over patterned stitch in one color, provided you check the multiple of stitches required for the pattern and change the number of stitches and cast on accordingly. The total quantity of yarn given will be a guide to the amount required, but remember that a scarf knitted in a patterned stitch may need more yarn.

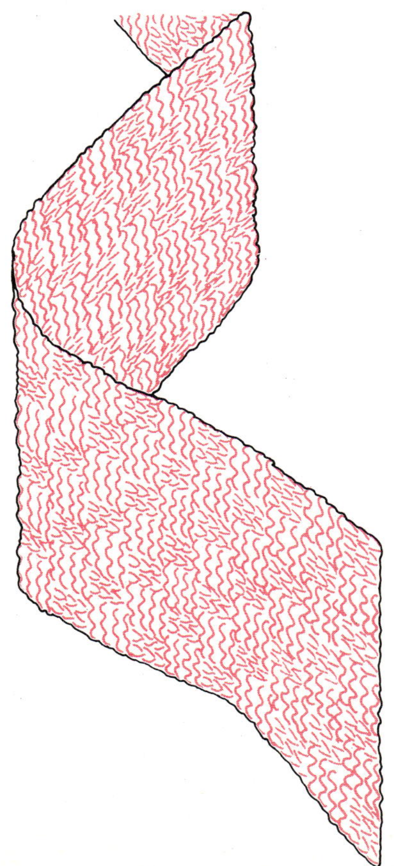

Scarf knitted in all-over patterned stitch.

Size

9in wide by 60in long

Gauge

22 sts and 28 rows to 4in in stockinette stitch (st st) worked on No.5 needles.

Materials

4 × 50 grm balls of Reynolds Classique in main color, A
4 balls of same in contrast color, B
Set of 4 No.5 double-pointed needles *or*
One No.5 circular knitting needle

Scarf

Using set of 4 No.5 needles or No.5 circular needle and A, cast on 100 sts. Work in rounds of st st, every round K, until piece measures 4in from beg. Break off A and join in B. Work a further 4in st st. Cont working stripes in this manner until piece measures 60in from beg. Bind off.

Finishing

Block under a damp cloth with a warm iron. Cut rem yarn into 12in lengths and knot fringe along each short end knotting the strands through double fabric and using A and B alternately. Trim ends.

Evening hood

We have used a glitter yarn and mohair to make this double sided hood for evening. Using a plain yarn and repeating the first pattern row only, a snug, daytime version can quite easily be made. The total quantity of yarn given will be a guide to the amount required, but make sure that you are getting the exact gauge.

Size
11in wide by 56in long

Gauge
16 sts and 28 rows to 4in in double fabric worked on No.5 needles

Materials
4 × 40 grm balls Reynolds Mohair No. 1 in main color, A
6 × 20 grm balls Reynolds Feu d'Artifice in contrast color, B
One pair No.5 double pointed needles
One pair No.3 needles

Evening hood
Using No.3 needles and A, cast on 88 sts. Change to No.5 needles.
1sr row (RS) Using A, *K1, yarn in front (yfwd), sl 1 as if to purl (P-wise), yarn in back (ybk), rep from * to end. Join in B.
(**Note:** When using one color, turn and rep this row throughout.)

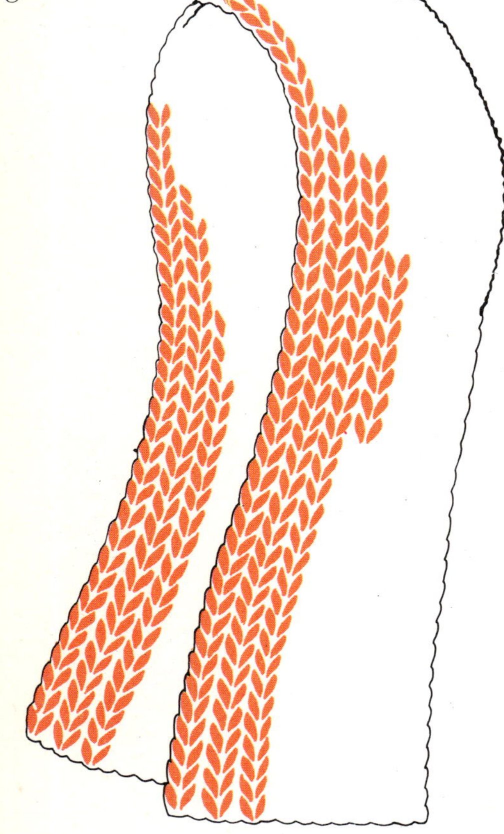

Hood worked in same yarn and color throughout

2nd row Do not turn work but return to beg of row. Using B, *sl 1 P-wise, yfwd, P1, ybk, rep from * to end. 44 sts each in A and B.
3rd row Turn work and cross A and B to close side edge, using B, *K1, yfwd, sl 1 P-wise, ybk, rep from * to end.
4th row Do not turn work but return to beg of row, using A, *sl 1 P-wise, yfwd, P1, ybk, rep from * to end. Turn and cross A and B to close side edge.
These 4 rows form the patt. Cont in patt until work measures 24in from beg, ending with a 2nd or 4th patt row.
Shape top
Next row Dec one st at beg of row in A and B by using both strands tog and (K2 tog) twice, patt to end.
Next 3 rows Patt to end.
Rep last 4 rows 13 times more. 30 sts each in A and B.
Next row Using A and B tog, (inc in next st) twice, patt to end.
Next 3 rows Patt to end.
Rep last 4 rows 13 times more. 44 sts each in A and B.
Cont in patt without shaping until work measures 24in from last inc row. Bind off K2 tog across row.

Finishing
Do not block. Join back shaping seam and 6in of straight edges.

GLOVES AND MITTENS

When knitting in rounds to produce gloves, mittens, socks and stockings, the most difficult part to master is the shaping required to give a perfect fit to fingers and thumbs or heels and toes.

At a given point in the pattern some of the stitches will be left unworked and held in abeyance on a stitch holder, while the first section is completed. Then the unworked stitches will be picked up, together with additional stitches in some instances, to complete the work correctly.

All these shaping details should be given out in full in any pattern, and in the sequence in which they are to be worked. This chapter deals with gloves and mittens, which can be worked entirely in rounds without seaming, and includes a pair of mittens for a baby – ideal for a first attempt.

Both the designs given here begin at the wrist, where a firm ribbed edge is needed to give a snug fit, and stockinette stitch has been used for the main sections. They can both be made in one color only but, as a way of using up small amounts of the same quality yarn, we have worked the wrist and thumb of the mittens in a contrasting color, and the wrist, thumb, and each finger of the gloves in a different color, for a fun effect.

Babies' mittens

Size

To fit 9/18 months

Gauge

28 sts and 36 rows to 4in in stockinette stitch (st st) worked on No.3 needles

Materials

1 × 1oz ball of 3 ply yarn in main color, A
Small amount of contrast color, B
Set of 4 No.3 double-pointed needles
Set of 4 No.1 double-pointed needles

Mittens

Using set of 4 No.1 needles and B, cast on 36 sts, 12 on each of 3 needles. Mark beg of round with colored thread.

1st round *K1, P1, rep from * to end.

Rep this round until work measures 1in from beg. Break off B. Join in A. Change to set of 4 No.3 needles. Beg with a K round and work in rounds of st st until work measures $1\frac{1}{2}$in from beg.

Shape thumb

Next round K17, pick up loop lying between sts and K tbl – called inc 1 –, K2, inc 1, K17.

Next round K to end.

Next round K17, inc 1, K4, inc 1, K17. 40 sts.

Next round K to end.

Cont inc in this way on next and every alt round until there are 46 sts.

Divide for thumb

Next round K18, sl next 10 sts on to holder and leave for thumb, turn and cast on 2 sts, turn and K18. 38 sts.

Cont in rounds of st st until work measures $4\frac{1}{4}$in from beg.

Shape top

Next round K1, sl 1, K1, psso, K13, K2 tog, K2, sl 1, K1, psso, K13, K2 tog, K1. 34 sts.

Next round K to end.

Next round K1, sl 1, K1, psso, K11, K2 tog, K2, sl 1, K1, psso, K11, K2 tog, K1. 30 sts.

Cont dec 4 sts in this way on every alt round until 14 sts rem. Arrange sts on 2 needles and bind off tog or weave them.

Thumb

Using set of 4 No.3 needles, B and with RS of work facing, arrange 10 thumb sts on 3 needles, then K 2 sts from base of cast on sts. 12 sts.

Cont in rounds of st st until thumb measures $\frac{3}{4}$in from beg.

Shape top

Next round *K2 tog, rep from * to end. 6 sts. Rep last round once more.

Break off yarn, thread through rem sts, draw up and fasten off.

Children's gloves

Size
To fit $6\frac{1}{4}$in around hand

Gauge
30 sts and 38 rows to 4in in stockinette stitch (st st) worked on No.2 needles.

Materials
1× 1oz ball of 3 ply yarn in main color, A
1 ball each, or small amounts of contrast colors, B, C, D, E and F
Set of 4 No.2 double-pointed needles
Set of 4 No.1 double-pointed needles

Gloves
Using set of 4 No.1 needles and B, cast on 48 sts and divide on 3 needles.
Mark beg of round with colored thread. Work $2\frac{1}{2}$in rib as for mittens.
Break off B. Join in A. Change to set of 4 No.2 needles.
Work 4 rounds st st.
Shape thumb
Next round K23, inc 1 as for mittens, K2, inc 1, K23.
Work 3 rounds st st without shaping.
Next round K23, inc 1, K4, inc 1, K23.
Cont inc in this way on every foll 4th round until there are 60 sts, ending with 3 rounds st st after last inc round.

Divide for thumb
Next round K24, sl next 12 sts on to holder and leave for thumb, turn and cast on 2 sts, turn and K24. 50 sts.
Cont in st st until work measures 6in from beg.

First finger
Next round Sl first 18 sts of round on to holder, join C to next st and K14, turn and cast on 2 sts, leave rem 18 sts on 2nd holder.
Cont in st st on these 16 sts until finger measures $2\frac{1}{4}$in from beg.
Shape top
Next round K1, *K2 tog, K1, rep from * to end. 11 sts.
Next round K to end.
Next round K1, *K2 tog, rep from * to end. 6 sts.
Break off yarn, thread through rem sts, draw up and fasten off.

Second finger
Next round Using D and with RS of work facing, leave first 11 sts on holder and K across last 7 sts on first holder, pick up and K 2 sts from base of first finger, K across next 7 sts on 2nd holder, turn and cast on 2 sts. 18 sts.
Cont in st st until finger measures $2\frac{1}{2}$in from beg.
Shape top
Next round *K1, K2 tog, rep from * to end. 12 sts.
Next round K to end.
Next round *K2 tog, rep from * to end. Complete as for first finger.

Third finger
Next round Using E and with RS of work facing, leave first 6 sts on holder and K across last 5 sts on first holder, pick up and K 2 sts from base of 2nd finger, K across next 5 sts on 2nd holder, turn and cast on 2 sts. 14 sts.
Cont in st st until finger measures $2\frac{1}{4}$in from beg.
Shape top
Next round K1, *K2 tog, K1, rep from * to last st, K1. 10 sts.
Complete as for 2nd finger.

Fourth finger
Next round Using F and with RS of work facing, K across rem 6 sts on first holder, pick up and K 2 sts from base of 3rd finger, K across rem 6 sts on 2nd holder. 14 sts.
Cont in st st until finger measures 2in from beg.
Shape top
Work as for 3rd finger.

Thumb
Next round Using B and with RS of work facing, K across 12 thumb sts, then pick up and K 4 sts from base of cast on sts. 16 sts.
Cont in st st until thumb measures $1\frac{3}{4}$in from beg.
Shape top
Work as for first finger.

SOCKS AND STOCKINGS

The previous chapter dealt with knitting in rounds to produce gloves and mittens, where the complete design can be worked without seaming. This chapter shows how simple it is to make socks and stockings, where the leg and foot can be worked in rounds and the stitches are divided at the heel and worked in rows, to produce the heel gusset shaping.

A plain basic sock design can be adapted in a variety of ways, either by using stripes for the leg and instep, keeping the top, heel and sole in a plain color, or by introducing a patterned stitch for the leg and instep but, in this event, making sure that the pattern chosen will divide evenly into the total number of stitches cast on. Alternatively, men's socks look most effective when a small, two-color motif is used as a clock on either side of the leg.

Here we give instructions for a pair of durable socks for children and a fashion accessory for women – a pair of beautiful, lacy stockings.

Socks

Sizes

To fit 7in foot

Length of leg from top of heel, 8in

Gauge

32 sts and 40 rows to 4in in stockinette stitch (st st) worked on No.1 needles

Materials

3 × 1oz balls of Brunswick Fore 'n Aft Sport Yarn

Set of 4 No.1 double-pointed needles

Socks

Using set of 4 No.1 needles cast on 56 sts and arrange on 3 needles. Mark end of round.

1st round *K1, P1, rep from * to end.

Rep this round until work measures $1\frac{1}{2}$in from beg. Beg with a K round cont in rounds of st st until work measures 3in from beg.

Shape leg

Next round K1, sl 1, K1, psso, K to last 3 sts, K2 tog, K1. Work 4 rounds st st without shaping. Rep last 5 rounds until 42 sts rem. Cont without shaping until work measures 8in from beg. Break off yarn.

Divide for heel

Next row Sl first and last 11 sts of round on to one needle, rejoin yarn and P to end. 22 sts.

Beg with a K row work 16 rows st st, ending with a P row.

Turn heel

Next row K14 sts, sl 1, K1, psso, turn.

Next row P7 sts, P2 tog, turn.

Next row K7 sts, sl 1, K1, psso, turn.

Next row P7 sts, P2 tog, turn.

Rep last 2 rows until all sts are on one needle.

Next round K4 sts, using 2nd needle K rem 4 heel sts, K 10 sts down side of heel, using 3rd needle K across 20 sts of instep, using 4th needle K 10 sts up other side of heel then complete heel by knitting the first 4 sts on to this needle.

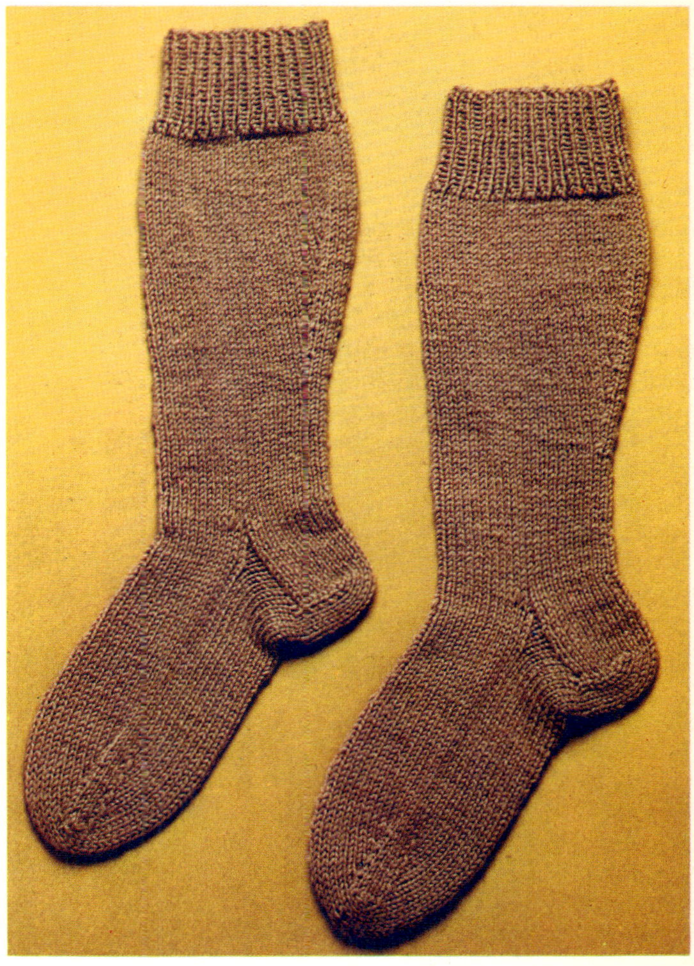

Shape instep

1st round K to end.

2nd round 1st needle K to last 3 sts, K2 tog, K1; 2nd needle K to end; 3rd needle K1, sl 1, K1, psso, K to end. Rep last 2 rounds until 42 sts rem. Cont without shaping until work measures 4in from where sts were picked up at heel.

Shape toe

1st round 1st needle K to last 3 sts, K2 tog, K1, 2nd needle K1, sl 1, K1, psso, K to last 3 sts, K2 tog, K1; 3rd needle K1, sl 1, K1, psso, K to end.

Work 2 rounds st st without shaping. Rep last 3 rounds until 22 sts rem, then K across sts on 1st needle. Bind off sts tog or weave sts.

Lacy stockings

Sizes

Directions are to fit $8\frac{1}{2}$in foot. Changes for $9\frac{1}{2}$in foot are in brackets [].

Leg length to toe of heel 28in adjustable.

Gauge

28 sts and 30 rows to 4in over patt worked on No.11 needles.

Materials

3 × 1oz balls Reynolds Gleneagles Fingering Yarn
Set of 4 No.8 double-pointed needles
Set of 4 No.6 double-pointed needles
Set of 4 No.4 double-pointed needles
Set of 4 No.3 double-pointed needles

Stockings

Using set of 4 No.8 needles cast on 68 sts very loosely and arrange on 3 needles. Mark beg of round with colored thread. Work 8 rounds K1, P1, rib. Start patt.

1st round *(K2 tog) 3 times, yfwd, (K1, yfwd) 5 times, (K2 tog tbl) 3 times, rep from * to end.

2nd and 3rd rounds K to end.

4th round P to end.

These four rounds form patt being sure that sts are divided on needles as necessary. Rep 4 patt rounds 17 times more, adjusting length at this point and noting that work will stretch to 32in. Change to set of 4 No.6 needles and rep patt rounds 16 times. Change to set of 4 No.4 needles and rep patt rounds 16 times. Change to set of 4 No.3 needles and rep patt rounds 8 times.

Shape heel

Next round K15, K into front and back of next st – called inc 1 –, K1, patt 34 sts, inc 1, K16.

Next round K18, patt 34, K18.

Next round K16, inc 1, K1, patt 34, inc 1, K17.

Next round K19, patt 34, K19.

Keeping heel sts in st st and center 34 sts in patt, cont to inc in this way on next and every alt round until there are 80 sts, then work 4 rounds without shaping.

Next round Still keeping center 34 sts in patt, K21, K2 tog, patt 34, sl 1, K1, psso, K21.

Next round K22, patt 34, K22.

Next round K20, K2 tog, patt 34, sl 1, K1, psso, K20.

Next round K21, patt 34, K21.

Cont dec in this way on next and every alt round until 56 sts rem, then cont without shaping until foot measures 7[8]in from center of heel, or desired length less $1\frac{1}{2}$in.

Shape toe

Next round K12, K2 tog, sl 1, K1, psso, K24, K2 tog, sl 1, K1, psso, K12.

Next round K to end.

Next round K11, K2 tog, sl 1, K1, psso, K22, K2 tog, sl 1, K1, psso, K11.

Next round K to end.

Cont dec in this way on next and every alt round until 20 sts rem. K sts from 3rd needle on to 1st needle and weave sts.

MOTIFS IN ROUNDS

We have already explained how knitting in rounds produces seamless, tubular fabric. This section deals with knitt ng in rounds using fine cotton yarn to form flat, circular motif shapes with a variety of uses.

Simple hexagonal motif
Using set of 4 double-pointed needles cast on 6 sts, having 2 sts on each of 3 needles. Join needles into a round and K all sts through back loop (tbl) to keep center flat Start patt.

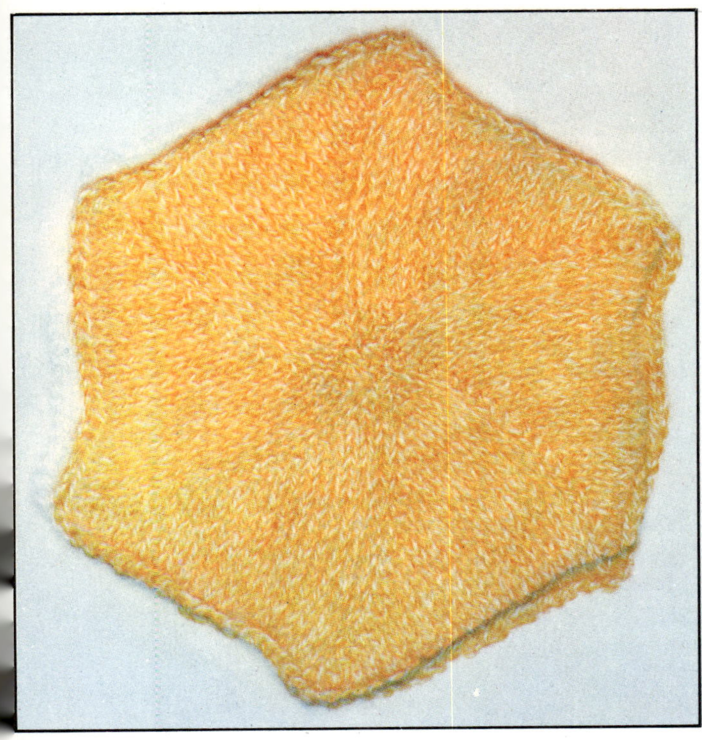

1st round *K into front then into back of next st – called inc 1–, rep from * to end. 12 sts.
2nd round *Inc 1, K1, rep from * to end. 18 sts.
3rd round *Inc 1, K2, rep from * to end. 24 sts.
4th round *Inc 1, K3, rep from * to end. 30 sts.
5th round *Inc 1, K4, rep from * to end. 36 sts.
6th round *Inc 1, K5, rep from * to end. 42 sts.
Cont inc 6 sts in this way on every round until motif is desired size. Bind off loosely.

To make a throw pillow cover
Size
16in diameter

Gauge
24 sts and 32 rows to 4in in stockinette stitch (st st) worked on No.5 needles

Materials
1× 50grm ball each of Reynolds Classique in 4 contrast colors, A, B, C and D
Set of 4 No.5 double-pointed needles
One No.5 circular needle
16in diameter circular cushion form
Buttons (optional)

Cover
Work as for hexagonal motif, working 2 rounds each in A, B, C and D throughout and changing to circular needle when required, until work measures 16in diameter. Bind off loosely. Make another hexagonal motif in same way.

Finishing
Block each piece under a damp cloth with a warm iron. With RS facing, join motifs tog leaving an opening to insert pillow form. Turn RS out. Insert form and complete seam. Sew one button to center of each side, if desired.

To make a circular lace table mat
Size
10in in diameter

Materials
1× 300yd ball Clark's Big Ball Mercerized Crochet Cotton No.20
Set of 4 No.1 double-pointed needles

Table mat
Using set of 4 No.1 needles cast on 8 sts, having 2 sts on 1st needle and 3 sts each on 2nd and 3rd needles. Join needles into a round and K all sts tbl to keep center flat. Commence patt.
1st round *Yfwd, K1, rep from * to end. 16 sts.
2nd and every alt round K to end.
3rd round *Yfwd, K2, rep from * to end. 24 sts.
5th round *Yfwd, K3, rep from * to end. 32 sts.
7th round *Yfwd, K4, rep from * to end. 40 sts.
9th round *Yfwd, K5, rep from * to end. 48 sts.
11th round *Yfwd, K6, rep from * to end. 56 sts.
13th round *Yfwd, K1, K2 tog, yarn round needle twice – called y2rn –, K2 tog, K2, rep from * to end.
Note that on next and subsequent rounds where y2rn has been worked on previous round, you must K1 then P1 into the new stitches.
15th round *Yfwd, K8, rep from * to end.
17th round *Yfwd, K9, rep from * to end.
19th round *Yfwd, K1, K2 tog, y2rn, (K2 tog) twice, y2rn, K2 tog, K1, rep from * to end.

21st round *Yfwd, K11, rep from * to end.
23rd round *Yfwd, K12, rep from * to end.
25th round *Yfwd, K5, K2 tog, y2rn, K2 tog, K4, rep from * to end.
27th round *Yfwd, K4, K2 tog, y2rn, (K2 tog) twice, y2rn, K2 tog, K2, rep from * to end.
29th round *Yfwd, K7, K2 tog, y2rn, K2 tog, K4, rep from * to end.
31st round *Yfwd, K1, yfwd, K2 tog, K3, K2 tog, y2rn, (K2 tog) twice, y2rn, K2 tog, K2, rep from * to end.
33rd round *Yfwd, K1, K2 tog, yfwd, K2 tog, K4, K2 tog, y2rn, K2 tog, K4, rep from * to end.
35th round *Yfwd, K1, yfwd, K2, yfwd, K1, yfwd, K2 tog, K11, rep from * to end.
37th round *Yfwd, K2, yfwd, K1, K2 tog, yfwd, K1, K2 tog, yfwd, K2 tog, K10, rep from * to end.
39th round *Yfwd, K1, yfwd, K2 tog, K1, yfwd, K2 tog, K1, yfwd, K2 tog, yfwd, K1, yfwd, (K2 tog) twice, y2rn, (K2 tog) twice, y2rn, K2 tog, K1, rep from * to end.
41st round *Yfwd, K2 tog, K1, yfwd, K1, K2 tog, yfwd, K2 tog, K1, yfwd, (K2 tog) twice, yfwd, K2 tog, K8, rep from * to end.
43rd round *Yfwd, K1, K2 tog, yfwd, (K2 tog) twice, yfwd, K1, K2 tog, yfwd, K1, K2 tog, yfwd, K2 tog, K7, rep from * to end.
45th round *Yfwd, K1, yfwd, K2 tog, K1, yfwd, K2 tog, K1, yfwd, K2 tog, K1, yfwd, K2 tog, yfwd, K1, yfwd, (K2 tog) twice, y2rn, K2 tog, K2, rep from * to end.
47th round *(Yfwd, K2 tog, K1) 3 times, yfwd, K1, K2 tog, yfwd, K2, yfwd, K2 tog, yfwd, K2 tog, K5, rep from * to end.
49th round *Yfwd, (K2 tog) twice, yfwd, K2 tog, (K1, yfwd, K2 tog) 3 times, K1, yfwd, K2, yfwd, K2 tog, K4, rep from * to end.
51st round *Yfwd, (K2 tog) twice, (yfwd, K2 tog, K1) 5 times, yfwd, K2 tog, K3, rep from * to end.
53rd round *Yfwd, (K2 tog) twice, (yfwd, K2 tog, K1) 5 times, yfwd, K2 tog, K2, rep from * to end.
55th round *Yfwd, K3 tog, K1, (yfwd, K2 tog, K1) 5 times, yfwd, K2 tog, K1, rep from * to end.
57th round *Yfwd, (K2 tog) twice, (yfwd, K2 tog, K1) 5 times, yfwd, K2 tog, rep from * to end.
58th round As 2nd.
Bind off loosely.

Edging
Using 2 No.1 needles cast on 9 sts.
1st row Sl 1, K1, yfwd, K2 tog, K1, yfwd, K2 tog, yfwd, K2.
2nd and every alt row K to end.
3rd row Sl 1, K1, yfwd, K2 tog, K2, yfwd, K2 tog, yfwd, K2.
5th row Sl 1, K1, yfwd, K2 tog, K3, yfwd, K2 tog, yfwd, K2.
7th row Sl 1, K1, yfwd, K2 tog, K1, yfwd, K2 tog, K1, yfwd, K2 tog, yfwd, K2.
9th row Sl 1, K1, yfwd, K2 tog, K2, yfwd, K2 tog, K5.
10th row Bind off 4 sts, K to end.
Rep 1st to 10th rows until edging fits around table mat. Bind off.

Finishing
Block under a damp cloth with a warm iron. Sew cast on edge of edging to bound off edge. Sew around table mat. Block.

More motifs

The same technique which produces flat, circular shapes can be used to form other geometric motifs, such as triangles, squares and octagons. It is simply a matter of working out how many sides you need and spacing the shaping on each side to increase the size of the motif.
Because you are working on 3 needles with numbers of stitches which will not always divide by 3, the number of stitches cast on to each needle will not always be equal. When the number of stitches become too many to hold comfortably on 3 needles, change to a circular needle.
Always mark the beginning of the round with a colored marker and, if you find it easier, cast on the full number of stitches onto one needle and knit each stitch through the back of the loop before dividing them onto 3 needles.

Triangular motif
Using set of 4 needles cast on 6 sts, having 2 sts on each needle.
Join needles into a round and K all sts through back loops (tbl) to keep center flat.

1st round *K into front then into back of next st – called inc 1 –, rep from * to end. 12 sts.
2nd round *Inc 1, K2, inc 1, rep from * to end. 18 sts.
3rd round *Inc 1, K4, inc 1, rep from * to end. 24 sts.
4th round *Inc 1, K6, inc 1, rep from * to end. 30 sts.
5th round *Inc 1, K8, inc 1, rep from * to end. 36 sts.
Cont inc 6 sts in this way on every round until motif is desired size.
Bind off loosely.

Square motif
Using set of 4 needles cast on 8 sts, having 2 sts on 1st needle and 3 sts each on 2nd and 3rd needles. Join needles into a round and K all sts tbl to keep center flat. Commence patt.
1st round *K into front then into back of next st – called inc 1 –, rep from * to end. 16 sts.

2nd and every alt round K to end.
3rd round *Inc 1, K2, inc 1, rep from * to end. 24 sts.
5th round *Inc 1, K4, inc 1, rep from * to end. 32 sts.
7th round *Inc 1, K6, inc 1, rep from * to end. 40 sts.
8th round K to end.
Cont inc 8 sts in this way on next and every alt round until motif is desired size. Bind off loosely.

Octagonal motif
Cast on and work 1st and 2nd rounds as given for square motif.
3rd round As 1st. 32 sts.
4th and 5th rounds K to end.
6th round *Inc 1, K2, inc 1, rep from * to end. 48 sts.
7th and 8th rounds K to end.
9th round *Inc 1, K4, inc 1, rep from * to end. 64 sts.
10th and 11th rounds K to end.

12th round *Inc 1, K6, inc 1, rep from * to end. 80 sts.
13th and 14th rounds K to end.
Cont inc 16 sts in this way on next and every foll 3rd round until motif is desired size. Bind off loosely.

Bath mat
Size
20in wide by 30in long

Gauge
Each octagonal motif measures 5in diameter worked on No.5 needles and using 2 strands of yarn.

Materials
6 × 155yd balls of Lily Sugar 'n Cream Cotton Yarn in main color, A
2 × 155yd balls of contrast color, B
Set of 4 No.5 double-pointed needles

Note
Yarn is used double throughout.

Bath mat
Using set of 4 No.5 needles and A, make 24 octagonal motifs, working 14 rounds only for each one.
Using set of 4 No.5 needles and B, make 15 square motifs, working 8 rounds only for each one.

Finishing
Block each piece under a damp cloth with a warm iron. Join motifs as shown in diagram. When complete, block again.
Another way of using instructions for the bath mat would be to use up left-over pieces of knitting worsted yarn in as many colors as possible to make a cheerful and practical carriage cover.

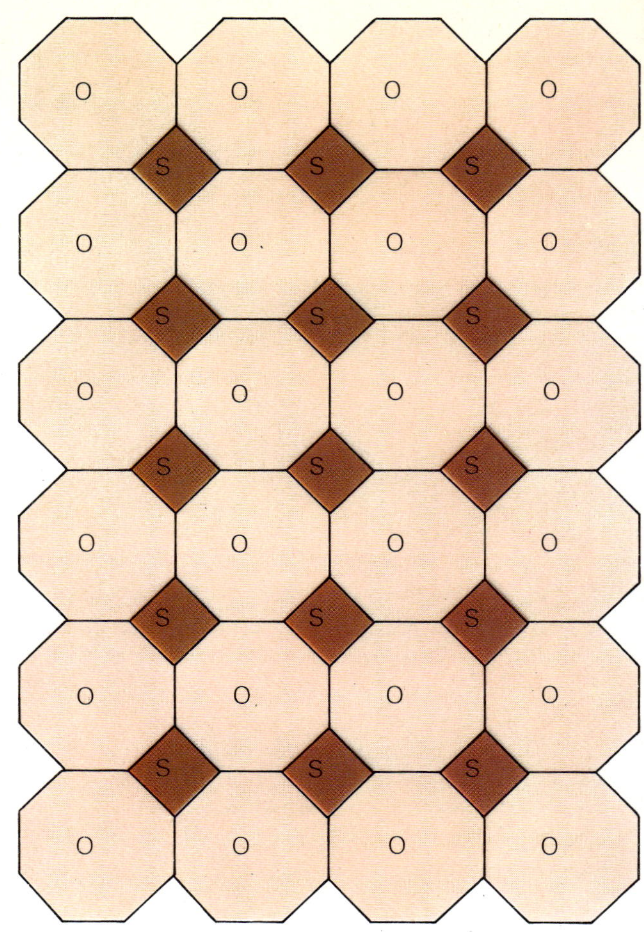

24 octagonal motifs=O
15 square motifs=S

ADJUSTING PATTERNS

Making changes to an existing pattern is quite an easy matter, provided you take the time to work out the correct positioning of your alterations before starting any knitting. A plain cardigan can be given an entirely different look by the addition of picot edgings instead of ribbed edges. Slimming bust darts may be incorporated into a basic pullover to achieve a better fit for the fuller figure. With a little care even the proportions of armholes and shoulders may be altered to suit your own individual requirements. Once you have the know-how, it is a simple matter to apply it and so gain even greater satisfaction from your knitting.

Edges

With knitting, the same basic shape can always be worked in a variety of different stitches (see Bobble stitches). Similarly, an existing pattern for a plain pullover or cardigan does not always need to have ribbed edges. Instead, try a picot edging on the waist, cuffs and neckband of a sweater, or even the front bands of a cardigan. For example, on a straight edge first check the number of stitches for each piece of the original pattern, after the ribbing has been completed. This will be the correct number of stitches to cast on to begin the picot edging. Beginning with a knit row work the desired depth for a turned-under hem, say 1in, ending with a purl row. On the next row make a picot edge by knitting two stitches together, then bring the yarn forward and over the needle to make a stitch and continue in this way to the end of the row, being sure that you end with the correct number of stitches. Beginning with a purl row work one row less than the hemline to complete the edging, then either continue in stockinette stitch or pattern as directed in the instructions, remembering to adjust the total length which will have taken the ribbing into account.

Where picot edges need to be joined at right angles, such as the corner where the hem or neckband meet the front bands on a cardigan, these edges must be mitered to fit correctly. To do this simply increase one stitch at the joining edge on the 2nd and every following row, work the picot row, then decrease one stitch at the same edge on every row for the completion of the edging until the original number of cast on stitches remains.

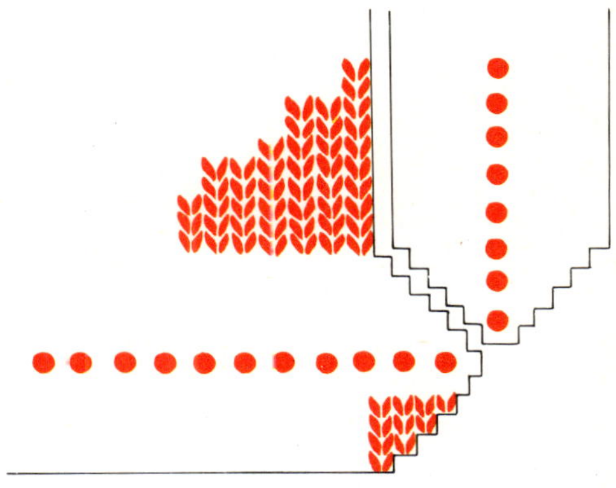

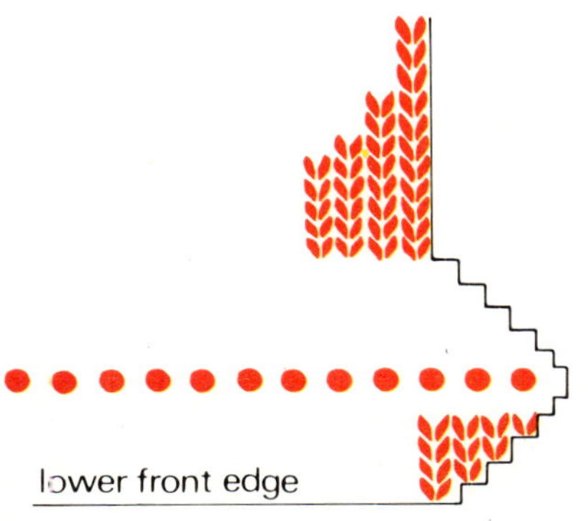

Another alternative is to work turned-under stockinette stitch hems or facing in place of ribbing. To do this on a straight hem, work as for the picot edging but end with a knit row, then instead of working the next row as a picot row, knit each stitch through the back of the loop to form the hemline. From this point you can continue in stockinette stitch or pattern as desired.

To use this method for edges which need to be joined at right angles, you must again miter the corners where the hem or neckband meet the front band.

As an example, say the original number of cast on stitches for the main section is 54 and an additional 8 stitches are needed for the front band, making a total of 62 stitches for the full width. If you are working a turned-under hem of 9 rows and are increasing one stitch at the front edge for the mitered corner on the 2nd and every following row, you will increase

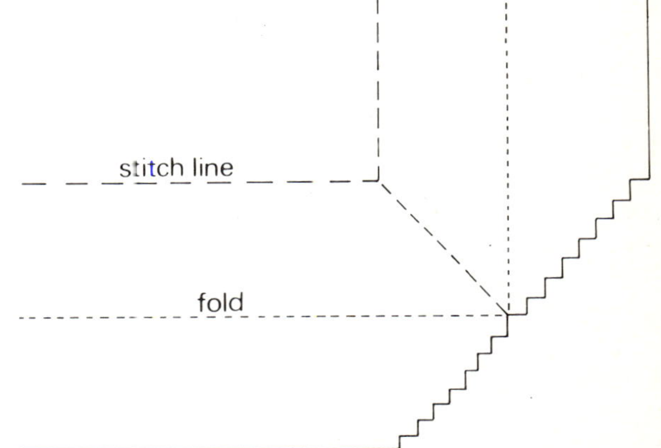

8 stitches on this edge and therefore need to cast on 8 stitches less than the total given number, in this case, 54 stitches in place of 62 stitches. Work the turned-under hem and the hemline row, increasing as shown, then continue increasing one stitch at the same edge on every row until you have a total of 70 stitches, which will give 8 extra stitches for the turned-under facing. Slip the last stitch of the main fabric on every right side row to form a fold line. When turned under the increased stitches on the hems and front facing will join into a neat mitered corner.

Bust darts

For the fuller figure, slimming bust darts can be incorporated into a plain stockinette stitch sweater to give extra depth across the bust without altering the underarm length of the garment.
Measure the exact underarm position for the darts, which should start between $1\frac{1}{2}$in and $2\frac{1}{2}$in below the beginning of the armhole shaping. The fuller the figure, the greater the number of rows needed for shaping the darts and the 12 row example given here is suitable for a 38/40in bust size. Work the front of the sweater until the position for the bust darts is reached, ending with a knit row, then start the dart shaping.

1st row P to last 5 sts, turn.
2nd row Sl 1, K to last 5 sts, turn.
3rd row Sl 1, P to last 10 sts, turn.
4th row Sl 1, K to last 10 sts, turn.
5th row Sl 1, P to last 15 sts, turn.
6th row Sl 1, K to last 15 sts, turn.
7th row Sl 1, P to last 20 sts, turn.
8th row Sl 1, K to last 20 sts, turn.
9th row Sl 1, P to last 25 sts, turn.
10th row Sl 1, K to last 25 sts, turn.
11th row Sl 1, P to end of row.
12th row K to end of row, closing holes between groups of 5 sts by picking up loop under the 5th st of each group and K this loop tog with next st on left hand needle.
This completes the dart shaping. Continue until the position for the armhole shaping is reached, remembering to measure on the side seam and not over the bust darts.

Changing proportions of armholes and shoulders
For a narrow shouldered figure it is a simple matter to change underarm and shoulder shaping. If this is desired, first work out the exact number of extra stitches which need to be decreased, based on the gauge given. Mark these alterations on the pattern so that you can work the complete armhole and shoulder section without further calculations.

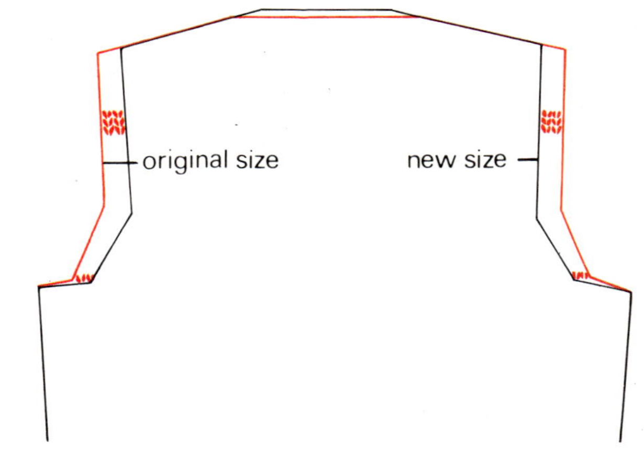

As an example, say you need to lose a further 8 stitches on the back of a sweater to achieve a narrower fit. Decrease half of this total at the underarm point, binding off 2 extra stitches at each side, then work 2 more decreasing rows to lose the remaining 4 stitches, thus arriving at the required total. At the shoulder line bind off 3 stitches less than the given number on the last 2 rows and allow for 2 stitches less than the given number for the remaining center back neck stitches. When working the front remember to make the same adjustments at the underarm and shoulder line and allow for 2 stitches less than the given number for the remaining center front neck stitches. The top of the sleeve shaping must also be changed to correspond to the underarm shaping.

ADJUSTING LENGTHS

With a little care and patience, horizontal hems can quite easily be lengthened or shortened, to contend with fashion changes or a growing family. Skirt, bodice or cuff lengths can be altered in this way and when making children's garments, it is always useful to buy one or two extra balls of yarn in the same dye lot to put aside for the day when such adjustments can be made quickly and inexpensively.

When you shorten a garment no extra yarn is required – in fact, a quantity of the original yarn will become available. Instead of wasting this, wind it into hanks and hand wash it, then hang it up to dry to remove

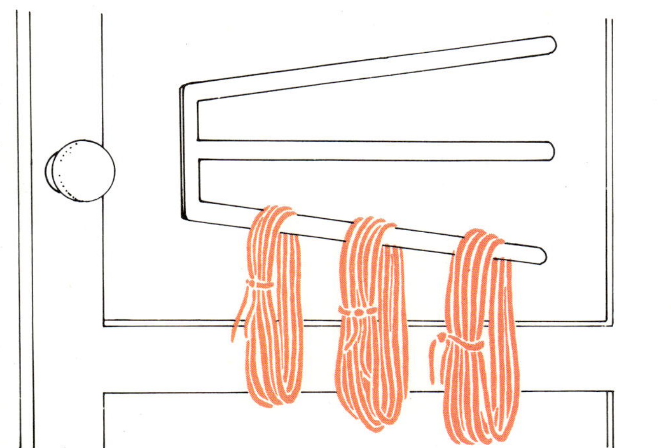

the kinks and lay it aside for some future use.

If a design needs to be lengthened, however, extra yarn is needed but it does not necessarily have to be the original yarn. Odd pieces of the same ply can be used to add a striped hem to a skirt or waist of a sweater and if the neckband is also unraveled and re-knitted in the same stripes, the whole effect will give a

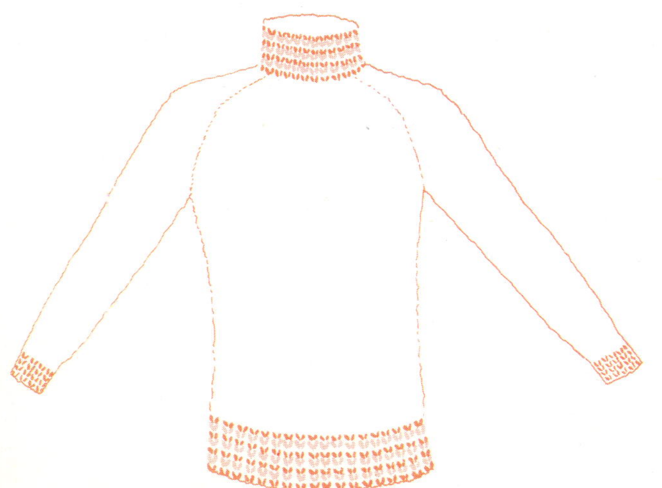

completely new look to the garment. Before beginning any adjustment, check the garment to find the best position for the lengthening or shortening. For example, if the body or sleeves of a sweater need lengthening and it already has a ribbed waistband or cuff 2in long, then the work must be picked up and re-knitted above that waistband or cuff. If a skirt needs shortening and it has a turned under hem, the adjustment must be made above the existing hemline. It is not advisable to attempt these alterations on a fabric which has used a very complicated stitch unless you are quite certain that you will be able to pick up the original number of stitches in their correct sequence, but stockinette stitch, garter stitch or any simple pattern can be altered quite easily in this way.

Lengthening a garment

Make sure that you have some additional yarn on hand. Check the garment and mark both the position where the garment is to be unraveled and a further point 1in above this, then count the exact number of rows between each point. Prepare the work by

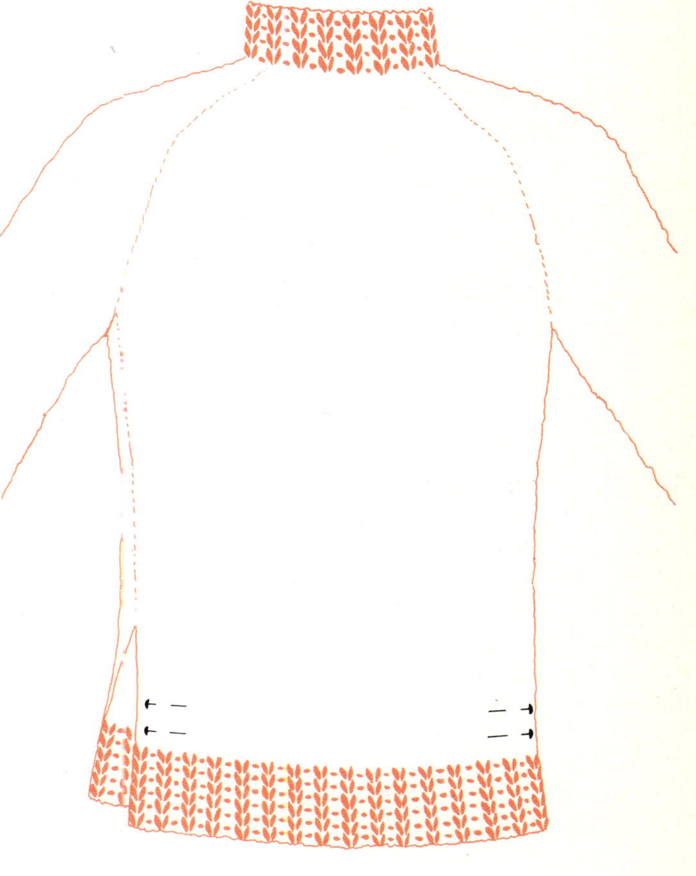

ripping out any hems and side seams to approximately 2in above the last marked point, to allow for freedom in manipulating the needles when re-knitting, taking great care not to cut into the fabric.
With the right side of the fabric facing and the correct needle size, pick up a loop with a needle at the marked row above the required adjustment point, and pull this up tight. Cut through this loop and carefully

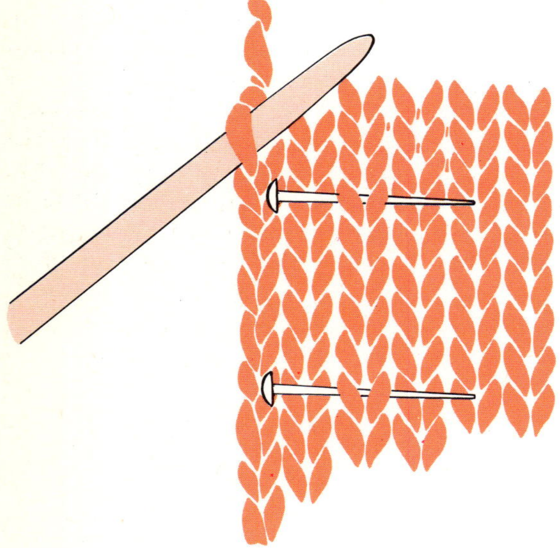

pull the fabric apart until two sets of stitches are exposed. Pull the cut end of yarn tight again and cut it, easing the fabric apart. Continue in this way until

the fabric is in two separate sections, then pick up the stitches of the main section with a knitting needle, making sure that the original number of stitches are on the needle and that each stitch is lying in the correct direction and has not become twisted. Unravel the remaining yarn, winding it into a neat ball ready for use for re-knitting. **. Join the yarn at the

beginning of the row and continue knitting for the required number of rows calculated between the two marked points, then continue knitting to give the extra length desired. Complete the garment by working the original number of rows in ribbing for a waistband or cuff, or by working the exact number of rows used for the original hem on a skirt. Bind off very loosely, then work any other sections in the same way. Re-seam any edges or hems and check whether the new knitting can be blocked, then proceed accordingly.

Shortening a garment
Check and prepare the garment and work as for lengthening to **. Join the yarn at the beginning of the row and continue knitting for the required number of rows calculated between the two marked points.
Bind off very loosely and finish the garment as for lengthening.

Words of caution
When unraveling seams great care must be taken not to cut into the fabric itself only the yarn used for sewing. Never rush this stage, just gently ease the seam apart until you are quite sure which is the exact strand to be cut.
Once the fabric has been divided into two separate sections, check at which end of the work the unraveled yarn finishes, to ascertain whether the next row to be knitted is a right or wrong side row. Only then pick up the stitches with a knitting needle, making sure that each stitch lies in the correct position and that the needle point is facing the correct end, ready to rejoin the yarn. Using a double-pointed needle can help at this stage. Don't panic if a few of the stitches begin to run! These can quite easily be picked up to the correct depth, using a crochet hook. Because the yarn has already been knitted up once, it will not re-knit to the exact even fabric as the original. If the yarn does not require blocking but looks rather uneven, simply wash and dry the garment in the recommended way when it is completed to even out the fabric.

TUCKS AND TRIMS

The more you know about knitting, the more fascinating it becomes. Once you have mastered the basic techniques, it is the small finishing touches that make all the difference in any design.
This chapter deals with four ideas which can be applied to almost any basic design – and they are fun to work. Two of these trimmings are worked in with the actual knitting, one is worked as part of the finishing and the last can be applied when the garment is completed.
Try incorporating one of these suggestions to lift your knitting from the ordinary to the couture class and, at the same time, setting your own individual stamp on any design.

Tucks
Horizontal tucks are easy to work and can be incorporated into the skirt or bodice of almost any plain garment. They look most effective when worked in stockinette stitch with a picot edge – imagine the skirt of a little girl's dress embellished with two or three layers of tucks, or the yoke of a plain sweater finished with two rows of tucking at underarm level. Remember that tucks will use yarn over and above the quantity stated and allow for one or two extra balls before beginning any design.

To work horizontal tucks: Mark the position on the pattern where the tucks are to be incorporated and work to this point, ending with a purl row. Mark each end of the last row with a colored thread. Depending on the depth of tuck required, work a further 5 to 9 rows in stockinette stitch, ending with a knit row. On the next row either knit all the stitches through the back of the loops to mark the foldline of the tuck, or work a row of eyelet holes by knitting 2 together, then bringing the yarn forward to make a stitch, all along the row. Beginning with a knit row work a further 4 to 8 rows stockinette stitch, ending with a purl row. Using a spare needle, return to the row marked with colored thread and pick up the correct number of stitches all along the row on the wrong side of the work, so that the points of the spare needle and the left hand needle holding the stitches are both facing in the same direction. Hold the spare needle behind the left hand needle and knit to the end of the row, working one stitch from the left hand needle together with one stitch from the spare needle. This forms one tuck and can be repeated as desired.

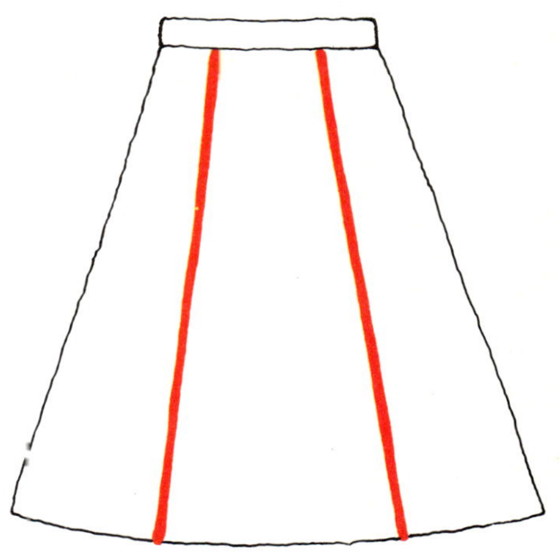

To work vertical tucks: These can be used to highlight any dart shapings on a design and, again, look their best against a plain stockinette stitch background. The continuity of the tucks must be kept throughout the whole length of the design and an additional 2 stitches should be cast on at the beginning for each tuck required. As an example, if the front of a skirt has two dart shapings which begin below hip level, read through the pattern to ascertain the place in the row where these shapings are first worked and allow 2 extra stitches on the right hand side of the first dart and 2 extra stitches on the left hand side of the second dart. Cast on 4 stitches at the beginning of the skirt and work as follows:
1st row K to within 2 sts of the position for the first dart, sl the next 2 sts P-wise keeping the yarn at the back of the work, work the first dart shaping, K to and then work the second dart shaping, sl the next 2 sts P-wise keeping the yarn at the back of the work, K to end.
2nd row P to end.
These 2 rows form the pattern and are repeated throughout, even after the dart shaping has been completed.

Lapped seams

These are worked at the finishing stage and are referred to in dressmaking as run and fell seams, such as you would see on a man's shirt. To look most effective they should be worked on a smooth fabric, such as stockinette stitch. For example, a plain raglan sleeved sweater on which lapped seams are used to join the side, sleeve and raglan seams would look quite original.

To work lapped seams: Depending on the position of the seam and the yarn being used, cast on an additional 2 or 3 stitches for each vertical seam and work a further 3 or 4 rows for each horizontal seam. When the pieces are completed, block as given in the instructions then place the two pieces to be joined with right sides together, with the underneath piece extending about $\frac{1}{2}$in beyond the edge of the upper piece. Work a firm back stitch seam along this edge. Turn the pieces to the right side and carefully back stitch the loose edge of the seam through both thicknesses of the fabric, about $\frac{1}{2}$in from the first seam. Block seam.

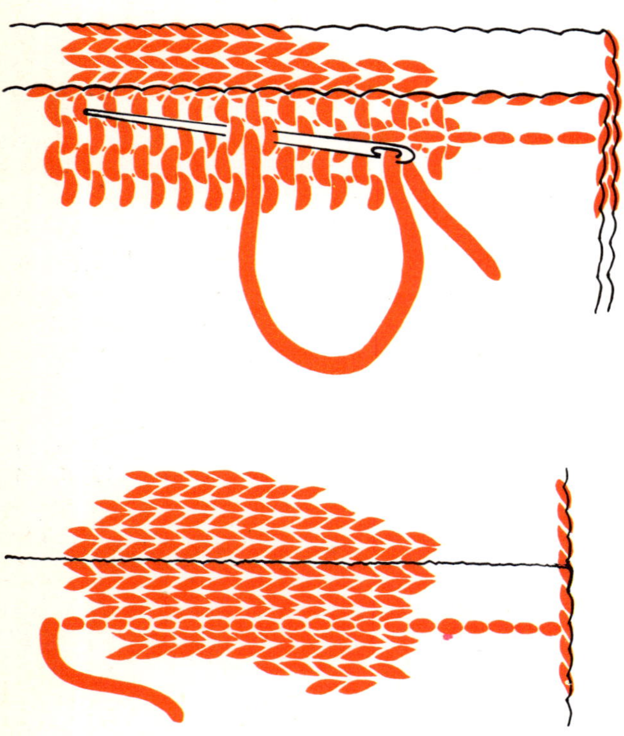

Piping cords

Most knitters will have experimented as children with French knitting, or horse-rein knitting. The round piping produced by this method can be thick or thin, depending on the yarn used and looks most attractive as a straight length of trimming sewn around the neck of a pullover, or on either side of the front bands of a cardigan. Also, separate lengths can be worked, then wound around and stitched to form flat, circular motifs. These motifs could be stitched at random on the bodice of a child's dress or used as a band above the ribbing and cuffs on a plain sweater. Any odd pieces of yarn will do – but think how colorful this piping would look in variegated yarn. The possibilities are endless and fun to work.

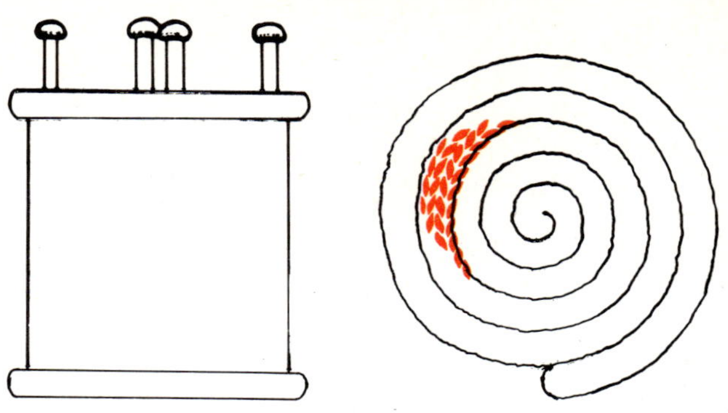

To work piping cord: Either purchase a horse-rein spool or use a wooden spool to make a bobbin, spacing 4 large, round-headed tacks evenly and firmly around the center hole at one end of the spool. Thread the yarn to be used through the center hole of the bobbin or spool, from the opposite end to the tacks, leaving an end free. Working in a clockwise direction throughout, wind the yarn around each of the 4 tacks and work as follows:

1st round Take the yarn once more around all 4 tacks without looping it around the tacks. Placing the yarn above the first round and using a fine crochet hook, lift the first loop over the second strand of yarn from the outside to the center and over the head of the tack. Repeat on all 4 tacks.

Continue repeating this round until the piping is the required length, pulling the cord down through the center hole of the bobbin or spool as it is formed. When the cord is the required length, break off the yarn, leaving an end, thread this end through a blunt ended needle, insert needle through loop on tack and lift loop off tack, repeat on all 4 tacks, pull up yarn and fasten off securely.

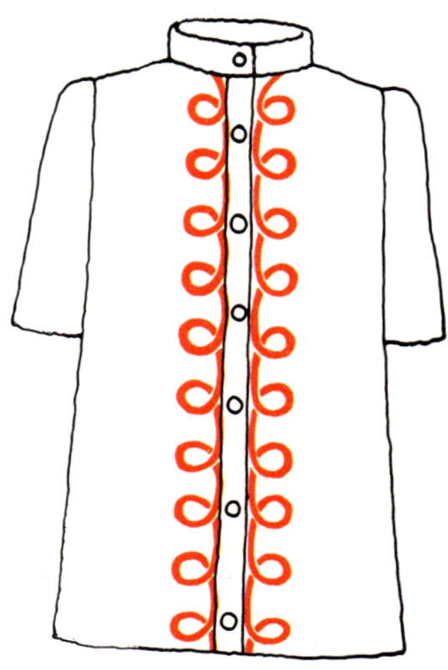

PLEATS

A swirling pleated skirt is a most useful and adaptable knitted garment, which can form the basis of a mix-and-match wardrobe of skirt, pullover, jacket and hat all worked in co-ordinated colors and contrasting patterns or stitch textures.
The method of working the pleats can be a simple, mock version or the inverted type, both of which give such a graceful swing to any skirt. They can be knitted vertically in stripes to form an even more striking variation and this is another ideal way of using up odd pieces of yarn of the same thickness to make a warm and practical skirt for a toddler. Use a yarn which will retain its shape without sagging, for all versions.

Planning pleats
The mock version is the most economical and is based on the width which is required around the hem of the skirt. Use this measurement and the gauge obtained with the yarn chosen to calculate the number of stitches which should be cast on. This number must be divisible by 8, so adjust the total if necessary by adding a few more stitches.
For inverted pleats, work out the required waist measurement and multiply this by three to arrive at the correct hem measurement. Use this measurement to determine the number of stitches to be cast on at the hem, again based on the gauge obtained. This number must be divisible by 12, plus 8, and the total can be adjusted by adding a few more stitches.
For vertical pleats you must measure the length required from waist to hem, plus an allowance of approximately 1in for a turned-under hem. Use this measurement and the gauge obtained to arrive at how many stitches must be cast on, having an even number of stitches, and work from side edge to side edge.

Mock pleats
These can be worked on two needles, either in two separate sections to form the back and the front of the skirt with a seam at each side, or in one piece with a center back seam.
Cast on the required number of stitches.
1st row (RS) *K7, P1, rep from * to end.
2nd row K4, *P1, K7, rep from * to last 4 sts, P1, K3.
These 2 rows form the pattern and are repeated for the required length. Bind off.
To work mock pleats without a seam, use a circular needle and cast on the required number of stitches.
1st round *K7, P1, rep from * to end of round.
2nd round P3, K1, *P7, K1, rep from * to last 4 sts, P4.
These 2 rounds form the pattern and are repeated for the required length. Bind off.
To complete the skirt, cut a piece of elastic to the

proper waist measurement and sew inside the waist edge, using casing stitch. As an alternative, cast on the number of stitches needed to form a separate waistband, allowing enough extra stitches for ease in pulling the skirt on and off, and work $2\frac{1}{4}$in st st. Bind off. Sew waistband to waist edge of skirt, fold in half to WS and sew in place. Thread elastic through waistband, sew ends neatly and fasten off.

Inverted pleats
This method requires a set of 4 double-pointed needles to close the pleats. Because the total number of stitches required is high it is easier to work the skirt in two separate sections, with a seam at each side.

Using two of the needles, cast on the required number of stitches.

1st row (RS) *K8, P1, K2, sl 1 as if to purl, rep from * to last 8 sts, K8.

2nd row *P11, K1, rep from * to last 8 sts, P8.

These 2 rows form the pattern and are repeated for the desired length, less 2in for the waistband. To close the pleats you will need to use all 4 needles.

Last row (waist edge) K4, *sl next 4 sts on to first extra needle, sl next 4 sts on to 2nd extra needle, place first extra needle behind 2nd extra needle and hold both extra needles behind the left hand needle, (K tog one st from all 3 needles) 4 times, rep from * to last 4 sts, K4.

Bind off.

To complete the skirt join seams, overlapping 4 sts at beg of row over 4 sts at end of row to complete pleating. Make a separate waistband and complete as you would for mock pleats.

Vertical pleats

This method is worked on two needles to a length that is twice as long as the waist measurement, with one seam at the center back. If you are working in stripes, carry the yarn not in use loosely up the side edge until it is required again. For neatness, this edge will become the waist edge, so that the strands of yarn can be sewn inside the waistband when the skirt is completed.

Cast on the required number of stitches, allowing approximately 1in extra for the hem.

1st row (RS) K to end.

2nd row P to end.

Rep 1st and 2nd rows 5 times more, then 1st row once more.

14th row P across sts for hem, *yo, P2 tog, rep from * to end.

Rep 1st and 2nd rows twice more, then 1st row once more.

20th row P across sts for hem, K tbl all sts to end.

These 20 rows form the pattern. Continue until work measures twice the required waist measurement, ending with a 20th row. Bind off.

To complete the skirt, join cast on edge to bound off edge to form center back seam. Turn hem at lower edge to WS and sew in place. Tack pleats in position along waist edge, folding each pleat at picot row to form inner fold and at knit row to form outer fold. Make separate waistband and complete as you would for mock pleats.

Toddler's striped skirt

Size

To fit 20in waist, adjustable
Length, 10in

Gauge

30 sts and 36 rows to 4in in stockinette stitch (st st) worked on No.3 needles

Materials

4 × 1oz balls 3 ply Fingering Yarn in main color, A
2 balls of contrast color, B
One pair No.3 needles
Waist length of elastic

Skirt

Using No.3 needles and A, cast on 76 sts. Keeping 8 sts at lower edge for hem, work as for vertical pleats, working first 14 patt rows in A and next 6 rows in B throughout, until work measures 40in from beg, or desired length. Bind off.

Waistband

Using No.3 needles and A, cast on 180 sts. Work 2in st st. Bind off.

Finishing

Block as directed on label. Finish as for vertical pleats.

BASIC TECHNIQUES

Designing your own clothes can be the most rewarding of all aspects of hand knitting. Details have already been given in previous chapters of the important part gauge plays in any designing, together with the compositions of various yarns and the structure of numerous stitches. These three factors form the basis of all successful hand knitted designs.

Before you can begin any design you need to know the exact measurements of the garment you have in mind. Don't tackle anything too complicated for a first attempt – something as simple as the skirt shown here would be ideal, as it does not entail a great deal of shaping.

Each section must be calculated exactly to the required width and length, based on the gauge obtained with any given yarn and needle size. To these measurements you must then add an additional number of stitches which will give sufficient tolerance for ease of movement and also allow for multiples of stitches which will work out correctly in the pattern which has been chosen. An over all tolerance of 2 inches is sufficient for most garments, although something as bulky as a casual jacket which is intended to be worn over another garment will obviously require more tolerance than a sleekly-fitting fine ply pullover.

Measurements

For something as simple as a skirt, five accurate measurements are required.

a The waist measurement in width.
b The hip measurement in width.
c The measurement from waist to hip in depth.
d The measurement from hipline to hemline in depth.
e The width of hemline at lowest point.

The exact shape of the desired skirt must then be determined. It can have almost straight sides, with the hem and hip measurement being about the same, then gently curving from the hipline into the waist. If you want a flared hemline, this must be shaped into the hips, before shaping from the hips to the waist. Whatever the style of skirt you choose, it can be worked in two separate sections, the back and front being exactly the same. To the measurements you now have to add the over all tolerance needed to give an easy-fitting garment, allowing half this additional measurement for the front and half for the back.

At this point, decide whether you want a separate waistband or the waist edge knitted in with the main fabric and finished with casing stitch worked over elastic. If the skirt is to be very slim-fitting you will also need to make provision for a zipper on the side seam. Plan the sort of hem you desire and take this into your calculations – most skirts hang better with a turned up hem, so you will need to add an additional 1 inch to the length.

Gauge

You must now decide on the type of yarn you wish to use. Check the gauge obtained on needles of your choice, which will produce a smooth, even fabric, neither too hard and tight nor too loose and open. Work a sample swatch, using a basic stitch such as stockinette stitch to begin with, and measure this accurately. If you do not measure this sample exactly, or feel that half a stitch difference to 1 inch is unimportant, you will not be able to produce the exact shape you desire. In printed patterns this procedure has already been overcome, as the yarn is specified and a guide to the needle size has been given. When designing for yourself, however, you are no longer limited to the gauge which has been obtained by the original designer but can decide for yourself what gauge will produce the effect you desire.

Making a diagram

Now that you have established the measurements needed and the gauge which will produce the type of fabric you have in mind, you must put all this information down on paper in the form of a diagram.

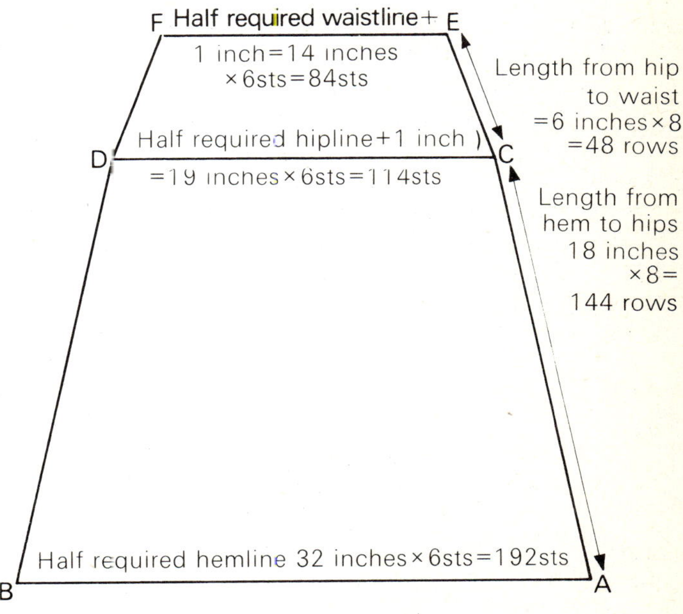

This does not have to be drawn to scale, as with a dressmaking pattern, but is simply used as a guide. The diagram shown here has been based on measurements to give a 36 inch hip size and has been calculated on a gauge of 6 stitches and 8 rows to 1 inch, worked in knitting worsted yarn on No.5 needles. Remember that with most knitted stitches the right side of the work is facing you, therefore your first knitted row will be worked from the right hand edge to the left hand edge. Our example has been worked in rice stitch, where the first, or right side row, is knitted and the second, or wrong side row is worked in single rib. It has also been worked from the hemline to the waist edge, decreasing as required to give the final waist measurement.

Hemline: This is the point marked A–B on the diagram.
Hipline: This is the point marked C–D on the diagram.
Waist: This is the point marked E–F on the diagram.

Calculating the number of stitches and rows
The measurements shown in the diagram given here now have to be multiplied by the number of stitches and rows to 1 inch which have been obtained in your gauge sample. The hemline width is 32 inches and when multiplied by 6 stitches, this gives a total of 192 stitches. Before the hipline point is reached, this width must be decreased to give 18 inches plus 1 inch tolerance, multiplied by 6 stitches to give a total of 114 stitches. Similarly, the depth from the hipline to the waist must be decreased to give 13 inches plus 1 inch tolerance, multiplied by 6 stitches to give a total of 84 stitches.
If you are working a straight skirt, the required number of stitches can be decreased at the side edges only. A flared skirt, however, has considerably more stitches to begin with and these will need to be decreased as carefully spaced darts as well as at the side edges. Calculate the number of rows which will be worked to give the required length from the hemline to the hipline, then work out how many decrease rows are needed to arrive at the correct number of stitches for the hip measurement, then how many rows are required between each set of decreases to give the correct length.

Skirt
Sizes
To fit 36in hips
Length, 25in

Gauge
24 sts and 32 rows to 4in in stockinette stitch (st st) worked on No.5 needles

Materials
10 × 2oz balls Brunswick Pomfret Sport Yarn
One pair No.5 needles
One pair No.4 needles

Waist length of 1in wide elastic

Back
Using No.5 needles cast on 192 sts. Beg with a K row work 7 rows st st.
Next row K all sts tbl to form hemline.
Next row K to end.
Next row *K1, P1, rep from * to end.
The last 2 rows form patt. Cont in patt until work measures 6 inches from hemline, ending with a WS row.

Shape darts
Next row Sl 1, K1, psso, K61, sl 1, K2 tog, psso, K60, sl 1, K2 tog, psso, K61, K2 tog. 186 sts.
Work 7 rows patt without shaping.
Next row Sl 1, K1, psso, K59, sl 1, K2 tog, psso, K58, sl 1, K2 tog, psso, K59, K2 tog. 180 sts.
Work 7 rows patt without shaping.
Cont dec in this way on next and every foll 8th row until 114 sts rem, then on every foll 6th row until 84 sts rem. Cont without shaping until work measures 24in from hemline, ending with a WS row.
Change to No.4 needles. Work 1in K1, P1 rib. Bind off in rib.

Front
Work as given for back.

Finishing
Join side seams. Turn hem at lower edge to WS and sew in place. Sew elastic inside waistband using casing stitch.

MORE ABOUT DESIGNING

This chapter continues with the necessary know-how required for designing your own clothes. As explained in the previous chapter, you need to know the exact measurements plus tolerance allowance for each section of the garment and the gauge obtained with the yarn, pattern stitch and needle size of your choice.
To plan the shape of the garment you can either make a diagram of each section and use this as a guide or, if the design you have in mind is rather complicated, you may find it easier to draft the garment out on squared graph paper, where each square represents one stitch and each line of squares shows a complete row of knitting. Most professional designers use the last method as it forms a detailed record of the design which can be checked against the written instructions.
Neither of these methods will be to the exact scale of the completed garment.
The pullover shown here has been worked to the same gauge as the skirt featured in the previous chapter, that is, 6 stitches and 8 rows to 1in in stockinette stitch worked on No.5 needles. With this knowledge you can make a diagram or knitting chart which will give you the exact measurements you require, but if you alter the yarn or needle size, you must first determine the gauge you will achieve before you can begin your design.

Basic pullover measurements
The diagrams and charts shown here represent the measurements and details of the shaping required

for the body and sleeves of a plain, round-necked pullover.

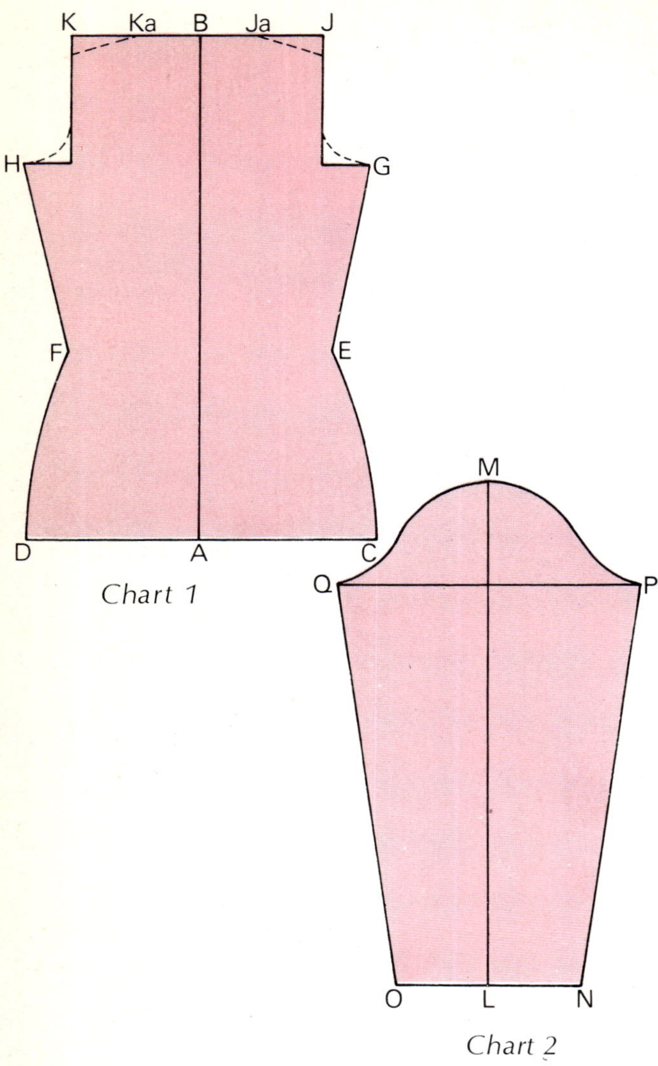

Chart 1

Chart 2

The center line on Chart 1, from the points marked A–B, represents the total length required from the lower edge to the back neck on the back of the pullover. The points marked C–D give the hemline measurements, E–F the waist measurements, G–H the bust measurement before shaping the armholes and J–K the shoulders and back neck width.

The center line on Chart 2, from the points marked L–M, shows the outside sleeve measurement from the wrist to the shoulder line. The points marked N–O represent the total wrist measurement and P–Q, the underarm sleeve width before shaping the cap of the sleeve.

Calculate the number of stitches and rows needed to give these measurements by multiplying the total number of inches from point to point by the number of stitches and rows obtained from your gauge sample.

Using graph paper

Charts 1 and 2 show the basic measurements needed when planning a pullover design, although the waist shaping on the body is not always essential and has been omitted on the pullover shown here. However, it is easier to show details of the graduated shaping required for each section on squared graph paper. The symbols used are a form of shorthand and are in standard use throughout all knitting charts.

Armhole shaping: Where a set in sleeve is required, the shaping takes place in the first 2/3in above the points marked G–H on Chart 1 in a gradual curve,

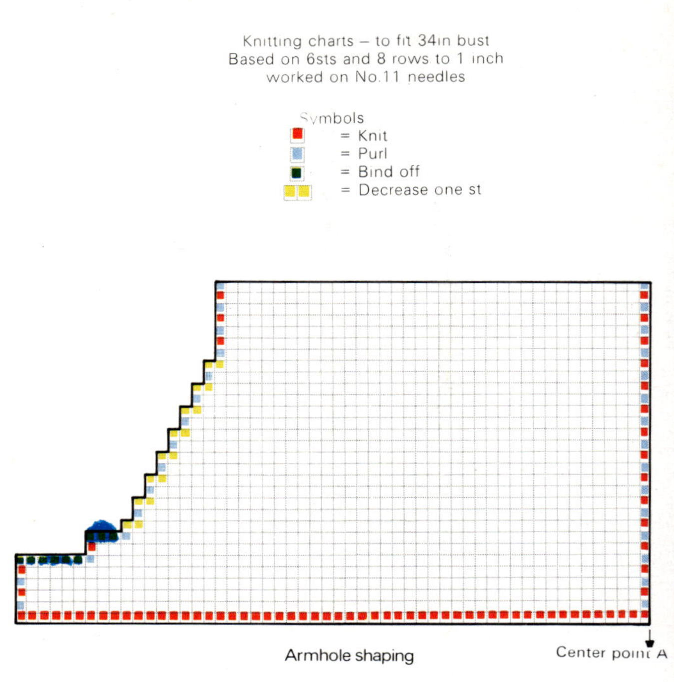

Armhole shaping

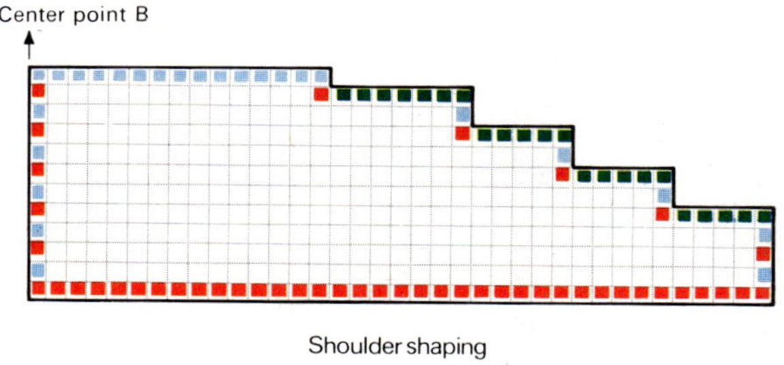

Shoulder shaping

which is more acute at the beginning to give a neat underarm shape. On a raglan sleeve, the same underarm shaping is required but the remaining stitches are then steadily decreased until only the number needed to form the back neck remain on the needle.

Shoulder shaping: For a set in sleeve, measure the shoulder seam length required from the points marked J–Ja and K–Ka on Chart 1 and start the shoulder shaping approximately 1in below the total length given from points marked A–B on Chart 1.

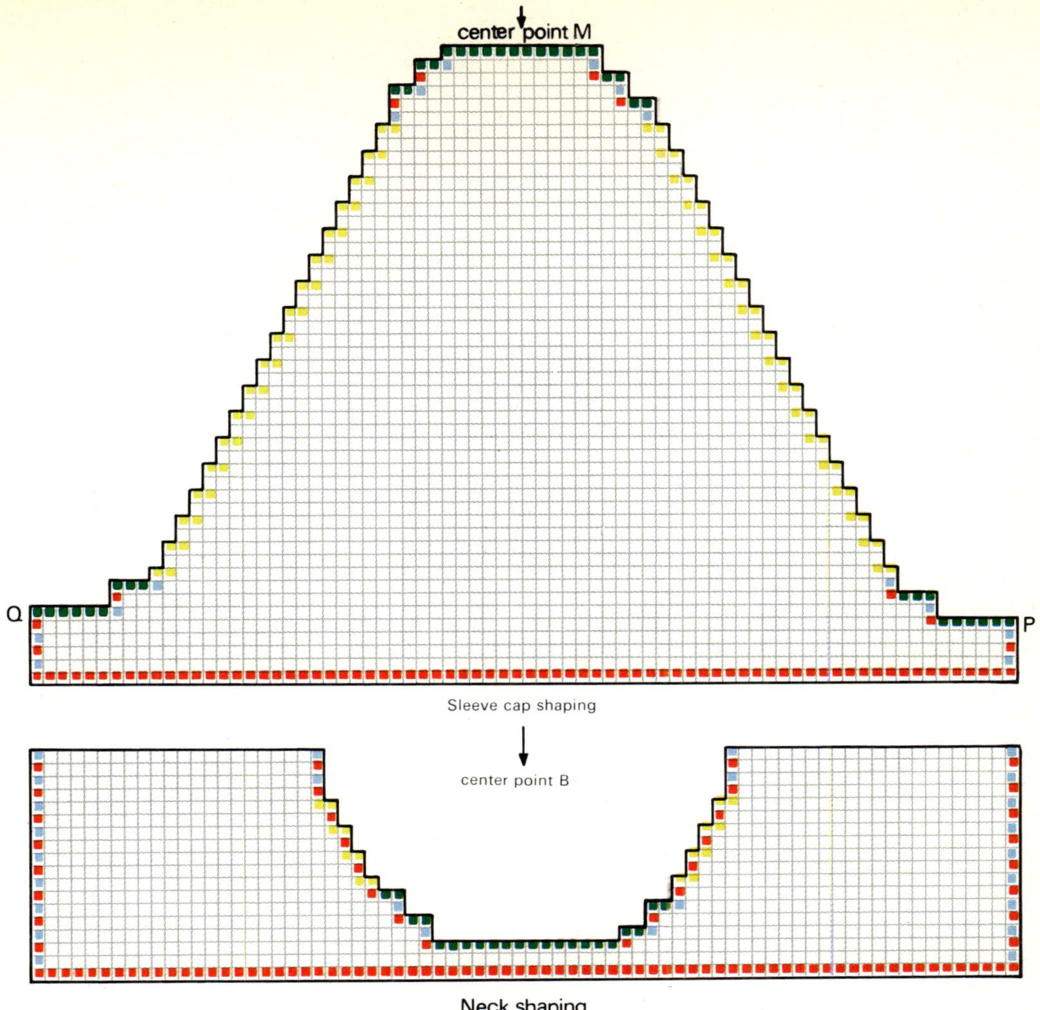

Sleeve cap shaping

Neck shaping

A raglan sleeve does not require shoulder shaping, as the cap of the sleeve is continued to form the shoulder line.

Sleeve shaping: All sleeves, whether long, short, set in or raglan, need to be shaped from the lower edge to the underarm to give a good fit. For a set in sleeve the cap must be shaped in a gradual curve, which is always more acute at the beginning to match the underarm shaping on the body. The number of remaining stitches on the last row of the sleeve should be less than 3in in width, to fit well across the shoulder line, and the final shape will depend on how the stitches are decreased to leave the correct number on the last row. After shaping the underarm, one stitch should be decreased at each end of the next 4–8 rows, depending on the row gauge being worked, and then on every other row to soften the curve until the sleeve is approximately 1in less than the total length from points marked L–M on Chart 2. The remaining stitches can then be bound off evenly at the beginning of the last few rows until the correct number remain for the final row.
Raglan sleeves should be shaped at the underarm, then decreased until sufficient stitches remain to form the side neck edge only.

Neck shaping For a round neck the back and front body sections are exactly the same, except for the shaping of the front neck. This point should be approximately 2in lower than the back neck and the stitches need to be divided at this point and each shoulder worked separately. You will have established how many stitches are required to work each shoulder on the back and this total should be deducted from the stitches which remain after the armhole shaping has been completed. The remaining stitches are used to shape the neck in a gradual curve before the shoulder shaping is started.
A V-neck will be divided at a lower point, either at the same time as the armhole shaping is started or after this section has been completed, depending on the final depth required. Each shoulder is again completed separately, decreasing evenly at the front neck edge until the number of stitches needed to complete the shoulder remain.
The neckband can be completed in a variety of ways, either as a crew neck, turtleneck or ribbed V-neck.

A BASIC DESIGN PROJECT

The two previous chapters have explained how easy it is to design your own basic garments for a desired shape and size. With this knowledge you can begin to combine all the skills and techniques which are given in this course to make the most exciting and original designs – all to your own personal taste.

Once you know how to plan a basic shape, you can begin to experiment with different patterns and textures. If you work with colored patterns, this need not be an expensive trial run as you can use up all sorts of odds and ends of the same thickness of yarn in a variety of ways. Keep to a fairly simple shape to begin with but use as many colors and patterns as you like, so that all the interest of the design is in the fabric and not in the shape. Remember to check the multiple of stitches which are required for each pattern and, if necessary, adjust the row beginnings and endings to insure that each pattern works out correctly over the total number of stitches.

All the stitches, methods and techniques used for the pullover shown here are given in the book.

Rainbow pullover

Sizes

To fit 34/36in bust
Length to shoulder, 25in
Sleeve seam, 17in

Gauge

24 sts and 32 rows to 4in in stockinette stitch (st st) worked on No.5 needles

Materials

Total of 12 × 2oz balls of Brunswick Pomfret Sport Yarn in 12 contrast colors, or as desired
One pair No.5 needles

Note

Colors may be used in any sequence and are not coded.

Pullover body

Using No.5 needles and any color, cast on 112 sts for lower edge. K9 rows garter stitch (g st).

Work 22 rows Greek key pattern, working one extra st at each end of row, see Mosaic patterns later. K6 rows g st.

Work in stripes of 2 rows, 1 row, 3 rows, 1 row, 4 rows, 1 row, 3 rows, 1 row and 2 rows. K6 rows g st.

Bind off loosely. Make another piece in same way, working same color sequence.

Using No.5 needles and any color, cast on 112 sts for main body. K6 rows g st.

Work in diagonal stripes of 2 sts in each of 2 colors for 10 rows, see horizontal stripes later. K6 rows g st.

Work in chevron pattern for 20 rows, having multiples of 11 sts plus 2 instead of 13 stitches plus 2, keeping 3 sts at each side of shaping, see chevron stripes later. K6 rows g stitch.

Work in patchwork pattern across 2nd, 1st, 5th and 3rd patches, or 4 complete patches of 28 sts, for 30 rows, see patchwork later. K6 rows g st.

Work in lattice stitch, omitting 1st row and working one extra st at each end of row for 32 rows, see lattice stitch later.

Shape shoulders

Cont in g st only, bind off at beg of next and every row 10 sts 6 times. K3 rows g st on rem sts.

Bind off loosely. Make another piece in same way, working same color sequence.

Diamond panel

**Using No.5 needles and any color, cast on 2sts. K1 row. Cont in g st, inc one st at each end of next and every alt row until there are 28 sts. K3 rows g st. **.

Dec one st at each end of next and every alt row until 2 sts rem. K1 row. Bind off. Make 7 more diamonds in same way, varying colors.

Make 16 half diamonds working from ** to ** and varying colors. Bind off.

Sleeves

Using No.5 needles and any color, cast on 49 sts. K9 rows g st, inc one st in every st on last row. 98 sts. Omitting diamond panel and chevron pattern, work in body patterns, with 6 rows g st between each pattern and ending with 6 rows g st. Bind off loosely.

Finishing

Block each piece under a damp cloth with a warm iron. Join shoulder seams of main sections and side seams of lower sections. Join side seams of main body leaving 8in open at top for armholes. Join diamonds and half-diamonds as shown in diagram. Sew bound off edge of lower edge of body to lower edge of diamond panel, then sew cast on edge of main body to top edge of diamond panel. Sew in sleeves. Join sleeve seams. Block seams.

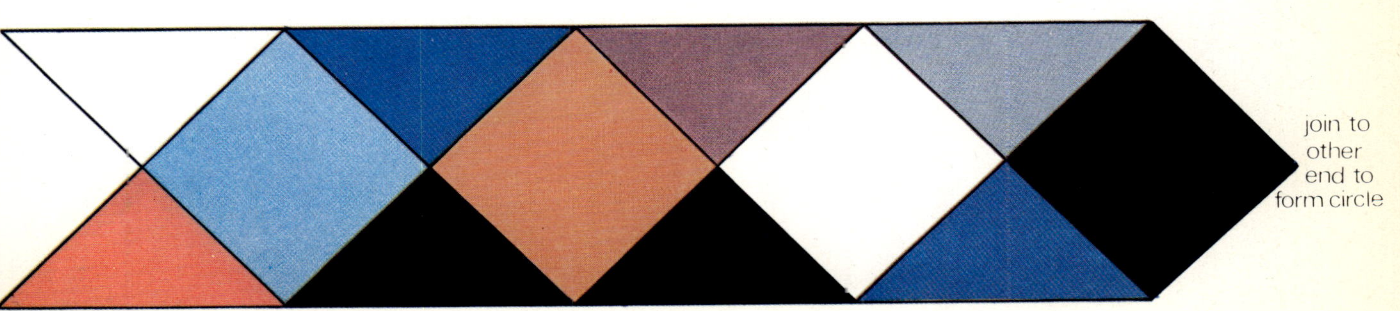

FINISHING TOUCHES

Unusual trimmings and finishing touches on a garment are the easiest way of achieving fashion flair and turning an otherwise simple design into an original which no one else will have. It may just mean the addition of a belt to a dress or tunic, or your own initials embroidered on the shoulder of a plain sweater. These know-how ideas are invaluable and you will have great fun both in trying them out and applying them.

Twisted cords
These are simple to make and have a variety of uses, depending on their thickness and length. They can be used instead of ribbon on a baby garment – saving additional expense as well as using up any odds and ends of left over yarn. Also thick cord trimmed with tassels makes a most attractive belt and avoids the problem of trying to match colors.
The number of strands of yarn required will vary according to the thickness of the cord needed and the yarn being used. As a guide, try using 4 strands for a baby garment and up to 12 strands for a thick belt. Take the required number of strands and cut them into lengths 3 times the length of the finished cord. For example, for a cord 20in long you will need lengths of 60in. Enlist the aid of another person but, if this is not possible, then one end of the strands may be fastened over a convenient hook. Knot each end of the strands together before beginning. If you are working with another person, each should insert a knitting needle into the knot and twist the strands in a clockwise direction, until they are tightly twisted. Do not let go of the strands but, holding them taut, fold them in half at the center and knot the 2 ends together. Holding the knot, let go of the folded end and give the cord a sharp shake, then smooth it down from the knot to the folded end to even out the twists. Make another knot at the folded end, cut through the folded loops, and ease out the ends.

Braided belt
Here is another idea for a highly original belt. In addition to the yarn you will need 12 small wooden beads. Cut 12 lengths of yarn, preferably knitting worsted, 90in long. Take 2 ends together at a time and knot at one end, then slide a bead down to the knot and make 6 strands in this way. Tie these strands together about 10in above the beaded ends. Form into 3 strands having 4 lengths in each strand and braid together, taking the left hand strands over the center strands, then the right hand strands over the center strands and continue in this way to within 16in of the other end. Knot all 12 strands together at this point. Now take 2 ends together and thread a bead on to them, then knot them at the end to hold the bead. Make 5 more strands in this way. Trim ends.

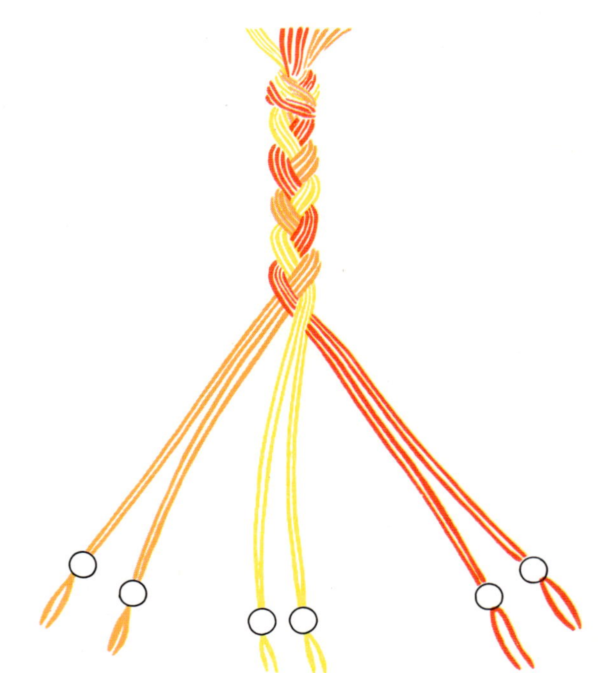

Pompons
These are a most attractive way of trimming a hat, with 2 or more in contrasting colors placed just above the brim, or one enormous loopy pompon placed on the top of a beret.
Round pompon Cut 2 circles of cardboard the size desired for the finished pompon, then cut out a circle from the center of each. Place the 2 pieces of cardboard together and wind the yarn evenly around them and through the center hole until the hole is nearly filled. Break off the yarn, leaving a long end, thread this through a blunt ended needle and use this

to thread the last turns through the hole until it is completely filled. Cut through the yarn around the outer edge of the circles, working between the 2 pieces of cardboard. Take a double length of yarn and tie very securely around the center of the pompon, between the 2 pieces of cardboard, leaving an end long enough to sew to the garment. Pull out the cardboard, then fluff the pompon and trim it into shape.

Loopy pompon Cut a strip of very thin cardboard about 8in long by 4in wide, depending on the size of pompon desired. Leave a short end of yarn free, then wind the yarn very loosely along the length of cardboard for the thickness desired. **. Cut the yarn leaving an end about 12in long and thread this into a blunt-ended needle. Insert the needle under the loops at one edge of the cardboard, going under 3 or 4 loops at a time, then bring the needle up and back over these loops to form a firm back stitch. Continue along the length of the cardboard until all the loops are secured in this way, then work another row of back stitch if desired. Bend the cardboard slightly and remove it from the loops, then insert the needle through all the loops at once being careful not to pull up too tightly. Now bring one end of the secured loops around in a circle to meet the other end and fasten off securely, tying the first short end of yarn to secure it and using the remainder of the yarn to sew the pompon onto the garment.

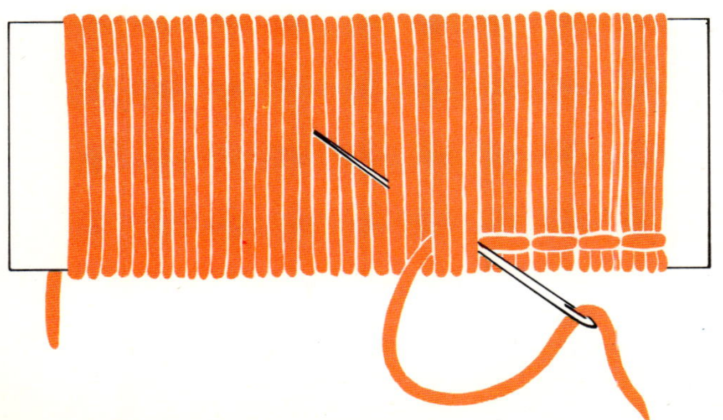

Tassels

Work as for the loopy pompon to **, then cut the yarn. Using a blunt ended wool needle threaded with yarn, insert the needle at one edge of the cardboard under all the strands and fasten off securely. Cut through the strands of yarn at the other untied edge of the cardboard. Finish the tassel by winding an end of yarn several times around the top folded ends, about $\frac{1}{2}$in down and fasten off securely, leaving an end long enough to sew on the tassel.

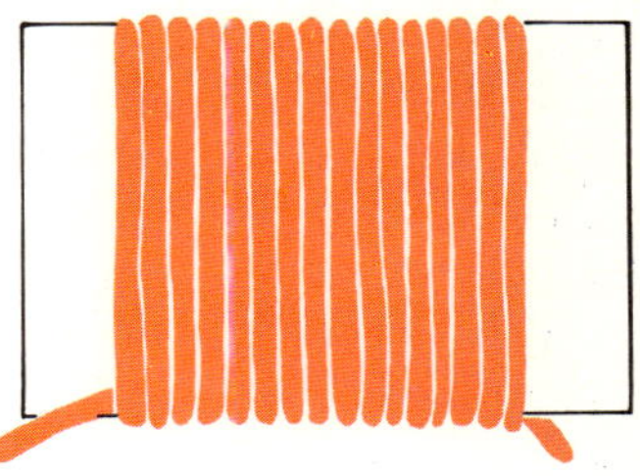

Swiss darning

For this type of embroidery it is advisable to use yarn of the same thickness as the knitted fabric. If the embroidery yarn is too thin the knitting will show through and if it is too thick, it will look clumsy.

Working from the chart, use a blunt ended needle threaded with the embroidery yarn and begin at the lower right hand corner of the design to be applied, working from right to left. Bring the needle through from the back to the front at the base of the first stitch to be embroidered and draw yarn through; insert the needle from right to left under the 2 loops of the same stitch one row above and draw yarn through; insert the needle back into the base of this stitch, along the back of the work, then into the base of the next stitch to the left from the back to the front and draw the yarn through. Taking great care to keep the loops at the same gauge as the knitting continue along the row in this way. At the end of the row, insert the needle into the base of the last stitch worked, then up in the center of this same stitch, which will form the base of the same stitch on the next row above. Now insert the needle from left to right under the 2 loops of this stitch on the row above, and continue working as before from left to right.

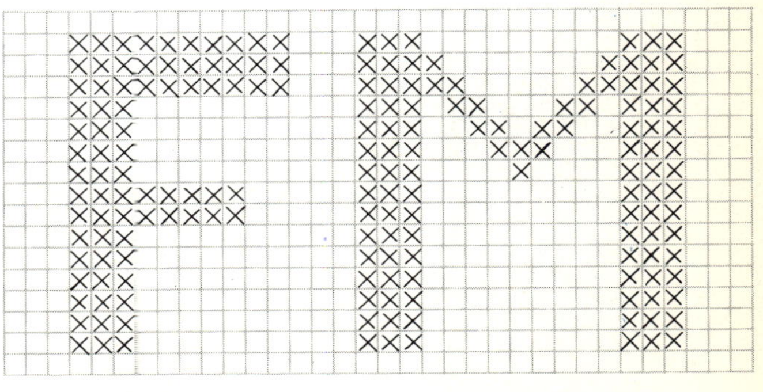

APPLIED EMBROIDERY

Embroidery can quite easily be applied to knitting without the need for charts or transfers. Quite apart from Swiss darning which gives a jacquard effect and is worked from a chart, see previous page, simple embroidery stitches such as cross stitch and chain stitch can be used to highlight a seam, or as a border pattern. Because of the amount of 'give' in most knitted fabrics, smocking, either knitted in as part of the main fabric or applied when the garment is completed, is particularly effective.

The following suggestions can be incorporated in a variety of ways, but a certain amount of planning is needed before beginning any garment. With the exception of smocking, they can all be worked on a plain stockinette stitch background, although care must be taken in working out the exact position for each stitch. Smocking, either applied or as part of the fabric, needs a ribbed background, and the pattern for any garment using this method will give detailed instructions for the correct placing. However, if you wish to try some smocking – perhaps on the bodice of a little girl's dress or around the cuffs of a plain pullover – remember to check and make sure that the number of stitches at the desired point will allow for the correct multiple of stitches.

Knitted-in smocking

Work as part of the main fabric over P3, K1 rib. The background color will be used for the main fabric, coded as A, and a contrast color of the same type will be used to work the smocking, coded as B. Either

cast on or make sure that you have a number of stitches divisible by 8+3. This allows for the knit stitches of the rib to be drawn together with the contrast color, alternating the position to give the smocked effect.

1st row (RS) Using A, *P3, K1, rep from * to last 3 sts, P3.
2nd row *K3, P1, rep from * to last 3 sts, K3.
Rep 1st and 2nd rows once more.
5th row Using A, P3, *K1, P3, K1, sl these last 5 sts onto a cable needle and hold at front of work, join in B at back of work, pass B in front of sts on cable needle to back of work then around to front and back again in a counter-clockwise direction, leaving B at back sl 5 sts onto right hand needle – called S5 –, P3 A, rep from * to end. Do not break off B.
6th row As 2nd.
Rep 1st and 2nd rows once, then 1st row once more.
10th row Using A, K3, P1, *K3, S5 by P1, K3, P1, holding cable needle at back of work and winding yarn around in a clockwise direction, rep from * to last 7 sts, K3, P1, K3. Do not break off B.
These 10 rows form the pattern.

Applied smocking

Work the background rib as for knitted-in smocking until the garment or piece to be trimmed is completed. Using a blunt ended needle threaded with B, *insert needle from back to front of the work after the 2nd knitted st of the 5th row, pass the needle across the front of the knit st, the next 3 purl sts and the next knit st, insert it from front to back after this knit st and pull yarn through, carry the yarn across the back of the work through to the front and around the 5 sts again through to the back, carry the yarn across the back of the work, skip (P3, K1) twice, rep from * to end. On the 10th row with the WS of the work facing, * work round the 2nd knit st of the first smocked sts, the next 3 purl sts and the first knit st of next smocked sts, then skip (K3, P1) twice, rep from * to the end. Continue in this way for the desired depth of smocking.

Applied bows

Work the stockinette stitch background and mark the positions for the bows on the RS of the work, allowing 5 sts and 5 rows for each bow and an additional 5 sts between each bow. Using a blunt ended needle threaded with contrast yarn, *insert the needle from back to front at the first marked st of the 1st row and pull yarn through. Working from right to left insert the needle under the 3rd st of the 3rd row and draw yarn through, insert the needle from front to back after the 5th st of the 1st row and draw yarn through; carry yarn across back of work, insert needle from back to front at first marked st of 2nd row and draw yarn through, insert needle under same 3rd st of 3rd row and draw yarn through, insert needle from front to back after 5th st of 2nd row and draw yarn through; carry yarn across back, insert needle from back to front at first marked st of 3rd row and draw yarn through, under the same 3rd st of 3rd row and draw yarn through, insert needle from front to back after 5th st of 3rd row and draw yarn through; carry yarn across back, insert needle from back to front at first marked st of 4th row and draw yarn through, under same 3rd st of 3rd row and draw yarn through, insert needle from front to back after 5th st of 4th row and draw yarn through, carry yarn across back, insert needle from back to front at first marked st of 5th row and draw yarn through, under same 3rd st of 3rd row and draw yarn through, insert needle from front to back after 5th st of 5th row and draw yarn through, carry yarn across back to next position and rep from * to end.

The next time the bows are worked, on 5 rows above, work them over 5 sts in between each bow of previous row.

Applied chain stitch

This looks most effective if it is worked in a contrast color on a stockinette stitch background where wide stripes of the main color and narrow stripes of the contrast color have been used to give a checked effect. Mark the positions for vertical chains depending on the size of check desired, allowing one stitch, one above the other, on every row.

Using a blunt ended needle threaded with contrast color, begin at lower edge of first marked position and insert needle from back to front in center of marked st and draw yarn through, *hold the yarn down with the thumb of the left hand, insert the needle into the same st and up into the next st above, drawing the yarn through. Rep from * to end and fasten off. Repeat on each marked st as desired.

Applied cross stitch

Work the stockinette stitch background and mark positions for the cross sts on the RS of work, allowing 3 sts and 4 rows for each cross st, with an additional 3 sts between each cross st. Using a blunt ended needle threaded with one or two thicknesses of contrast color begin at lower edge, *insert needle from back to front at side of first marked st and draw yarn through, then working from right to left insert needle from front to back after 3rd st on 4th row above and draw yarn through, carry yarn across back of work, insert needle from back to front after first st on 4th row and draw yarn through, insert needle from front to back after 3rd st of 1st row and draw yarn through, carry yarn across back to next position and rep from * to end. The next line of cross sts are worked 4 rows above, working them over 3 sts in between each cross st of previous row.

COVERED BUTTONS

Just as untidy buttonholes can mar the effect of an otherwise perfect garment, buttons which do not match exactly or coordinate with the yarn used for a design can spoil the whole appearance.
Sometimes it is impossible to find suitable buttons. The economical and simple answer to this problem is to cover button molds with knitting to achieve a perfect match.
Here we give a selection of buttons to suit all garments.

Bouclé yarn button
Using No.1 needles cast on 4 sts. Working in st st, inc one st at each end of every row until there are 12 sts. Work 6 rows without shaping. Dec one st at each end of every row until 4 sts rem. Bind off. Gather around wooden mold.

Reverse stockinette stitch button
Using No.1 needles and 3 ply yarn, work as for bouclé yarn button, beg with a P row. This will cover a $\frac{7}{8}$in mold.

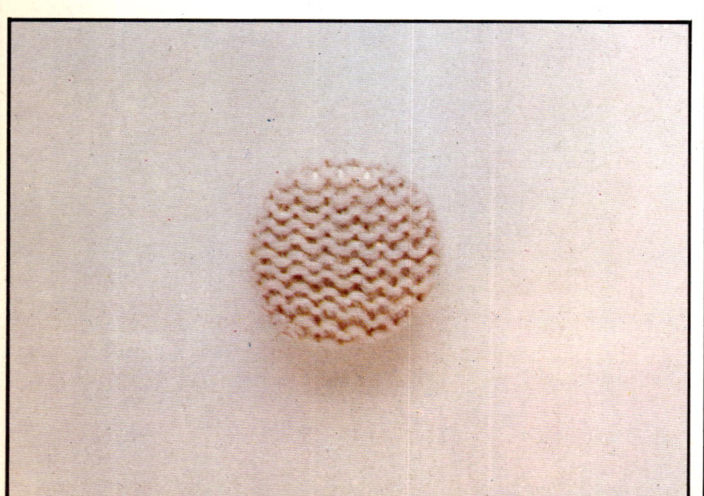

Single rib button
Using No.1 needles and 3 ply yarn, work in K1, P1 rib as for reverse st st button. This will cover a $\frac{7}{8}$in mold.

Bobble button
Using No.1 needles and 3 ply yarn, cast on 3 sts. Working in st st, inc one st at each end of every row until there are 11 sts. Work 3 rows without shaping.
Next row K5, K into front and back of next st 5 times, K5.
Next row P5, K5 tog, P5.
Work 2 rows without shaping. Dec one st at each end of every row until 3 sts rem. Bind off. This will cover $\frac{7}{8}$in mold.

Continental stockinette stitch button
Using No.1 needles and 3 ply yarn, cast on and work as for reverse st st button, working in foll patt:
1st row K into back of each st to end.
2nd row P to end.
Bind off. This will cover a $\frac{7}{8}$in mold.

Tweed stitch button
Using No.1 needles and 3 ply yarn, cast on and work as given for reverse st st button, working in foll patt:
1st row *K1, yfwd, sl 1 P-wise, ybk, rep from * to end.
2nd row P to end.
3rd row *Yfwd, sl 1 P-wise, ybk, K1, rep from * to end.
4th row P to end.
Bind off. This will cover a $\frac{7}{8}$in mold.

Two-color button
Using No.1 needles and 3 ply yarn in 2 colors, A and B, cast on and work as for reverse st st button, working in foll patt:
1st row (WS) Using A, *P1, sl 1 P-wise, rep from * to end.
2nd row Using A, K to end.
3rd row Using B, as 1st.
4th row Using B, as 2nd.
Bind off. This will cover a $\frac{7}{8}$in mold.

Embroidered button
Using No.1 needles and 3 ply yarn, cast on 6 sts. Work in st st inc one at each end of every row until there are 16 sts. Work 8 rows without shaping.
Dec one st at each end of every row until 6 sts rem. Bind off. Using 3 colors of 6-strand embroidery thread and chain st, work a flower motif in center of button. Gather over wooden mold.

Basket stitch button
Using No.2 needles and knitting worsted, cast on and work as for the bouclé yarn button, working in foll patt:
1st row *K2, P2, rep from * to end.
2nd row As 1st.
3rd row *P2, K2, rep from * to end.
4th row As 3rd.
Bind off. Gather over wooden mold.

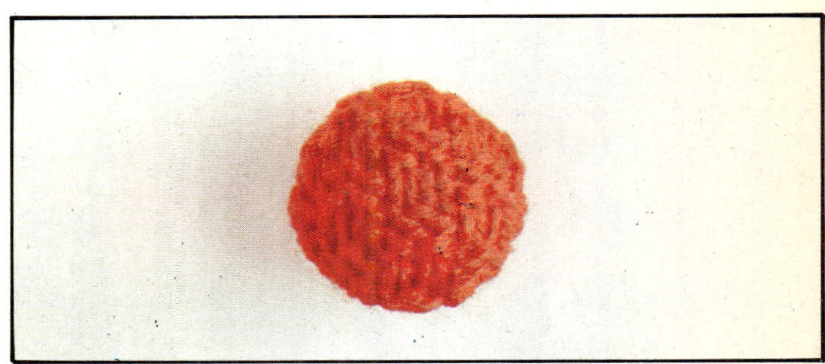

Woven basket stitch button
Using No.2 needles and knitting worsted, cast on and work as for the Basket stitch button, working in foll patt:
1st row *Pass right hand needle behind first st on left hand needle and K second st, then K first st in usual way, dropping both sts off needle tog, rep from * to end.
2nd row P1, *P second st on left hand needle then P first st and sl both sts off needle tog, rep from * to last st. P1.
Bind off. Gather over wooden mold.

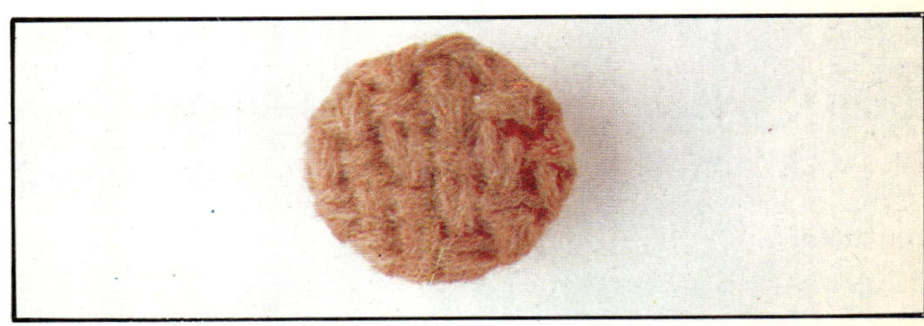

Beret button
Using No.1 needles and knitting worsted, cast on 11 sts.
1st and every alt row (WS) P to end.
2nd row K1, (K twice into next st, K1) 5 times. 16 sts.
4th row (K2, K twice into next st) 5 times, K1. 21 sts.
6th row (K2, K2 tog) 5 times, K1. 16 sts.
8th row (K1, K2 tog) 5 times, K1. 11 sts.
10th row (K2 tog) 5 times, K1. 5 sts.
Break off yarn, thread through rem sts, insert $1\frac{1}{4}$in wooden mold, draw up and fasten off.

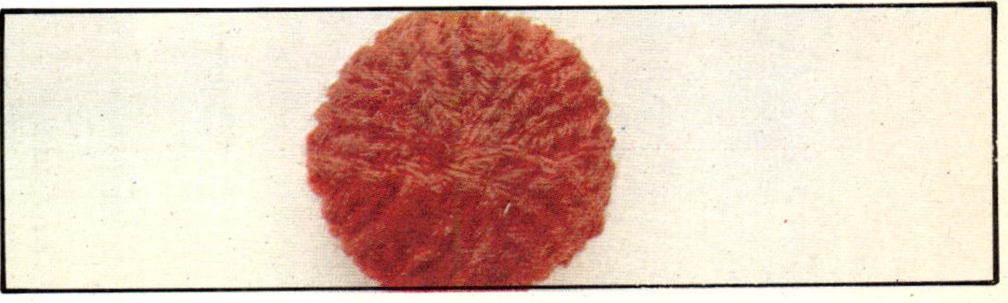

APPLIED EDGINGS

Knitted edgings
Although many beautiful and interesting forms of edgings are given in crochet patterns, reference is seldom made to the equally effective variations of knitted borders. These may be used to trim anything from baby clothes and fashion garments to household linens.
The correct choice of yarn for these borders is very important, depending upon the use to which they will be put. Something as fine as a 2 or 3 ply yarn would produce a delicate edging for a baby dress or shawl, a knitting worsted quality would give a firm, textured border for a fashion garment, or a crisp cotton would be ideal for household linens. All of the examples shown here are worked separately to the desired length, then sewn in place when the item is completed.

Simple lace edging
Cast on a number of stitches divisible by 5 plus 2.
1st row K1, yfwd and over needle to make one st, * K5, turn, lift 2nd, 3rd, 4th and 5th sts over the first st and off the needle, turn, yfwd, rep from * to last st, K1.
2nd row K1, *(P1, yon to make one st, K1 tbl) all into next st, P1, rep from * to end.
3rd row K2, K1 tbl, *K3, K1 tbl, rep from * to last 2 sts, K2.
Work 3 rows g st. Bind off.

Shell edging
Using thumb method, cast on a number of stitches divisible by 11 plus 2.
1st row P to end.
2nd row K2, *K1, sl this st back on to left hand needle and lift the next 8 sts on left hand needle over this st and off the needle, yfwd and round right hand needle twice to inc 2 sts, then K first st again, K2, rep from * to end.
3rd row K1, *P2 tog, drop extra loop of 2 new sts on previous row, and into this long loop work (K1, K1 tbl) twice, P1, rep from * to last st, K1.
Work 5 rows g st. Bind off.

Leaf edging
Cast on a number of stitches divisible by 13 plus 2.
1st row K1, *K2, sl 1, K1, psso, sl 2, K3 tog, p2sso, K2 tog, K2, rep from * to last st, K1.

2nd row P4, *yrn, P1, yrn, P6, rep from * ending last rep with P4 instead of P6.
3rd row K1, yfwd, *K2, sl 1, K1, psso, K1, K2 tog, K2, yfwd, rep from * to last st, K1.
4th row P2, *yrn, P2, yrn, P3, yrn, P2, yrn, P1, rep from * to last st, P1.
5th row K2, *yfwd, K1, yfwd, sl 1, K1, psso, K1, sl 1, K2 tog, psso, K1, K2 tog, yfwd, K1, yfwd, K1, rep from * to last st, K1.
6th row P to end.
7th row K5, *yfwd, sl 2, K3 tog, p2sso, yfwd, K7, rep from * ending last rep with K5 instead of K7.
Work 4 rows g st. Bind off.

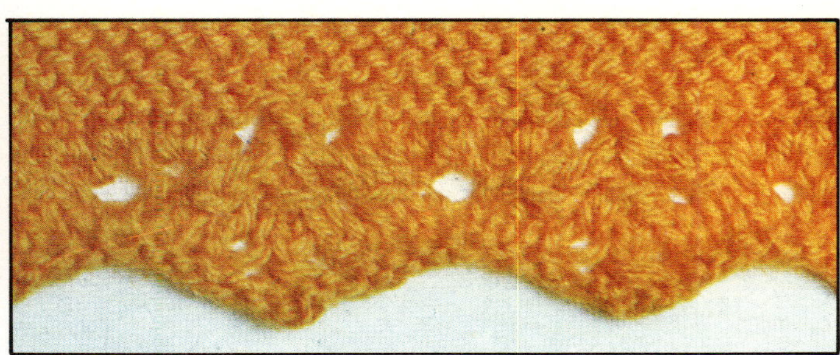

Chain edging
Using 2 needle method and working into each st instead of between sts, cast on a number of stitches divisible by 29.
1st row *K3 tbl, (pick up loop lying between sts and K tbl – called inc 1 –, drop 3 sts off left hand needle, K2 tog tbl) 4 times, inc 1, drop 3 sts off left hand needle, K3, rep from * to end.
2nd row P to end.
3rd row *K2 tbl, (sl 1, K1, psso) twice, sl 1, K2 tog, psso, (K2 tog) twice, K2, rep from * to end.
4th row P to end.
Work 3 rows g st. Bind off.

Serrated edging
Cast on 8 sts loosely.
1st row K to last 2 sts, K twice into next st, yfwd and hold at front of work, sl 1 P-wise. 9 sts.
2nd row K1 tbl, K1, (yfwd and over needle – called M1 –, sl 1, K1, psso, K1) twice, yfwd, sl 1 P-wise.
3rd row K1 tbl, K to end, turn and cast on 3 sts.
4th row K1, K twice into next st, K2, (M1, sl 1, K1, psso, K1) twice, M1, K1, yfwd, sl 1 P-wise.
5th row K1 tbl, K to last 2 sts, K twice into next st, yfwd, sl 1 P-wise.
6th row K1 tbl, K twice into next st, K2, (M1, sl 1, K1, psso, K1) 3 times, K1, yfwd, sl 1 P-wise.
7th row K1 tbl, K to last 2 sts, K2 tog.
8th row Sl 1 P-wise, ybk, K1, psso, sl 1, K1, psso, K4, (M1, sl 1, K1, psso, K1) twice, yfwd, sl 1 P-wise.
9th row K1 tbl, K to last 2 sts, K2 tog.
10th row Cast off 3 sts, K2, M1, sl 1, K1, psso, K1, M1, sl 1, K1, psso, yfwd, sl 1 P-wise, 9 sts.
Rows 3 to 10 inclusive form pattern. Repeat pattern rows until edging is desired length. Bind off.

Fan edging
Cast on 13 sts loosely.
1st row (RS) Sl 1, K1, yfwd, K2 tog, K5, yfwd, K2 tog, yfwd, K2.
2nd and every alt row Yrn to inc 1, K2 tog, K to end.
3rd row Sl 1, K1, yfwd, K2 tog, K4 (yfwd, K2 tog) twice, yfwd, K2.
5th row Sl 1, K1, yfwd, K2 tog, K3, (yfwd, K2 tog) 3 times, yfwd, K2.
7th row Sl 1, K1, yfwd, K2 tog, K2, (yfwd, K2 tog) 4 times, yfwd, K2.
9th row Sl 1, K1, yfwd, K2 tog, K1, (yfwd, K2 tog) 5 times, yfwd, K2.
11th row Sl 1, K1, yfwd, K2 tog, K1, K2 tog, (yfwd, K2 tog) 5 times, K1.
13th row Sl 1, K1, yfwd, K2 tog, K2, K2 tog, (yfwd, K2 tog) 4 times, K1.
15th row Sl 1, K1, yfwd, K2 tog, K3, K2 tog, (yfwd, K2 tog) 3 times, K1.
17th row Sl 1, K1, yfwd, K2 tog, K4, K2 tog, (yfwd, K2 tog) twice, K1.
19th row Sl 1, K1, yfwd, K2 tog, K5, K2 tog, yfwd, K2 tog, K1.
20th row Yrn, K2 tog, K11.
These 20 rows form the pattern. Repeat pattern rows until edging is desired length. Bind off.

SHAPED EDGINGS

Knitted borders
The last chapter dealt with straight knitted edgings, either worked over a multiple of stitches in rows to give the desired length, or from side edge to side edge on a set number of stitches for the desired length. Where a border is required to fit a rectangular, square or circular shape, however, provision must be made for working corners or shaping the border so that the outer edge is wider than the inner edge.
The circular border given here is used to trim a baby's shawl, where the center is knitted in stockinette stitch to a circular shape, but if it is worked in a fine cotton yarn, the same border would most effectively trim a circular fabric tablecloth.
The border with corner shaping, used here to trim a fabric place mat, would also be ideal for trimming a pillow case, a tablecloth or a delicate evening stole.

Shawl center
Using set of 4 double-pointed needles, cast on 6 sts.
1st round *K into front then into back of next st, rep from * to end. 12 sts.
2nd round K1, *yfwd to make one, K2, rep from * to last st, yfwd, K1. 18 sts.
3rd round K1, *K into front then into back of yfwd of previous round, K2, rep from * to last 2 sts, K into front then into back of yfwd, K1. 24 sts.
4th round K2, *yfwd, K4, rep from * to last 2 sts, yfwd, K2. 30 sts.
5th round K2, *K into front then into back of yfwd, K4, rep from * to last 3 sts, K into front then into back of yfwd, K2. 36 sts.
6th round K3, *yfwd, K6, rep from * to last 3 sts, yfwd, K3. 42 sts.
7th round K3, *K into front then into back of yfwd, K6, rep from * to last 4 sts, K into front then into back of yfwd, K3.
Cont inc 6 sts on every round in this way until center is desired diameter. Bind off very loosely.

Shawl border
Cast on 52 sts loosely.
1st row K2, (K2 tog, yfwd to inc one – called M1 –, K2) 3 times, K2 tog, K11, K2 tog, (K2 tog, M1, K2) 3 times, K2 tog, (M1, K2 tog) 4 times. 49 sts.
2nd row P10, turn and leave 39 sts unworked.
3rd row K2 tog, (M1, K2 tog) 4 times.
4th row P8, (K2 tog, M1, K2) 3 times, P13, (K2 tog, M1, K2) 3 times, K3.
5th row K3, (K2 tog, M1, K2) 3 times, (K2 tog) twice, (M1, K1) 5 times, M1, (K2 tog) twice, (K2 tog, M1, K2) 3 times, K1, (M1, K2 tog) 3 times, M1, K1.
6th row P9, (K2 tog, M1, K2) 3 times, P15, (K2 tog, M1, K2) 3 times, K3.
7th row K3, (K2 tog, M1, K2) 3 times, K2 tog, K11, K2 tog, (K2 tog, M1, K2) 3 times, K2, (M1, K2 tog) 3 times, M1, K1.
8th row P10, (K2 tog, M1, K2) 3 times, P12, turn and leave 16sts unworked.
9th row K1, K2 tog, (M1, K1) 5 times, M1, (K2 tog) twice, (K2 tog, M1, K2) 3 times, K3, (M1, K2 tog) 3 times, M1, K1.
10th row P11, (K2 tog, M1, K2) 3 times, P14, P2 tog, (K2 tog, M1, K2) 3 times, K3.

11th row K3, *K2 tog, M1, K1, sl next 3 sts on to cable needle and hold at back of work, K1, K2 tog from left hand needle, M1, K2 from cable needle, K next st on left hand needle and last st on cable needle tog, M1, K2, *, K2 tog, K11, K2 tog, rep from * to *, K4, (M1, K2 tog) 3 times, M1, K1.
12th row P13, turn and leave 39 sts unworked.
13th row K6, (M1, K2 tog) 3 times, M1, K1.
14th row *P13, (K2 tog, M1, K2) 3 times, rep from * once more, K3.
15th row K3, (K2 tog, M1, K2) 3 times, (K2 tog) twice, (M1, K1) 5 times, M1 (K2 tog) twice, (K2 tog, M1, K2) 3 times, K3, K2 tog, (M1, K2 tog) 4 times.
16th row P12, (K2 tog, M1, K2) 3 times, P15, (K2 tog, M1, K2) 3 times, K3.
17th row K3, (K2 tog, M1, K2) 3 times, K2 tog, K11, K2 tog, (K2 tog, M1, K2) 3 times, K2, K2 tog, (M1, K2 tog) 4 times.
18th row P11, (K2 tog, M1, K2) 3 times, P12, turn and leave 16 sts unworked.
19th row K1, K2 tog, (M1, K1) 5 times, M1, (K2 tog) twice, (K2 tog, M1, K2) 3 times, K1, K2 tog, (M1, K2 tog) 4 times.
20th row P10, (K2 tog, M1, K2) 3 times, P14, P2 tog, (K2 tog, M1, K2) 3 times, K3.
These 20 rows form patt. Cont in patt until inner edge of border fits around outer edge of center. Sew in place around shawl.

Place mat
Cut fabric to required size and hem round all edges.

Border
Cast on 9sts. Start patt.
1st row (RS) K to end.
2nd row K3, K2 tog, yfwd to inc one, K2 tog, yfwd, K1, yfwd, K1. 10 sts.
3rd and every alt row K to end.
4th row K2, K2 tog, yfwd, K2 tog, yfwd, K3, yfwd, K1. 11 sts.
6th row K1, K2 tog, yfwd, K2 tog, yfwd, K5, yfwd, K1. 12 sts.
8th row K3, yfwd, K2 tog, yfwd, K2 tog, K1, K2 tog, yfwd, K2 tog. 11 sts.
10th row K4, yfwd, K2 tog, yfwd, K3 tog, yfwd, K2 tog. 10 sts.
12th row K5, yfwd, K3 tog, yfwd, K2 tog. 9 sts.
These 12 rows form patt. Cont in patt until border is required length to first corner, ending with a 6th row.

Shape corner
1st row K10, turn.
2nd row Sl 1 K-wise, yfwd, K2 tog, yfwd, K2 tog, K1, K2 tog, yfwd, K2 tog. 11 sts.
3rd row K8, turn.
4th row Sl 1 K-wise, yfwd, K2 tog, yfwd, K3 tog, yfwd, K2 tog. 10 sts.
5th row K5, turn.

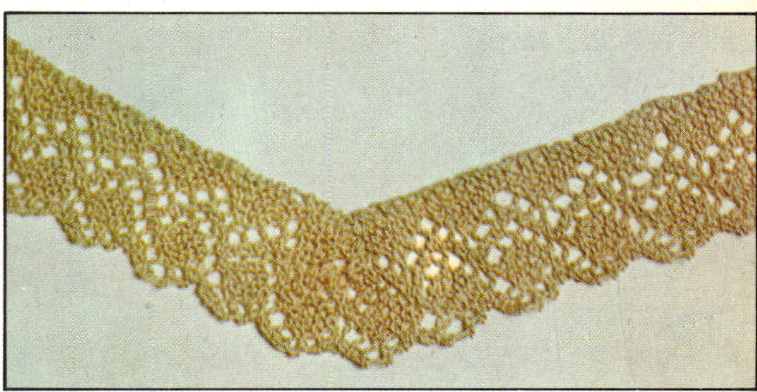

6th row Sl 1 K-wise, yfwd, K3 tog, yfwd, K2 tog. 9 sts.
7th row K6, turn.
8th row K2 tog, yfwd, K2 tog, yfwd, K1, yfwd, K1. 10 sts.
9th row K8, turn.
10th row K2 tog, yfwd, K2 tog, yfwd, K3, yfwd, K1. 11 sts.
11th row K10, turn.
12th row K2 tog, yfwd, K2 tog, yfwd, K5, yfwd, K1. 12 sts.
13th row K to end.
This completes corner shaping. Beg with an 8th patt row, cont in patt to next corner, then rep shaping rows. Cont in this way until border is completed. Sew in place around mat.

EDGINGS AND INSERTIONS

Knitted edgings and insertions can be used most effectively as a trim for fabric garments, or on household linens. They look their best when worked in a fine cotton, such as No.20, which is delicate and will also stand up to laundering without losing its shape.
The insertion pattern given here may be used by itself to form a panel on each side of the front of a fabric blouse, or it could be combined with any one of the edgings to form the yoke of a charming nightgown.
Alternatively, the insertion could be applied across the top of a sheet, which could then be finished off with an edging to transform a plain household linen into a family heirloom.

7th row K4, P2, K1, P4, K2, (yrn, P2 tog) twice, K1.
8th row K3, (yrn, P2 tog) twice, yon, K1 tbl, K1, K1, tbl, yfwd, sl 1, K2 tog, psso, yfwd, K5.
9th row K5, P7, K2, (yrn, P2 tog) twice, K1.
10th row K3, (yrn, P2 tog) twice, yon, K1 tbl, K3, K1 tbl, yfwd, K7.
11th row Bind off 4 sts, K2, P7 K2, (yrn, P2 tog) twice, K1.
The 2nd through 11th rows form the pattern.

Shell edging
Cast on 13 sts.
1st row (WS) P to end.
2nd row Sl 1, K1, yrn, P2 tog, K1, (yfwd, sl 1, K1, psso) 3 times, y2rn, K2 tog.

Leaf edging
Cast on 17 sts.
1st row (WS) K to end.
2nd row K3, (yrn, P2 tog) twice, yon, K1 tbl, K2 tog, P1, sl 1, K1, psso, K1 tbl, yfwd, K3.
3rd row K3, P3, K1, P3, K2, (yrn, P2 tog) twice, K1.
4th row As 2nd.
5th row As 3rd.
6th row K3, (yrn, P2 tog) twice, yon, K1 tbl, yfwd, K2 tog, P1, sl 1, K1, psso, yfwd, K4.

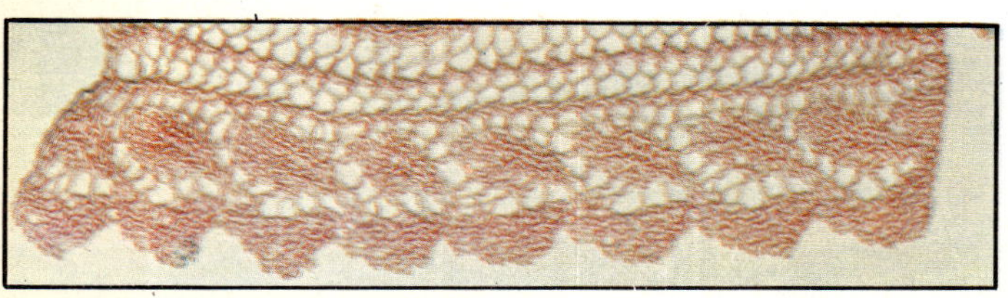

3rd row Yfwd to make 1, K2 tog, P9, yrn, P2 tog, K1, noting that the first K2 tog includes the first loop of

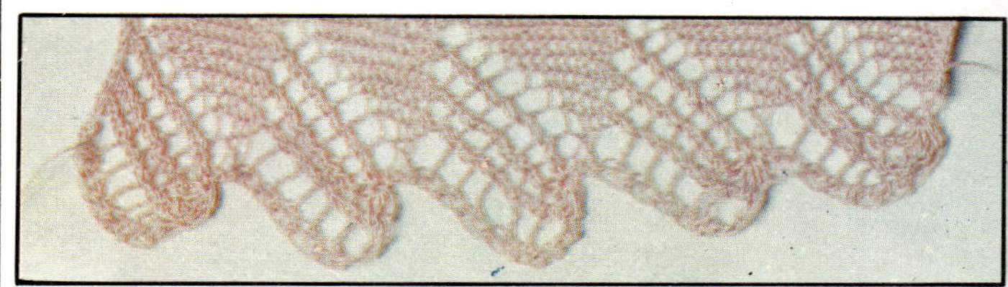

y2rn and the second loop forms the first P st.
4th row Sl 1, K1, yrn, P2 tog, K2, (yfwd, sl 1, K1, psso) 3 times, y2rn, K2 tog.
5th row Yfwd, K2 tog, P10, yrn, P2 tog, K1.
6th row Sl 1, K1, yrn, P2 tog, K3, (yfwd, sl 1, K1, psso) 3 times, y2rn, K2 tog.
7th row Yfwd, K2 tog, P11, yrn, P2 tog, K1.

8th row Sl 1, K1, yrn, P2 tog, K4, (yfwd, sl 1, K1, psso) 3 times, y2rn, K2 tog.
9th row Yfwd, K2 tog, P12, yrn, P2 tog, K1.
10th row Sl 1, K1, yrn, P2 tog, K5, (yfwd, sl 1, K1, psso) 3 times, y2rn, K2 tog.
11th row Yfwd, K2 tog, P13, yrn, P2 tog, K1.
12th row Sl 1, K1, yrn, P2 tog, K6, (yfwd, sl 1, K1, psso) 3 times, y2rn, K2 tog.
13th row Yfwd, K2 tog, P14, yrn, P2 tog, K1.
14th row Sl 1, K1, yrn, P2 tog, K7, (yfwd, sl 1, K1, psso) 3 times, y2rn, K2 tog.
15th row Yfwd, K2 tog, P15, yrn, P2 tog, K1.
16th row Sl 1, K1, yrn, P2 tog, K8, yfwd, K1, return last st to left hand needle and with point of right hand needle lift the next 7 sts one at a time over this st and off needle, then sl st back on to right hand needle.
17th row P2 tog, P9, yrn, P2 tog, K1.
The 2nd through 17th rows form the pattern.

Cockleshell edging
Cast on 16 sts.
1st row K to end.
2nd row Yfwd to make 1, K2 tog, K1, yfwd, K10, yfwd, K2 tog, K1.

3rd row K2, yfwd, K2 tog, K12, P1.
4th row Yfwd, K2 tog, K1, yfwd, K2 tog, yfwd, K9, yfwd, K2 tog, K1.
5th row K2, yfwd, K2 tog, K13, P1.
6th row Yfwd, K2 tog, K1, (yfwd, K2 tog) twice, yfwd, K8, yfwd, K2 tog, K1.
7th row K2, yfwd, K2 tog, K14, P1.
8th row Yfwd, K2 tog, K1, (yfwd, K2 tog) 3 times, yfwd, K7, yfwd, K2 tog, K1.
9th row K2, yfwd, K2 tog, K15, P1.
10th row Yfwd, K2 tog, K1, (yfwd, K2 tog) 4 times, yfwd, K6, yfwd, K2 tog, K1.
11th row K2, yfwd, K2 tog, K16, P1.
12th row Yfwd, K2 tog, K1, (yfwd, K2 tog) 5 times, yfwd, K5, yfwd, K2 tog, K1.
13th row K2, yfwd, K2 tog, K17, P1.
14th row Yfwd, K2 tog, K1, (yfwd, K2 tog) 6 times, yfwd, K4, yfwd, K2 tog, K1.
15th row K2, yfwd, K2 tog, K18, P1.
16th row Yfwd, K2 tog, K1, (yfwd, K2 tog) 7 times, yfwd, K3, yfwd, K2 tog, K1.
17th row K2, yfwd, K2 tog, K19, P1.
18th row Yfwd, (K2 tog) twice, (yfwd, K2 tog) 7 times, K3, yfwd, K2 tog, K1.
19th row As 15th.
20th row Yfwd, (K2 tog) twice, (yfwd, K2 tog) 6 times, K4, yfwd, K2 tog, K1.
21st row As 13th.
22nd row Yfwd, (K2 tog) twice, (yfwd, K2 tog) 5 times, K5, yfwd, K2 tog, K1.
23rd row As 11th.
24th row Yfwd, (K2 tog) twice, (yfwd, K2 tog) 4 times, K6, yfwd, K2 tog, K1.
25th row As 9th.
26th row Yfwd, (K2 tog) twice, (yfwd, K2 tog) 3 times, K7, yfwd, K2 tog, K1.
27th row As 7th.
28th row Yfwd, (K2 tog) twice, (yfwd, K2 tog) twice, K8, yfwd, K2 tog, K1.
29th row As 5th.
30th row Yfwd, (K2 tog) twice, yfwd, K2 tog, K9, yfwd, K2 tog, K1.
31st row As 3rd.
32nd row Yfwd, (K2 tog) twice, K10, yfwd, K2 tog, K1.
33rd row K2, yfwd, K2 tog, K11, P1.
The 2nd through 33rd rows form the pattern.

Diamond insertion panel
Cast on 21 sts.
1st and every alt row (WS) P to end.
2nd row K2, yfwd, sl 1, K1, psso, K1, yfwd, sl 1, K1, psso, K3, K2 tog, yfwd, K1, yfwd, sl 1, K1, psso, K6.
4th row K3, (yfwd, sl 1, K1, psso, K1) twice, K2 tog, yfwd, K3, yfwd, sl 1, K1, psso, K5.
6th row K4, yfwd, sl 1, K1, psso, K1, yfwd, K3 tog, yfwd, K2, yfwd, sl 1, K1, psso, K1, yfwd, sl 1, K1, psso, K4.

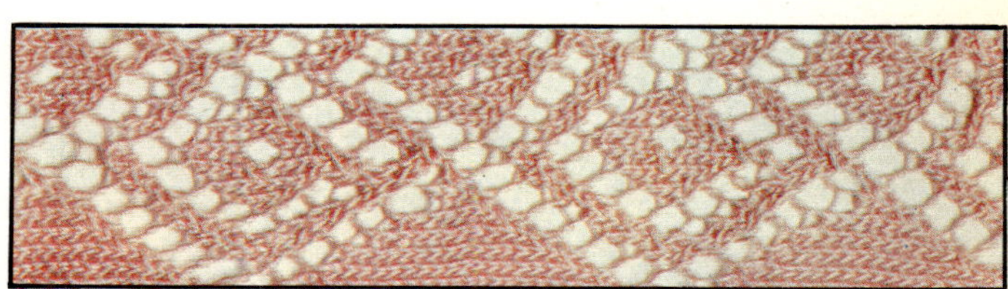

8th row K5, yfwd, sl 1, K1, psso, (K2 tog, yfwd, K1) twice, yfwd, sl 1, K1, psso, K1, yfwd, sl 1, K1, psso, K3.
10th row K6, yfwd, sl 1, K1, psso, K1, K2 tog, yfwd, K3, yfwd, sl 1, K1, psso, K1, yfwd, sl 1, K1, psso, K2.
12th row K7, yfwd, K3 tog, yfwd, K5, (yfwd, sl 1, K1, psso, K1) twice.
14th row K7, K2 tog, yfwd, K3, yfwd, sl 1, K1, psso, K2, yfwd, sl 1, K1, psso, K1, yfwd, sl 1, K1, psso.
16th row K6, K2 tog, yfwd, K1, yfwd, sl 1, K1, psso, K3, K2 tog, yfwd, K1, K2 tog, yfwd, K2.
18th row K5, K2 tog, yfwd, K3, yfwd, sl 1, K1, psso, (K1, K2 tog, yfwd) twice, K3.
20th row K4, K2 tog, yfwd, K1, K2 tog, yfwd, K2, yfwd, sl 1, K2 tog, psso, yfwd, K1, K2 tog, yfwd, K4.
22nd row K3, (K2 tog, yfwd, K1) twice, yfwd, sl 1, K1, psso, K1, yfwd, sl 1, K1, psso, K2 tog, yfwd, K5.
24th row K2, K2 tog, yfwd, K1, K2 tog, yfwd, K3, yfwd, sl 1, K1, psso, K1, K2 tog, yfwd, K6.
26th row (K1, K2 tog, yfwd) twice, K5, yfwd, sl 1, K2 tog, psso, yfwd, K7.
28th row K2 tog, yfwd, K1, K2 tog, yfwd, K2, K2 tog, yfwd, K3, yfwd, sl 1, K1, psso, K7.
These 28 rows form the pattern.

SEQUINS AND BEADS

Beaded and sequinned tops and jackets make glamorous and dazzling garments for evening wear and the technique is very simple to work. The beads or sequins are knitted in with the fabric and they can be used to form an all-over design, or as a most effective trimming.

Most chain stores sell packets of beads and sequins which will prove suitable for this type of knitting.

If you are using beads, they should not be too large or heavy, so they do not pull the fabric out of shape – small pearl beads are ideal. The hole in the center of the bead must be large enough to thread over the yarn being used.

Sequins also come in various sizes and shapes and must also have a hole large enough to be threaded over the yarn. This hole should be at the top of the sequin and not in the center so that the sequins do not stick out but hang flat against the knitted background.

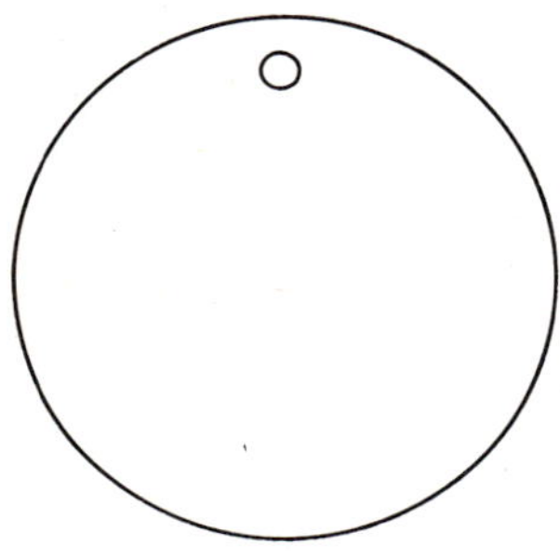

To thread beads or sequins onto a ball of yarn

Cut a 10in length of ordinary sewing thread and fold this in half. Thread both cut ends through a fine sewing needle, leaving a loop of thread as shown in diagram 1.

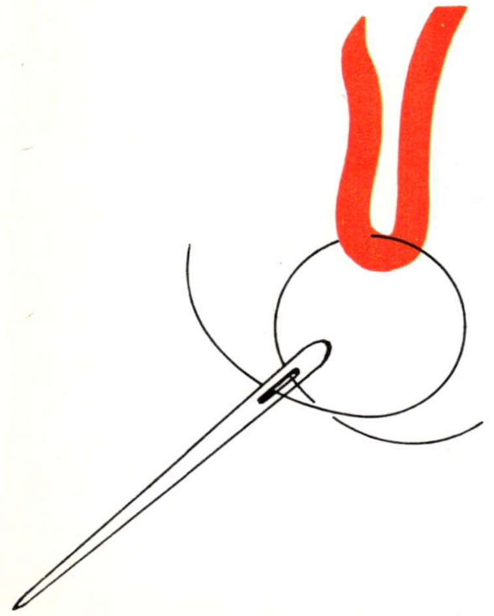

Thread the required number of beads or sequins on to the ball of yarn with which you are going to knit by passing approximately 6in of the end of this ball through the loop of sewing thread. Thread the beads or sequins on to the needle, then slide them down the thread and on to the ball of yarn, as shown in diagram 2.

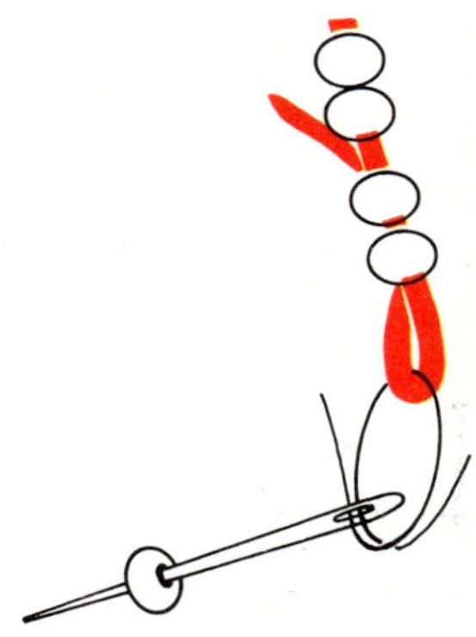

To knit in beads or sequins

Prepare a ball of yarn by threading on the required number of beads or sequins. These should be knitted in on a right side row against a stockinette stitch background, although they can be worked in panels and interspersed with a lace pattern, as shown in the evening top given here.

Knit until the position for the bead or sequin is reached, push one bead or sequin up the ball of yarn close to the back of the work, knit the next stitch through the back of the loop in the usual way, pushing the bead or sequin through to the front of the work with the loop of the stitch, and taking care not to split the yarn. Working this way allows the bead or sequin to lie flat against the fabric.

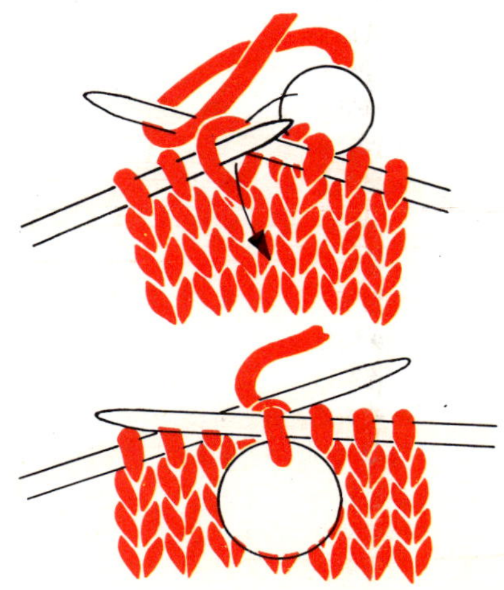

ening top

es
ections are to fit 32in bust. Changes for 34, 36, 38 d 40in bust are in brackets [].
ngth to center back, 14in

uge
sts and 36 rows to 4in in patt worked on No.4 edles

terials
10oz balls of Bucilla 3-ply Fingering Yarn
prox 700 sequins with hole at top
e pair No.4 needles
e pair No.3 needles

te
ead approximately 350 sequins onto each of 2 balls yarn

k
ng No.3 needles and ball of yarn which has not n threaded with sequins, cast on 94[100:106:112: sts. Work 6in K1, P1 rib. Break off yarn. Change to 4 needles. Join in ball threaded with sequins. Start t.
row (RS) K1, *K2, K2 tog, yarn round needle twice – called y2rn – K2 tog tbl, rep from * to last 3 sts, K3.
2nd row *P4, P into front then into back of y2rn, rep from * to last 4 sts, P4.
3rd row K1, *K1, K sequin in with next st through back loops (tbl) – called K1S –, K2 tog, y2rn, K2 tog tbl, rep from * to last 3 sts, K1, K1S, K1.
4th row As 2nd.
5th row As 1st.
6th row As 2nd.
7th row K1, *K1S, K1, K2 tog, y2rn, K2 tog tbl, rep from * to last 3 sts, K1S, K2.
8th row As 2nd.
These 8 rows form patt. Cont in patt until work measures 12in from beg, ending with a WS row.

Shape armholes
Maintaining patt, bind off 5[6:7:8:9] sts at beg of next 2 rows. Dec one st at each end of next and every alt row 8 times in all, ending with a WS row. 68[72:76:80:84] sts.

Shape neck
Next row Dec one st, patt 20[21:22:23:24] sts, bind off 24[26:28:30:32] sts, patt to last 2 sts, dec one st.
Complete left shoulder first.
Next row Patt to end.
Next row Dec one st, patt to last 2 sts, dec one st.
Rep last 2 rows until 3[2:3:2:3] sts rem K3[2:3:2:3] tog.
Fasten off.
With WS of work facing, rejoin yarn to rem sts and complete the right shoulder to correspond to the left shoulder.

Front
Work as for back.

Shoulder straps (make 2)
Using No.3 needles and ball of yarn which has not been threaded with sequins, cast on 11 sts.
1st row K1, *P1, K1, rep from * to end.
2nd row P1, *K1, P1, rep from * to end.
Rep these 2 rows until strap measures 20in from beg, or desired length to fit around armhole to shoulder.
Bind off.
Join cast on edge to bound off edge. Join side seams.
Pin straps in place around armhole.

Neck edging (make 2)
Work as for shoulder straps until edging fits down side of one shoulder strap, around center neck edge and up side of other shoulder strap.
Bind off.

Finishing
Do not block. Sew shoulder straps in place. Sew neck edging down inner edge of shoulder strap, around neck and along inner edge of other strap, then join shoulder seam. Fold straps and edging in half to WS and sew in place.

CHANGING COLORS

SIMPLE STRIPES

Striped patterns, using simple stitches and subtle combinations of colors, are the easiest way of achieving a colorful knitted fabric. A plain, basic sweater can be changed and given a completely new look by working regular or random stripes in three or four colors. This is, besides, a very useful way of using up odds and ends of yarn of the same thickness.

Twisting yarns to change color

When you work any form of horizontal stripe, there is no problem about joining in different colored yarns. As one color is finished with at the end of a row, the new one is brought in at the beginning of the next row. When each color has been brought into use, it is left until it is needed again, then carried loosely up the side of the work and twisted once around the last color used, before you begin to work with it again.

Vertical or diagonal stripes are a little more difficult to work, as the colors must be changed at several points within the same row. When you knit narrow vertical or diagonal stripes, it is best to twist each yarn with the last color used as it is brought into use, then carry the yarn not in use across the back of the work until it is needed again. For wider stripes however it is not advisable to use this method of carrying the yarn across the back of the work as, apart from the waste of yarn, there is a tendency to pull the yarn too tightly, which results in an unsightly puckering of the fabric and a loss of gauge. It is much better to divide each color into small separate balls before beginning to work and then use one ball of yarn for each stripe, twisting one color to the next at the back of the work when a change is made.

It is important to remember that stripes worked by twisting the yarn in changing colors give a fabric of normal thickness, while stripes worked by carrying the yarn across the back of the work produce a fabric of double thickness.

Horizontal stripes

These are usually worked in stockinette stitch and are achieved by changing color at the beginning of a knit row. This gives an unbroken line of color on the right side of the fabric. An even number of rows must be worked, either two, four, six and so on, and the same number of rows can be used for each color or varied to give a random striped effect.

The purl side of this fabric can also be used as the right side of the work. Where each new color is brought into use, it gives a broken line of color on the purl side which looks most effective.

Ribbed stitches can also be used to produce a striped fabric. If an unbroken line of color is needed on the right side of the fabric, the row where a change of color is made needs to be knitted each time, and the other rows of each stripe worked in ribbing. An interesting fabric is produced by working in ribbing throughout, irrespective of the color change which gives a broken line of color each time.

Fancy striped rib

Cast on a number of stitches divisible by 10 plus 5.

1st row P5, *K1, yfwd, sl 1, ybk, K1, yfwd, sl 1, ybk, K1, P5, rep from * to end.

2nd row K1, yfwd, sl 1, ybk, K1, yfwd, sl 1, ybk, K1, *P5, K1, yfwd, sl 1, ybk, K1, yfwd, sl 1, ybk, K1, rep from * to end.

These 2 rows form the pattern, changing colors as you wish.

Chevron stripes

Cast on a number of stitches divisible by 13 plus 2.

1st row *K2, pick up loop lying between needles and place it on the left hand needle then K this loop through the back – called inc 1 –, K4, sl 1 P-wise, K2 tog, psso, K4, inc 1, rep from * to last 2 sts, K2.

2nd row P to end.
These 2 rows form the pattern. Change colors as you wish on any row.

Vertical stripes

To work narrow or wide vertical stripes, the best effect is achieved in stockinette stitch with the knit side of the fabric as the right side. The yarn must be carried across or twisted at the back of the fabric.
To work a wide stripe it is necessary to use a separate ball of yarn for each color. Using two colors, the first color would be referred to as A and the second color as B.

Wide vertical stripe

Cast on 6 stitches with B, 6 with A, 6 with B and 6 with A, making a total of 24 stitches.
1st row *Using A, K6 sts, hold A to the left at the back of the work, pick up B and bring it towards the right at the back of the work and under the A thread no longer in use, K6 B, hold B to the left at the back of the work, pick up A and bring it towards the right at the back of the work and under the B thread no longer in use, rep from * to end.

2nd row (WS) *Using B, P6 sts, hold B to the left at the front of the work, pick up A and bring it towards the right at the front of the work and over the B thread no longer in use, P6 A, hold A to the left at the front of the work, pick up B and bring it towards the right at the front of the work and over the A thread no longer in use, rep from * to end.
These 2 rows form the pattern.

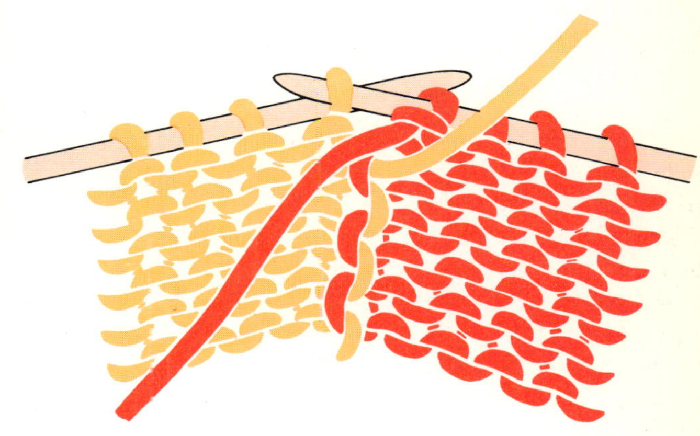

Diagonal stripes

Depending on the width of the stripes, the yarn can either be carried across the back of the work, or separate balls of yarn used for each color as for wide vertical stripes.

Narrow diagonal stripes

Cast on a number of stitches divisible by 5 plus 3, using two colors, A and B.
1st row (RS) K3 A, *pick up B and K2, pick up A and K3, rep from * to end.
2nd row Pick up B and P1, *pick up A and P3, pick up B and P2, rep from * to last 2 sts, pick up A and P2.
3rd row K1 A, *pick up B and K2, pick up A and K3, rep from * to last 2 sts, pick up B and K2.
4th row Pick up A and P1, pick up B and P2, *pick up A and P3, pick up B and P2, rep from * to end.
Continue working in this way, moving the stripes one stitch to the right on K rows and one stitch to the left on P rows.

TWO COLOR PATTERNS

By combining the working method for horizontal stripes with the clever use of slipped stitches colorful tweed fabrics can be quickly and easily made. These stitches can be worked in two or more colors, and on each change of color the yarn is merely carried up the side of the work and does not have to be carried across the back of the fabric as it does for the more difficult jacquard and Fair Isle patterns.

Bird's eye stitch
Using 2 colors coded as A and B, cast on a multiple of 2 stitches.
1st row Using A, *sl 1 P-wise, K1, rep from * to end.
2nd row Using A, P to end.
3rd row Using B, *K1, sl 1 P-wise, rep from * to end.
4th row Using B, P to end.
These 4 rows form the pattern.

Mock houndstooth stitch
Using 2 colors coded as A and B, cast on any multiple of 3 stitches.
1st row Using A, *sl 1 P-wise, K2, rep from * to end.

2nd row Using A, P to end.
3rd row Using B, *K2, sl 1 P-wise, rep from * to end.
4th row Using B, P to end.
These 4 rows form the pattern.

Crossed stitch
Using 2 colors coded as A and B, cast on a multiple of 2 plus 1.
1st row Using A, K to end.
2nd row Using A, K to end.
3rd row Using B, *K1, sl 1 P-wise, rep from * to last st, K1.
4th row Using B, *K1, yfwd, sl 1 P-wise, ybk, rep from * to last st, K1.
5th row Using A, K to end.
6th row Using A, K to end.
7th row Using B, *sl 1 P-wise, K1, rep from * to last st, sl 1 P-wise.
8th row Using B, *sl 1 P-wise, ybk, K1, yfwd, rep from * to last st, sl 1 P-wise.
These 8 rows form the pattern.

Bee stitch
Using 2 colors coded as A and B, cast any multiple of 2 stitches.
1st row Using A, K to end.
2nd row Using A, K to end.
3rd row Using B, *insert right hand needle into next stitch on the row below and K in usual way – called K1B –, K next st on left hand needle, rep from * to end.
4th row Using B, K to end.
5th row Using A, *K1, K1B, rep from * to end.

6th row Using A, K to end.
Rows 3 through 6 form the pattern.

Two color fuchsia stitch

Using 2 colors coded as A and B, cast on a multiple of 4 stitches.
1st row Using A, K to end.
2nd row Using A, P to end.
Rep 1st and 2nd rows once more.
5th row Using B, *K3, insert right hand needle into next st in first row of A and draw through a loop, K1 and pass the loop over K1, rep from * to end.
6th row Using B, P to end.
7th row Using B, K to end.
8th row Using B, P to end.
9th row Using A, *K1, insert right hand needle into next st in first row of B and draw through a loop, K1 and pass the loop over K1, K2, rep from * to end.
Rows 2 through 9 form the pattern.

Ladder stitch

Using 2 colors coded as A and B, cast on a multiple of 6 stitches plus 5.
1st row Using A, K2, *sl 1 P-wise, K5, rep from * to last 3 sts, sl 1 P-wise, K2.
2nd row Using A, P2, *sl 1 P-wise, P5, rep from * to last 3 sts, sl 1 P-wise, P2.
3rd row Using B, *K5, sl 1 P-wise, rep from * to last 5 sts, K5.
4th row Using B, *K5, yfwd, sl 1 P-wise, ybk, rep from * to last 5 sts, K5.
These 4 rows form the pattern.

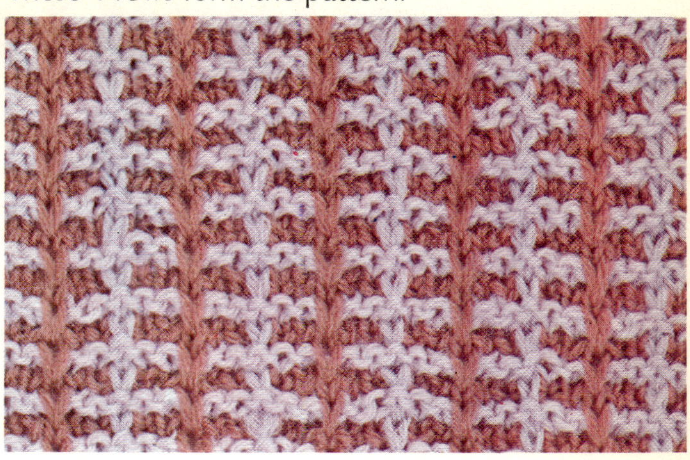

Brick stitch

Using 2 colors coded as A and B, cast on a multiple of 4 stitches.
1st row Using A, K to end.
2nd row Using A, K to end.
3rd row Using B, *K3, sl 1 P-wise, rep from * to end.
4th row Using B, *sl 1 P-wise, P3, rep from * to end.
5th row As 1st.
6th row As 2nd.
7th row Using B, K2, *sl 1 P-wise, K3, rep from * to last 2 sts, sl 1 P-wise, K1.
8th row Using B, P1, *sl 1 P-wise, P3, rep from * to last 3 sts, sl 1 P-wise, P2.
9th row As 1st.
10th row As 2nd.
11th row Using B, K1, *sl 1 P-wise, K3, rep from * to last 3 sts, sl 1 P-wise, K2.
12th row Using B, P2, *sl 1 P-wise, P3, rep from * to last 2 sts, sl 1 P-wise, P1.
13th row As 1st.
14th row As 2nd.
15th row Using B, *sl 1 P-wise, K3, rep from * to end.
16th row Using B, *P3, sl 1 P-wise, rep from * to end.
These 16 rows form the pattern.

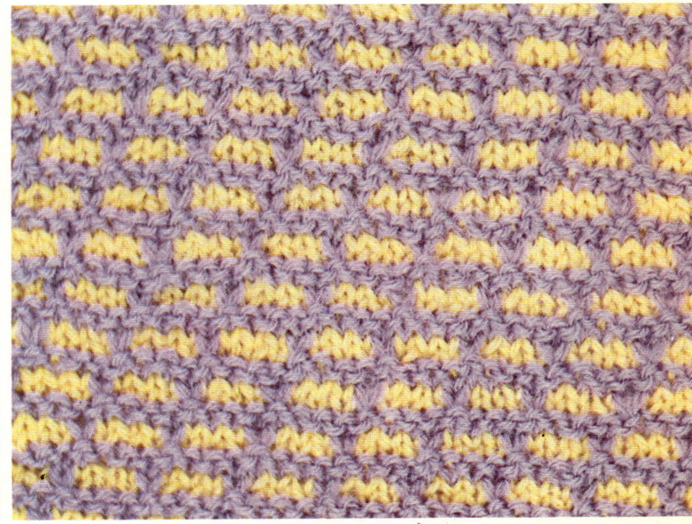

TEXTURED PATTERNS

Unlike patterns which produce a plain knitted fabric with colorful designs, such as Fair Isle (see later) patterns worked in stripes which also combine slipped stitches form textured fabrics which are further enhanced by the use of contrasting colors. Because these stitches do not need such careful regulation of the gauge, they do not necessarily need contrasting yarns of the same thickness. A wool yarn can be combined with many different materials, such as macramé cord, cotton, or metallic yarns to give an exciting and colorful effect.

All the stitches illustrated here are produced by working a set number of rows with one or more colors and, however complicated they may appear, the colors are changed at the end of the row just as for more usual striped patterns.

Ridged check stitch

Two colors of the same yarn have been used for this sample, coded as A and B. Cast on a number of stitches divisible by 4 plus 3 in A.

1st row (WS) Using A, P to end.
2nd row Using B, K3, *sl 1 P-wise keeping yarn at back of work – called sl 1B –, K3, rep from * to end.
3rd row Using B, P3, *sl 1 P-wise keeping yarn at front of work – called sl 1F –, P3, rep from * to end.
4th row As 2nd.
5th row Using B, P to end.
6th row Using A, as 2nd.
7th row Using A, as 3rd.
8th row Using A, as 4th.
These 8 rows form the pattern.

Fancy checked stitch

Two colors of contrasting yarn have been used for this sample, a plain yarn coded as A and a metallic yarn coded as B. Cast on a number of stitches divisible by 6 plus 5 in A.

1st row (RS) Using A, K to end.
2nd row Using A, P to end.
3rd row Using B, K2, *sl 1 P-wise keeping yarn at back of work – called sl 1B –, K1, rep from * to last st, K1.
4th row Using B, K1, *(K1, sl 1 P-wise keeping yarn at front of work – called sl 1F) twice, P1, sl 1F, rep from * to last 4 sts, K1, sl 1F, K2.
5th row Using A, K5, *sl 1B, K5, rep from * to end.
6th row Using A, P5, *sl 1F, P5, rep from * to end.
7th row As 5th.
8th row As 6th.
9th row Using A, as 1st.
10th row Using A, as 2nd.
11th row Using B, K1, *sl 1B, K1, rep from * to end.
12th row Using B, K1, *sl 1F, P1, (sl 1F, K1) twice, rep from * to last 4 sts, sl 1F, P1, sl 1F, K1.
13th row Using A, K2, *sl 1B, K5, rep from * to last 3 sts, sl 1B, K2.
14th row Using A, P2, *sl 1F, P5, rep from * to last 3 sts, sl 1F, P2.
15th row As 13th.
16th row As 14th.
These 16 rows form the pattern.

Ribbon stitch

Two colors of contrasting yarn have been used for this sample, a plain yarn coded as A and a macramé cord coded as B. Cast on a number of stitches divisible by 4 plus 3 in A.

1st row (WS) Using A, P to end.
2nd row Using B, K1, *sl 1 P-wise keeping yarn at back of work – called sl 1B –, K3, rep from * to last 2 sts, sl 1B, K1.
3rd row Using B, K1, *sl 1 P-wise keeping yarn at front of work – called sl 1F –, K1, K1 winding yarn 3 times around needle, K1, rep from * to last 2 sts, sl 1F, K1.
4th row Using A, K3, *sl 1B dropping extra loops, K3, rep from * to end.
5th row Using A, P3, *sl 1B, P3, rep from * to end.
6th row Using A, K3, *sl 1B, K3, rep from * to end.

7th row Using A, as 5th.
8th row Using A, as 6th.
These 8 rows form the pattern.

Tapestry stitch
Two colors of the same yarn have been used for this sample, coded as A and B. Cast on a number of stitches divisible by 4 plus 3 in A.
1st row (WS) Using A, P to end.
2nd row Using B, K1, sl 1 P-wise keeping yarn at front of work – called sl 1F –, K1, *sl 1 P-wise keeping yarn at back of work – called sl 1B –, K1, sl 1F, K1, rep from * to end.
3rd row Using B, P3, *sl 1F, P3, rep from * to end.
4th row Using A, K1, *sl 1B, K3, rep from * to last 2 sts, sl 1B, K1.
5th row Using A, P to end.
6th row Using B, K1, sl 1B, K1, *sl 1F, K1, sl 1B, K1, rep from * to end.
7th row Using B, P1, *sl 1F, P3, rep from * to last 2 sts, sl 1F, P1.
8th row Using A, K3, *sl 1B, K3, rep from * to end.
These 8 rows form the pattern.

Lattice stitch
Two colors of contrasting yarn have been used for this sample, a plain yarn coded as A and a metallic yarn coded as B. Cast on a number of stitches divisible by 6 plus 2 in A.
1st row (WS) Using A, K to end.
2nd row Using B, K1, sl 1 P-wise keeping yarn at back of work – called sl 1B –, *K4, sl 2B, rep from * to last 6 sts, K4, sl 1B, K1.
3rd row Using B, P1, sl 1 P-wise keeping yarn at front of work – called sl 1F –, *P4, sl 2F, rep from * to last 6 sts, P4, sl 1F, P1.
4th row Using A, as 2nd.
5th row Using A, K1, sl 1F, *K4, sl 2F, rep from * to last 6sts, K4, sl 1F, K1.
6th row Using B, K3, *sl 2B, K4, rep from * to last 5 sts, sl 2B, K3.
7th row Using B, P3, *sl 2F, P4, rep from * to last 5 sts, sl 2F, P3.
8th row Using A, as 6th.
9th row Using A, K3, *sl 2F, K4, rep from * to last 5 sts, sl 2F, K3.
Rows 2 through 9 form the pattern.

Pillow
Size
16in wide by 16in deep

Gauge
26 sts and 32 rows to 4in in patt worked on No.5 needles

Materials
2 × 2oz balls Dawn Wintuk Sport Yarn in main color, A
2 balls of contrast color, B
One pair No.5 needles
16in by 16in pillow form
2yd silk cord, optional
8in zipper

Pillow
Using No.5 needles and A, cast on 103 sts. Work in tapestry st until piece measures 16in from beg. Bind off. Make another piece in same way.

Finishing
Block each piece under a damp cloth with a warm iron. With RS facing, join 3 sides. Turn RS out. Insert pillow form. Join rem seam, inserting zipper in center. Sew cord around edges if desired, looping it at each corner.

MOSAIC PATTERNS

Mosaic patterns are worked in two colors, using the slip-stitch method to form complex and unusual geometric shapes. Although the patterns may appear to be complicated, the working method is very simple and is based on knitting two rows with one color and two rows with the second color.

What makes these designs so interesting is that bands of different patterns which require the same multiples of stitches can be worked together to form an overall fabric, using as many different colors as you like. This is another way of using up odds and ends of yarn which are of the same thickness.

You could use a basic pattern which gives the correct multiple of stitches required for each mosaic pattern to form a colorful and original child's sweater, a throw pillow or a warm and practical afghan or bed throw. Because the yarn is not carried across the back of the work as in Fair Isle knitting, the back of the fabric formed is not untidy and is of a single thickness.

Brick pattern

Two colors are used, coded as A and B. Using A, cast on a number of stitches divisible by 4 plus 3.

1st row (RS) Using A, K to end.

2nd row Using A, P to end.

3rd row Using B, K3, *sl 1, K3, rep from * to end.

4th row Using B, K3, *yfwd, sl 1, ybk, K3, rep from * to end.

5th row Using A, K2, *sl 1, K1, rep from * to last st, K1.

6th row Using A, P2, *sl 1, P1, rep from * to last st, P1.

7th row Using B, K1, *sl 1, K3, rep from * to last 2 sts, sl 1, K1.

8th row Using B, K1, *yfwd, sl 1, ybk, K3, rep from * to last 2 sts, yfwd, sl 1, ybk, K1.

9th and 10th rows As 1st and 2nd.

11th and 12th rows As 7th and 8th.

13th and 14th rows As 5th and 6th.

15th and 16th rows As 3rd and 4th.

These 16 rows form the pattern.

Double brick pattern

Two colors are used, coded as A and B. Using A, cast on a number of stitches divisible by 4 plus 3.

1st row (RS) Using A, K to end.

2nd row Using A, K to end.

3rd row Using B, K3, *sl 1, K3, rep from * to end.

4th row Using B, K3, *yfwd, sl 1, ybk K3, rep from * to end.

5th row Using A, K1, *sl 1, K3, rep from * to last 2 sts, sl 1, K1.

6th row Using A, K1, *yfwd, sl 1, ybk, K3, rep from * to last 2 sts, yfwd, sl 1, ybk, K1.

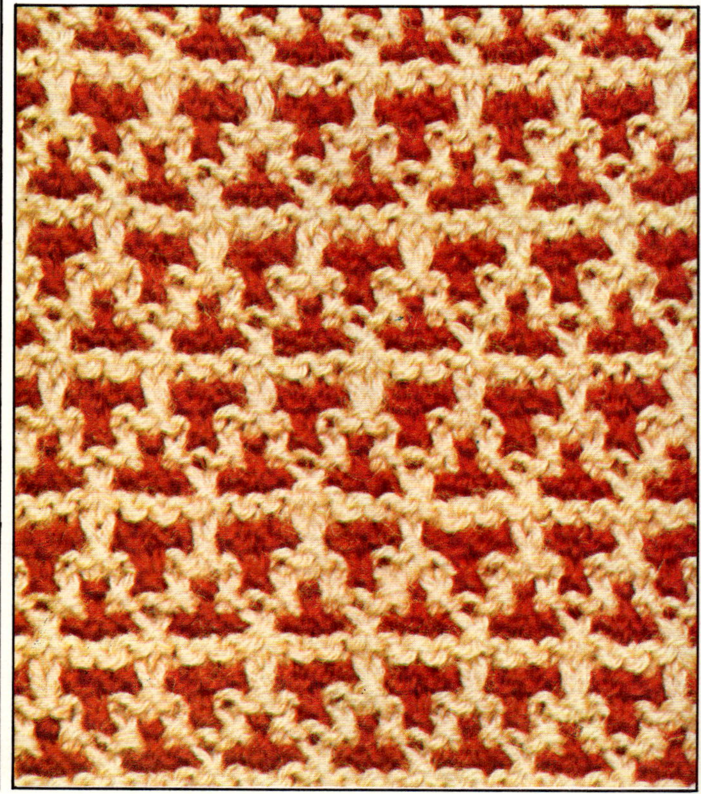

7th row Using B, K2, *sl 1, K1, rep from * to last st, K1.
8th row Using B, K2, *yfwd, sl 1, ybk, K1, rep from * to last st, K1.
9th and 10th rows Using A, as 3rd and 4th.
11th and 12th rows Using B, as 5th and 6th.
13th and 14th rows As 1st and 2nd.
15th and 16th rows As 11th and 12th.
17th and 18th rows As 9th and 10th.
19th and 20th rows As 7th and 8th.
21st and 22nd rows As 5th and 6th.
23rd and 24th rows As 3rd and 4th.
These 24 rows form the pattern.

Vertical chevron pattern
Two colors are used, coded as A and B. Using A, cast on a number of stitches divisible by 6 plus 2.
1st row (RS) Using A, *K5, sl 1, rep from * to last 2 sts, K2.
2nd and every alt row Using same color as previous row, keep yarn at front of work and P all K sts of previous row and sl all sl sts.
3rd row Using B, K2, * sl 1, K3, sl 1, K1, rep from * to end.
5th row Using A, K3, *sl 1, K5, rep from * to last 5 sts, sl 1, K4.
7th row Using B, K4, *sl 1, K1, sl 1, K3, rep from * to last 4 sts, (sl 1, K1) twice.
9th row Using A, K1, *sl 1, K5, rep from * to last st, K1.
11th row Using B, K2, *sl 1, K1, sl 1, K3, rep from * to end.
13th, 15th, 17th, 19th and 21st rows Rep 1st, 3rd, 5th, 7th and 9th rows in that order.
23rd, 25th, 27th and 29th rows Rep 7th, 5th, 3rd and 1st rows in that order.
31st, 33rd, 35th, 37th and 39th rows Rep 11th, 9th, 7th, 5th and 3rd rows in that order.
40th row As 2nd.
These 40 rows form the pattern.

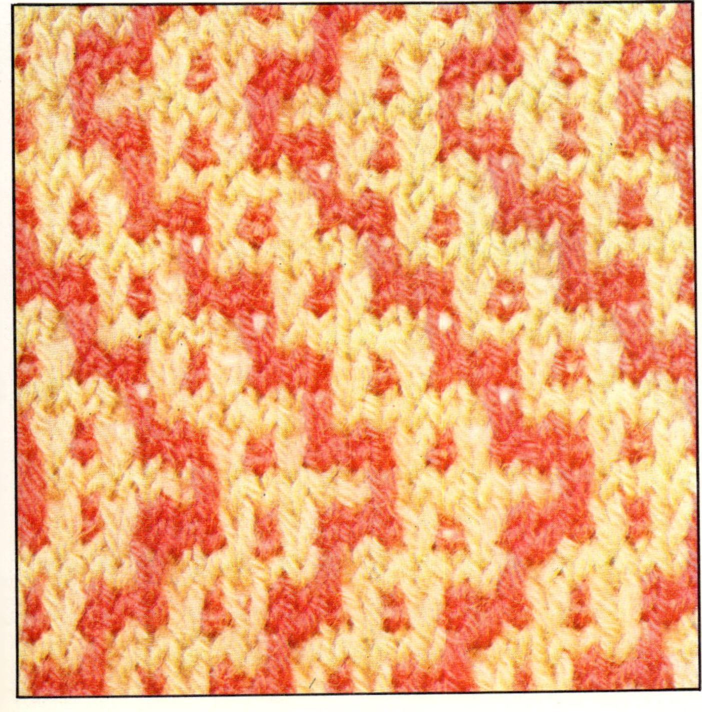

Greek key pattern
Two colors are used, coded as A and B. Using A, cast on a number of stitches divisible by 6 plus 2.
1st row (RS) Using A, K to end.
2nd row Using A, K to end.
3rd row Using B, K1, *sl 1, K5, rep from * to last st, K1.
4th and every alt row Using same color as previous row, keep the yarn at front of work and K all K sts of previous row and sl all sl sts.
5th row Using A, K2, *sl 1, K3, sl 1, K1, rep from * to end.
7th row Using B, K1, *sl 1, K3, sl 1, K1, rep from * to last st, K1.
9th row Using A, K6, *sl 1, K5, rep from * to last 2 sts, sl 1, K1.
11th and 12th rows Using B, as 1st and 2nd.
13th row Using A, K4, *sl 1, K5, rep from * to last 4 sts, sl 1, K3.
15th row Using B, *K3, sl 1, K1, sl 1, rep from * to last 2 sts, K2.
17th row Using A, K2, *sl 1, K1, sl 1, K3, rep from * to end.
19th row Using B, K3, *sl 1, K5, rep from * to last 5 sts, sl 1, K4.
20th row As 4th.
These 20 rows form the pattern.

Maze pattern
Two colors are used, coded as A and B. Using A, cast on a number of stitches divisible by 12 plus 3.
1st row (RS) Using A, K to end.
2nd row Using A, P to end.
3rd row Using B, K1, *sl 1, K11, rep from * to last 2 sts, sl 1, K1.
4th and every alt row Using same color as previous row, keep the yarn at front of work and P all K sts of previous row and sl all sl sts.

5th row Using A, K2, *sl 1, K9, sl 1, K1, rep from * to last st, K1.
7th row Using B, (K1, sl 1) twice, *K7, (sl 1, K1) twice, sl 1, rep from * to end omitting sl 1 at end of last rep.
9th row Using A, K2, sl 1, K1, sl 1, *K5, (sl 1, K1) 3 times, sl 1, rep from * to last 10 sts, K5, sl 1, K1, sl 1, K2.
11th row Using B, (K1, sl 1) 3 times, *K3, (sl 1, K1) 4 times, sl 1, rep from * to last 9 sts, K3, (sl 1, K1) 3 times.
13th row Using A, K2, *sl 1, K1, rep from * to last st, K1.
15th, 17th, 19th, 21st, 23rd and 25th rows Rep 11th, 9th, 7th, 5th, 3rd and 1st rows in that order.
27th row Using B, K7, *sl 1, K11, rep from * to last 8 sts, sl 1, K7.
29th row Using A, K6, *sl 1, K1, sl 1, K9, rep from * to last 9 sts, sl 1, K1, sl 1, K6.
31st row Using B, K5, *(sl 1, K1) twice, sl 1, K7, rep from * to last 10 sts, (sl 1, K1) twice, sl 1, K5.
33rd row Using A, K4, *(sl 1, K1) 3 times, sl 1, K5, rep from * to last 11 sts, (sl 1, K1) 3 times, sl 1, K4.
35th row Using B, K3, *(sl 1, K1) 4 times, sl 1, K3, rep from * to end.
37th row As 13th.
39th, 41st, 43rd, 45th and 47th rows Rep 35th, 33rd, 31st, 29th and 27th rows in that order.
48th row As 4th.
These 48 rows form the pattern.

Lattice window pattern
Two colors are used, coded as A and B. Using A, cast on a number of stitches divisible by 12 plus 3. K 1 row.
1st row (RS) Using B, K1, *sl 1, K11, rep from * to last 2 sts, sl 1, K1.
2nd and every alt row Using same color as previous row, keep the yarn at front of work and K all K sts of previous row and sl all sl sts.
3rd row Using A, K4, *(sl 1, K1) 3 times, sl 1, K5, rep from * to last 11 sts, (sl 1, K1) 3 times, sl 1, K4.
5th row Using B, K3, *sl 1, K7, sl 1, K3, rep from * to end.
7th row Using A, K2, *sl 1, K3, sl 1, K1, rep from * to last st, K1.
9th row Using B, K5, *sl 1, K3, sl 1, K7, rep from * to last 10 sts, sl 1, K3, sl 1, K5.
11th row Using A, K2, *sl 1, K1, sl 1, K5, (sl 1, K1) twice, rep from * to last st, K1.
13th row Using B, K7, *sl 1, K11, rep from * to last 8 sts, sl 1, K7.
15th and 16th rows As 11th and 12th.
17th and 18th rows As 9th and 10th.
19th and 20th rows As 7th and 8th.
21st and 22nd rows As 5th and 6th.
23rd and 24th rows As 3rd and 4th.
These 24 rows form the pattern.

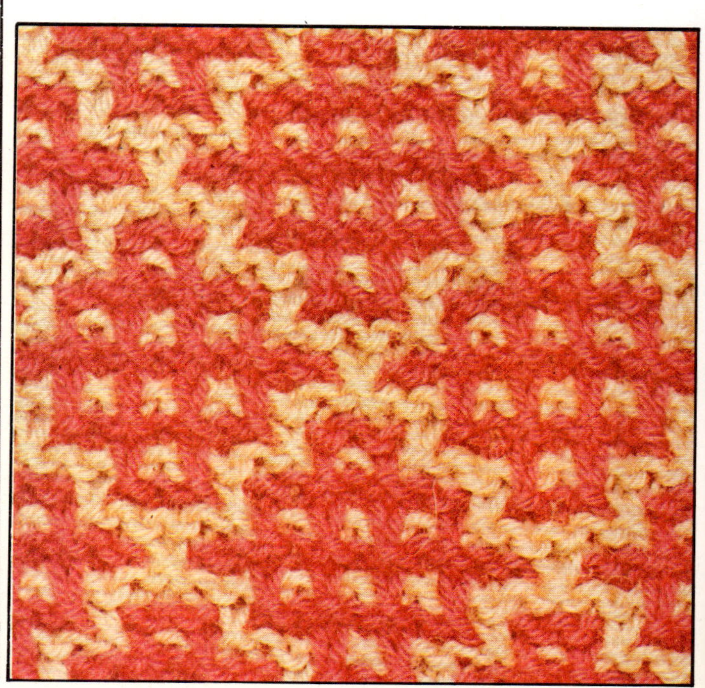

MOCK FAIR ISLE

Although they look rather complicated, Fair Isle patterns are quite simple to work as they rarely use more than two colors in one row at a time. The beautiful, multi-colored effects are achieved by varying the two combinations of colors.

A form of 'mock' Fair Isle, however, is even simpler to work as this only requires two colors throughout – a plain background color and an ombre yarn used for the contrast color. As the ombre yarn is worked, it changes its color sequence to give a most striking effect.

Unlike horizontal striped patterns, where the color is changed at the end of a row, two yarns will be in use during the course of a row. As only a few stitches are worked in one color, the yarn not in use can be carried loosely across the back of the work until it is required, then twisted around the last color before it is brought into use again.

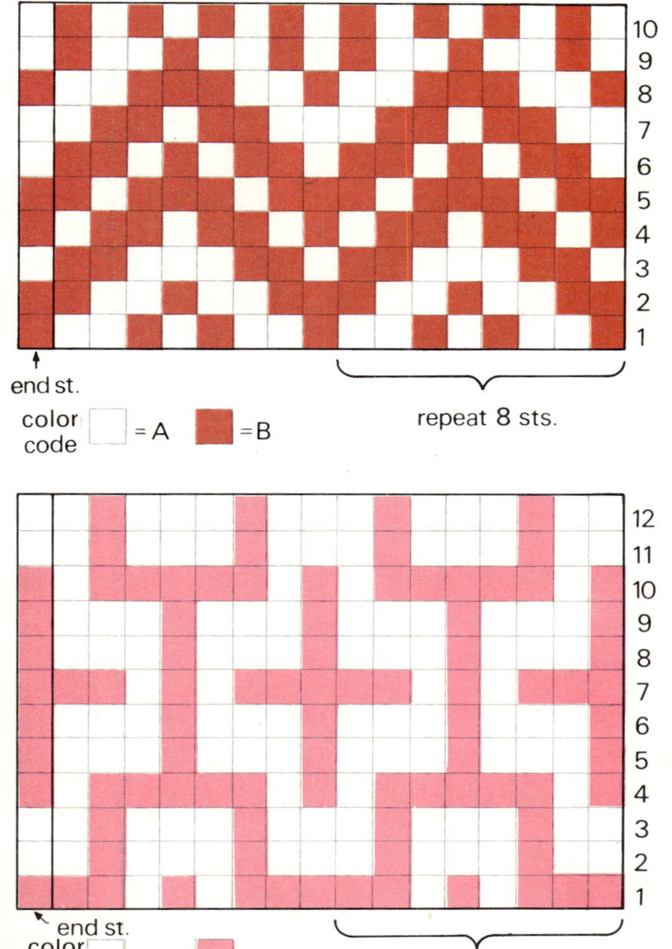

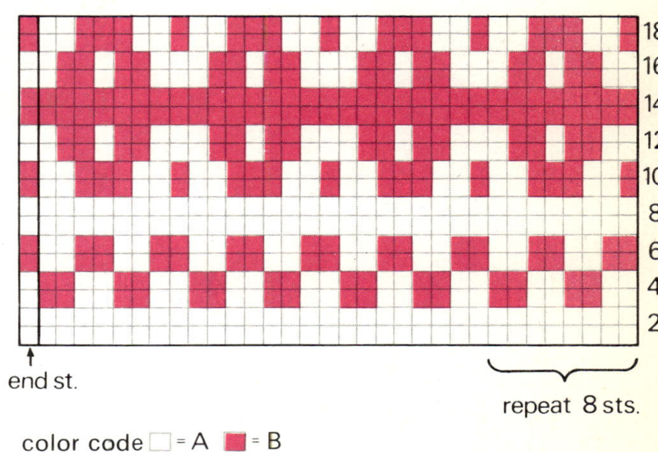

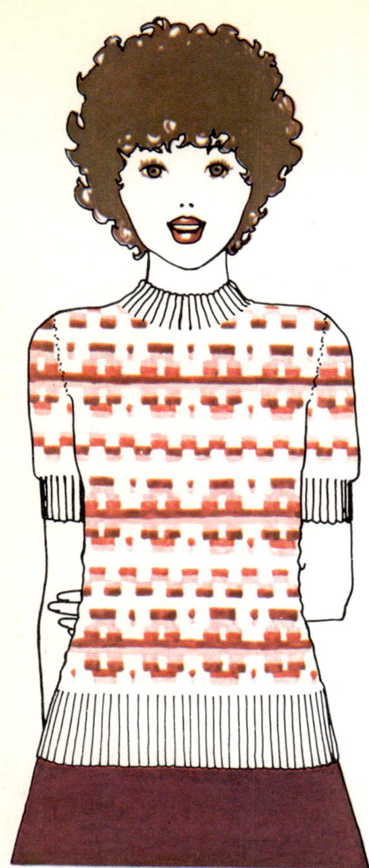

Three 'mock' Fair Isle patterns

We give three samples and charts here, any one of which can be used for the short sleeved pullover, as each pattern requires a multiple of 8 stitches plus one.

Mock Fair Isle pullover

Sizes

Directions are to fit 34in bust. Changes for 36, 38 and 40in bust are in brackets [].
Length to shoulder, 24[24½:26:26½]in
Sleeve seam, 4in

Gauge

26 sts and 32 rows to 4in in patt worked on No.4 needles

Materials

3[3:4:4] × 4oz balls Bucilla Win-Knit in main color, A
2[2:3:3] × 3½oz balls Bucilla Ombre Win-Kit in contrast color, B
One pair of No.4 needles
One pair of No.2 needles

Back

Using No.2 needles and A, cast on 113[121:129:137]sts.
1st row K1, *P1, K1, rep from * to end.
2nd row P1, *K1, P1, rep from * to end.
Rep these 2 rows 11 times more. Change to No.4 needles. Beg with a K row cont in st st, working in any patt from chart, until work measures 17[17:18:18]in from beg, ending with a WS row.

Shape armholes

Maintaining patt, bind off 6[7:8:9] sts at beg of next 2 rows. Dec one st at each end of next 8[9:10:11] rows. 85[89:93:97] sts. Cont in patt without shaping until armholes measure 7[7½:8:8½]in from beg, ending with a WS row.

Shape shoulders

Bind off at beg of next and every row 8[8:9:9] sts twice, 8[9:9:9] sts twice and 9[9:9:10] sts twice. Place rem 35[37:39:41] sts on holder for back neck.

Front

Work as for back until armhole shaping has been completed. 85[89:93:97] sts. Cont without shaping until armholes measure 5½[6:6½:7]in from beg, ending with a WS row.

Shape neck

Next row Work in patt across 32[33:34:35], turn and place rem sts on holder.
Complete this side first. Dec one st at neck edge on next and every row 7 times in all. 25[26:27:28] sts. Cont without shaping until front is same as back to shoulder, ending at armhole edge.

Shape shoulder

Bind off at beg of next and every alt row 8[8:9:9] sts once, 8[9:9:9] sts once and 9[9:9:10] sts once.
With RS of work facing, sl first 21[23:25:27] sts on holder for front neck, rejoin yarn to rem sts and patt to end. Complete to correspond to first side, reversing shaping.

Sleeves

Using No.2 needles and A, cast on 81[89:89:97] sts. Work 12 rows rib as for back. Change to No.4 needles. Beg with a K row cont in st st, working in any patt from chart and inc one st at each end of 3rd and every foll 6th row, until there are 87[95:95:103] sts. Cont without shaping until sleeve measures 4in from beg, ending with a WS row.

Shape top

Bind off 6[7:8:9] sts at beg of next 2 rows. Dec one st at each end of next and every foll alt row until 47[55:47:49] sts rem. Patt one row. Bind off 2 sts at beg of next 16[18:14:14] rows. Bind off rem 15[17:19:21] sts.

Neckband

Join right shoulder seam. Using No.2 needles, A and with RS of work facing, K18 sts down left front neck, K across front neck sts on holder, K19 sts up right front neck and K across back neck sts on holder. 87[91:95:99] sts. Work 12 rows rib as for back. Bind off loosely in rib.

Finishing

Block under a dry cloth with a warm iron. Join left shoulder and neckband seam. Set in sleeves. Join side and sleeve seams. Block seams.

Toddler's robe

The mock Fair Isle technique has been used for this front-opening toddler's robe. An even more interesting pattern has been achieved, however, by using a plain background with a contrasting ombre yarn for the first pattern repeat, then reversing the pattern by using a second ombre yarn as the background and a second plain color for the contrast for the next repeat.

Robe

Sizes

Directions are to fit 22in chest. Changes for 24in chest are in brackets [].

Length to shoulder, 22[24]in
Sleeve seam, $6\frac{1}{2}$[8]in

Gauge

28 sts and 36 rows to 4in in patt worked on No.3 needles

Materials

2[3] × 2oz balls Red Heart Wintuk Sport Yarn in 1st contrast, A
2[2] × $1\frac{3}{4}$oz balls Red Heart Wintuk Ombre Sport yarn in 2nd contrast, B
1[1] × 2oz ball Red Heart Wintuk Sport Yarn in 3rd contrast, C

1[2] × 1¾oz ball Red Heart Wintuk Ombre Sport Yarn in 4th contrast, D
One pair No.3 needles
One pair No.1 needles
8 buttons

Back and fronts
Using No.1 needles and A, cast on 162[175] sts and work in one piece to underarm. Beg with a K row work 9 rows st st.
Next row K all sts tbl to form hemline.
Change to No.3 needles. Beg with a K row cont in st st, join in B and work **22 rows from chart using A and B. Break off A and B. Join in C and D and work 22 rows from chart, using C for A and D for B. **.
Cont in patt from ** to ** until work measures 17[18¾]in from hemline, ending with a WS row.
Divide for armholes
Next row Patt 37[39] sts, bind off 6[8] sts, patt 76[81] sts, bind off 6[8] sts, patt 37[39] sts.
Complete left front first. Maintaining patt, dec one st at armhole edge on every row until 31[32] sts rem. Cont without shaping until armhole measures 3½[3¾]in from beg, ending at neck edge.
Shape neck
Bind off 5 sts at beg of next row. Dec one st at neck edge on every row until 20[20] sts rem. Cont without shaping until armhole measures 4½[4¾]in from beg, ending at armhole edge.
Shape shoulder
Bind off at beg of next and foll alt row 10 sts twice.
With WS of work facing, rejoin yarn to sts for back. Maintaining patt, dec one st at each end of every row until 64[67] sts rem. Cont without shaping until armholes measure same as left front to shoulder, ending with a WS row.
Shape shoulders
Bind off at beg of next and every row 10 sts 4 times and 24[27] sts once.
With WS of work facing, rejoin yarn to rem sts and complete right front to match left front, reversing shaping.

Sleeves
Using No.1 needles and A, cast on 44[48] sts. Work 10 rows K1, P1 rib, inc 19[15] sts evenly across last row. 63[63] sts. Change to No.3 needles. Cont in patt as for back until sleeve measures 6½[8]in from beg, taking care to beg with a patt row and color which will enable sleeve seam to be completed on same row as back and fronts at underarm, ending with a WS row.
Shape top
Bind off 3[4] sts at beg of next 2 rows. Dec one st at each end of next and every alt row until 39[41] sts rem, then at each end of every row until 27 sts rem. Dec 2 sts at each end of every row until 11 sts rem. Bind off.
Button band
Using No.1 needles and A, cast on 12 sts. Work in K1, P1 rib until band is long enough, when slightly stretched, to fit from hemline to beg of neck shaping. Place sts on holder. Sew button band in place on left front for a girl and right front for a boy from hemline to neck. Mark positions for 8 buttons on button band, the first to come in neckband with 7 more evenly spaced at 2in intervals, measured from base of previous buttonhole.

Buttonhole band
Work as for button band, making buttonholes as markers are reached, as foll:
1st row (buttonhole row) Rib 5 sts, bind off 2, rib to end.
2nd row Rib to end, casting on 2 sts above those bound off in previous row.
Place sts on holder.

Neckband
Join shoulder seams. Stitch buttonhole band in place. Using No.1 needles, A and with RS of work facing, sl 12 sts of band on to needle, K 59[63] sts evenly spaced around neck then rib across rem sts on holder. Work 1 row K1, P1 rib. Make buttonhole as before on next 2 rows. Work 3 more rows rib. Bind off in rib.

Finishing
Block each piece under a damp cloth with a warm iron. Join sleeve seams. Set in sleeves. Press seams. Turn hem to WS at lower edge and sew in place. Sew on buttons.

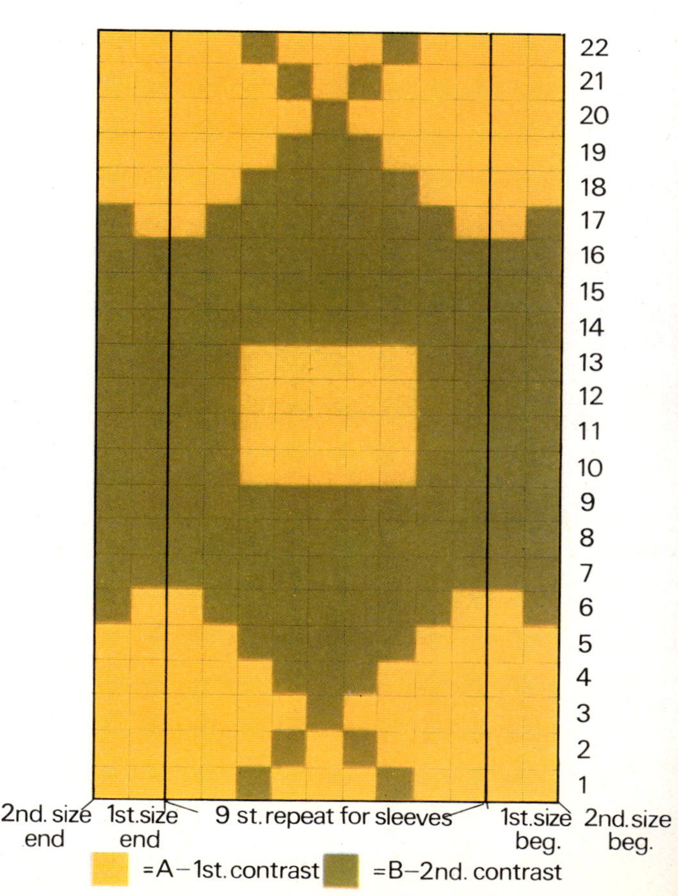

TRADITIONAL FAIR ISLE
Simple patterns

Traditional Fair Isle patterns produce beautiful designs and fabrics which are world-renowned for their subtle color combinations. Ideally, they should be worked in authentic, softly shaded yarns but they look just as effective when worked in bright, contrasting colors. These patterns may be used to form an all-over fabric or as a border to highlight the waist and sleeves of a basic pullover or cardigan. When the pattern is small and is repeated as an all-over design, it is a fairly simple matter to work from a chart, where each color in the pattern is shown as a separate symbol. Some knitters, however, experience difficulty in working from a chart when the pattern is large and fairly complex, particularly where shaping is required. In this event, it is preferable to work from a pattern which gives row-by-row instructions, where each separate color is coded with a letter, such as A, B or C.
To help you decide which of the methods you wish to follow, the patterns here have been given with row by row instructions.

Fair Isle pattern No. 1
Cast on a multiple of 12 stitches plus 6.
1st row *K3 A, 1 B, 5 A, 1 B, 2 A, rep from * to last 6 sts, K3 A, 1 B, 2 A.
2nd row *(P1 A, 1 B) twice, 2 A, rep from * to end.
3rd row *K1 A, 1 B, 3 A, 1 B, rep from * to end.
4th row As 2nd.
5th row *K1 B, 2 A, rep from * to end.
6th row *(P1 B, 1 A) twice, 2 B, rep from * to end.
7th row *K2 B, (1 A, 1 B) twice, rep from * to end.
Rep 6th and 7th rows once more.
10th row *P2 A, 1 B, rep from * to end.
11th row *K2 A, (1 B, 1 A) twice, rep from * to end.
12th row *P1 B, 3 A, 1 B, 1 A, rep from * to end.
13th row As 11th.
14th row *P2 A, 1 B, 5 A, 1 B, 3 A, rep from * to last 6 sts, 2 A, 1 B, 3 A.
15th row *K1 B, 5 A, rep from * to end.
16th row *P1 B, 3 A, 1 B, 1 A, rep from * to end.
17th row *K2 A, (1 B, 1 A) twice, rep from * to end.
18th row As 16th.
19th row *K1 B, 2 A, rep from * to end.
20th row *P1 A, 3 B, 1 A, 1 B, rep from * to end.
21st row *K1 B, 1 A, 3 B, 1 A, rep from * to end. Rep 20th and 21st rows once more.
24th row *P2 A, 1 B, rep from * to end.
25th row *K1 A, 1 B, 3 A, 1 B, rep from * to end.
26th row *(P1 A, 1 B) twice, 2 A, rep from * to end.
27th row As 25th.
28th row *P5 A, 1 B, rep from * to end.
These 28 rows form the pattern.

Fair Isle pattern No. 2
Cast on a multiple of 18 stitches plus 1.
1st row *K1 B, 1 A, rep from * to last st, 1 B.
2nd row Using A, P to end.
3rd row Using A, K to end.
4th row *P1 C, 1 A, 1 C, 6 A, 1 C, 6 A, 1 C, 1 A, rep from * to last st, P1 C.
5th row *K2 C, 1 A, 1 C, 4 A, 3 C, 4 A, 1 C, 1 A, 1 C, rep from * to last st, K1 C.
6th row *P1 C, 3 A, 1 C, 2 A, 2 C, 1 A, 2 C, 2 A, 1 C, 3 A, rep from * to last st, P1 C.
7th row *K1 C, 4 A, 1 C, 1 A, 5 C, 1 A, 1 C, 4 A, rep from * to last st, K1 C.
8th row *P1 A, 1 C, 4 A, 3 C, 1 A, 3 C, 4 A, 1 C, rep from * to last st, P1 A.
9th row *K1 B, 3 A, 3 B, 2 A, 1 B, 2 A, 3 B, 3 A, rep from

* to last st, 1 B.
10th row *P3 A, 4 B, (1 A, 1 B) twice, 1 A, 4 B, 2 A, rep from * to last st, 1 A.
11th row *K2 A, 2 B, (1 A, 1 B) 5 times, 1 A, 2 B, 1 A, rep from * to last st, 1 A.
Rep 10th to 1st rows. These 21 rows form border pattern, working 22nd row for all-over pattern.

Fair Isle pattern No. 3
Cast on multiples of 18 stitches plus 1.
1st row *K1 B, 1 A, rep from * to last st, 1 B.
2nd row *P1 A, 1 B, rep from * to last st, 1 A.
3rd row Using A, K to end.
4th row Using A, P to end.
5th row As 3rd.
6th row *P3 A, 1 C, 5 A, 1 C, 5 A, 1 C, 2 A, rep from * to last st, 1 A.
7th row *K2 A, 2 C, 4 A, 3 C, 4 A, 2 C, 1 A, rep from * to last st, 1 A.
8th row *P1 A, 3 C, 5 A, 1 C, 5 A, 3 C, rep from * to last st, 1 A.
9th row *K1 D, 2 C, 2 D, 3 C, 3 D, 3 C, 2 D, 2 C, rep from * to last st, 1 D.
10th row *P1 D, 1 C, 2 D, 3 C, 5 D, 3 C, 2 D, 1 C, rep from * to last st, 1 D.
11th row *K1 B, 2 E, 3 B, 3 E, 1 B, 3 E, 3 B, 2 E, rep from * to last st, 1 B.
12th row *P1 F, 2 B, 5 F, 3 B, 5 F, 2 B, rep from * to last st, 1 F.
Rep 11th to 3rd rows.
22nd row *P1 B, 1 A, rep from * to last st, 1 B.
23rd row *K1 A, 1 B, rep from * to last st, 1 A.
These 23 rows form border pattern, repeating 22 rows only for all-over pattern.

Fair Isle pattern No. 4
Cast on multiples of 28 stitches plus 1.
1st row *K2 B, 1 A, 1 B, rep from * to last st, 1 B.
2nd row *P1 B, 3 A, rep from * to last st, 1 B.
3rd row Using A, K to end.
4th row *P1 A, 2 C, 2 A, 2 C, 2 A, 2 C, 3 A, 1 C, 3 A, 2 C, 2 A, 2 C, 2 A, 2 C, rep from * to last st, 1 A.
5th row *K1 A, 1 C, (2 A, 2 C) twice, 3 A, 1 C, 1 A, 1 C, 3 A, (2 C, 2 A) twice, 1 C, rep from * to last st, 1 A.
6th row *P1 A, 1 C, 1 A, 2 C, 2 A, 2 C, 3 A, (1 C, 1 A) twice, 1 C, 3 A, 2 C, 2 A, 2 C, 1 A, 1 C, rep from * to last st, 1 A.
7th row *K1 A, 3 C, 2 A, 2 C, 3 A, 1 C, 1 A, 3 C, 1 A, 1 C, 3 A, 2 C, 2 A, 3 C, rep from * to last st, 1 A.
8th row *P1 A, 2 C, 2 A, 2 C, 3 A, 1 C, 2 A, 3 C, 2 A, 1 C, 3 A, 2 C, 2 A, 2 C, rep from * to last st, 1 A.
9th row *K1 A, 1 D, 2 A, 2 D, 3 A, 3 D, 2 A, 1 D, 2 A, 3 D, 3 A, 2 D, 2 A, 1 D, rep from * to last st, 1 A.
10th row *P1 A, 1 D, 1 A, 2 D, 3 A, 1 D, 2 A, 2 D, 1 A, 1 D, 1 A, 2 D, 2 A, 1 D, 3 A, 2 D, 1 A, 1 D, rep from *to last st, 1 A.
11th row *K1 A, 3 D, 3 A, 2 D, 3 A, 5 D, 3 A, 2 D, 3 A, 3 D, rep from * to last st, 1 A.
12th row *P1 A, 2 D, 3 A, 1 D, 1 A, 2 D, 3 A, 3 D, 3 A, 2 D, 1 A, 1 D, 3 A, 2 D, rep from * to last st, 1 A.
13th row *K1 A, 1 D, 3 A, 1 D, 3 A, 2 D, 3 A, 1 D, 3 A, 2 D, 3 A, 1 D, 3 A, 1 D, rep from * to last st, 1 A.
14th row *P1 A, 1 D, 2 A, 1 D, 1 A, 2 D, 2 A, 2 D, (1 A, 1 D) twice, 1 A, 2 D, 2 A, 2 D, 1 A, 1 D, 2 A, 1 D, rep from * to last st, 1 A.
15th row *K1 A, (1 B, 1 A) twice, 8 B, 1 A, 1 B, 1 A, 8 B, (1 A, 1 B) twice, rep from * to last st, 1 A.
Rep from 14th through 1st rows. These 29 rows form border pattern, working 30th row for all over pattern.

Snowflake patterns

The Scandinavian countries provide an endless source of what are loosely termed 'Fair Isle' designs, particularly variations of the delightful snowflake pattern. They are worked in the same way as the traditional Shetland designs but the patterns are usually bolder and the choice of color is more distinctive.

From the middle European countries and further east, more intricate and colorful designs are introduced, often involving the use of three or more colors at a time. These beautiful fabrics, often based upon traditional carpet designs, feature floral or symmetrical patterns in rich jewel colors.

To look most effective, the samples given here should not be used as over all patterns but as borders, pockets or cuff motifs.

Border pattern

This can either be worked as a horizontal or vertical

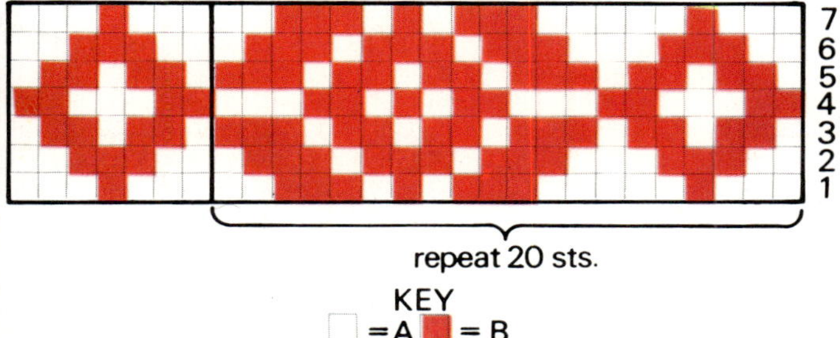

border. For a horizontal border cast on any multiple of 20 stitches plus 7 and work the 7 pattern rows from the chart. To work the border vertically, turn the chart sideways and work over 7 stitches for 20 rows.

Star pattern

This is another motif which can be used singly or as a horizontal border pattern.

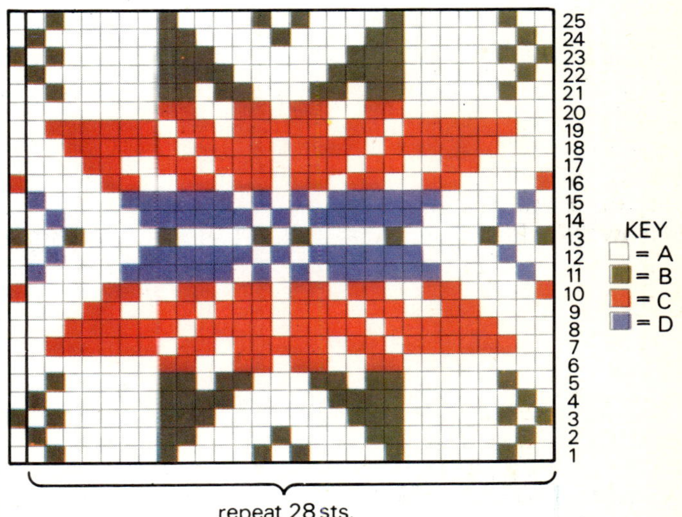

JACQUARD KNITTING

Whereas traditional Fair Isle knitting normally uses only two colors in any one row, jacquard, bobbin and patchwork knitting are all forms of the same technique, where more than two colors are used at a time in any one pattern row. These designs are best worked in stockinette stitch against a stockinette stitch background, although bobbin knitting may also combine many different stitches very effectively.

Unlike Fair Isle knitting this method is a little complicated and difficult to work, since more than one strand has to be carried across the back of the work until it is needed again although it is possible to work a jacquard design with a small repeat in this way, carrying the yarn not in use loosely across the back of the work. This method does, however, inevitably mean a variance in gauge against the main fabric. When using this method, it is therefore advisable to change to one size larger needles to work the pattern, reverting to the original needle size to work the main pattern.

The correct method of working all large multicolored patterns, motifs, wide vertical stripes and patchwork designs is to use small, separate balls of yarn for each color. In this way a fabric of single thickness is formed, without any strands of yarn across the back of the work. These patterns are usually worked from a chart, just as in Fair Isle knitting, with each different color coded with a symbol.

Use of bobbins

Before beginning to knit, wind all the colors which are to be used into small, separate balls around a bobbin. These are easy to handle and hang at the back of the work, keeping each color free from tangles.

To make a bobbin: Use a stiff piece of cardboard and cut to shape as shown in the diagram with a slit at the top of each bobbin. Wind the yarn around the center of the bobbin with the working end passing through the slit as illustrated.

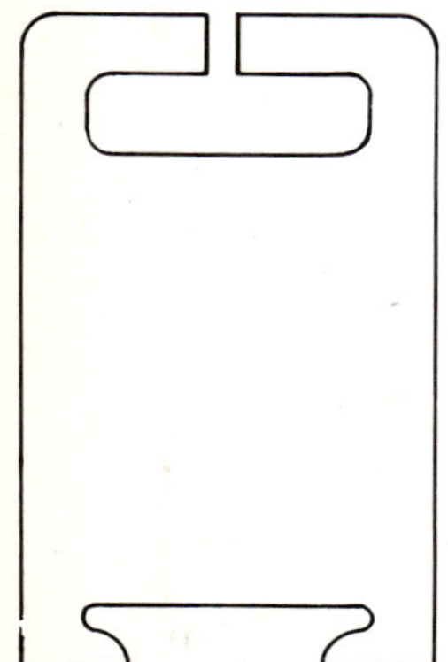

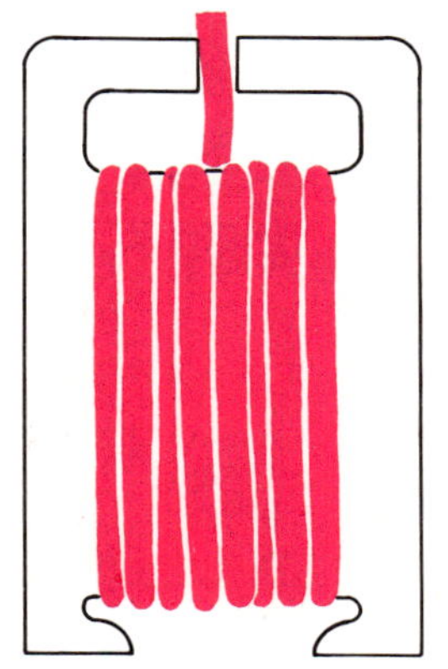

Joining in each new color

The next important point to remember is that knitting patterns of a geometric or random shape, such as diamonds or flower motifs, as opposed to straight vertical stripes, require the color to be changed by means of looping the two yarns around each other when on a right side row, to avoid gaps in the knitting. On the return purl row it is not so essential to loop the yarns around each other as the purl stitch will probably encroach into the pattern sequence and the yarns will automatically be looped. Vertical bands of color, however, must be looped on every row, as there will be no encroaching stitch to form a natural link in either direction.

To loop yarns on a knit row: Keep each ball of yarn at the back of the work until it is required. Knit the last stitch in the first color, then take this end of yarn over the next color to be used and drop it, pick up the next color under this strand of yarn and take it over the strand ready to knit the next stitch.

To loop yarns on a purl row: Keep each ball of yarn at the front of the work until it is required, purl the last stitch in the first color, then take this end of yarn over the next color to be used and drop it, pick up the next color under this strand of yarn and take it over the strand ready to purl the next stitch.

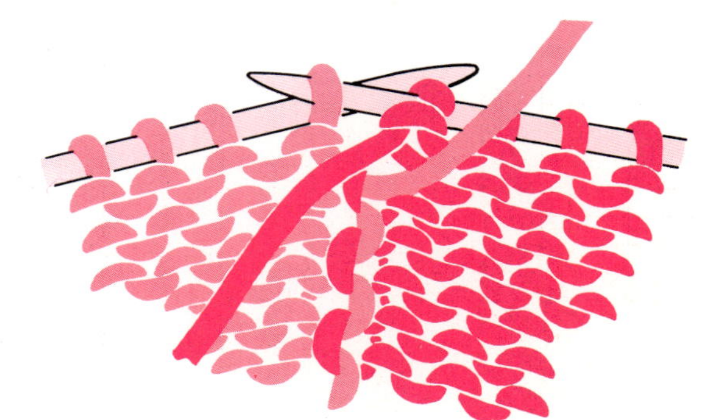

Jacquard borders

Begin by working something as simple as an all-over jacquard border pattern in three colors, carrying each color across the back of the work until it is required again.

In these charts, the background, or main color, is coded as A and shown as a blank square; the first contrast color is coded as B and the second contrast color coded as C.

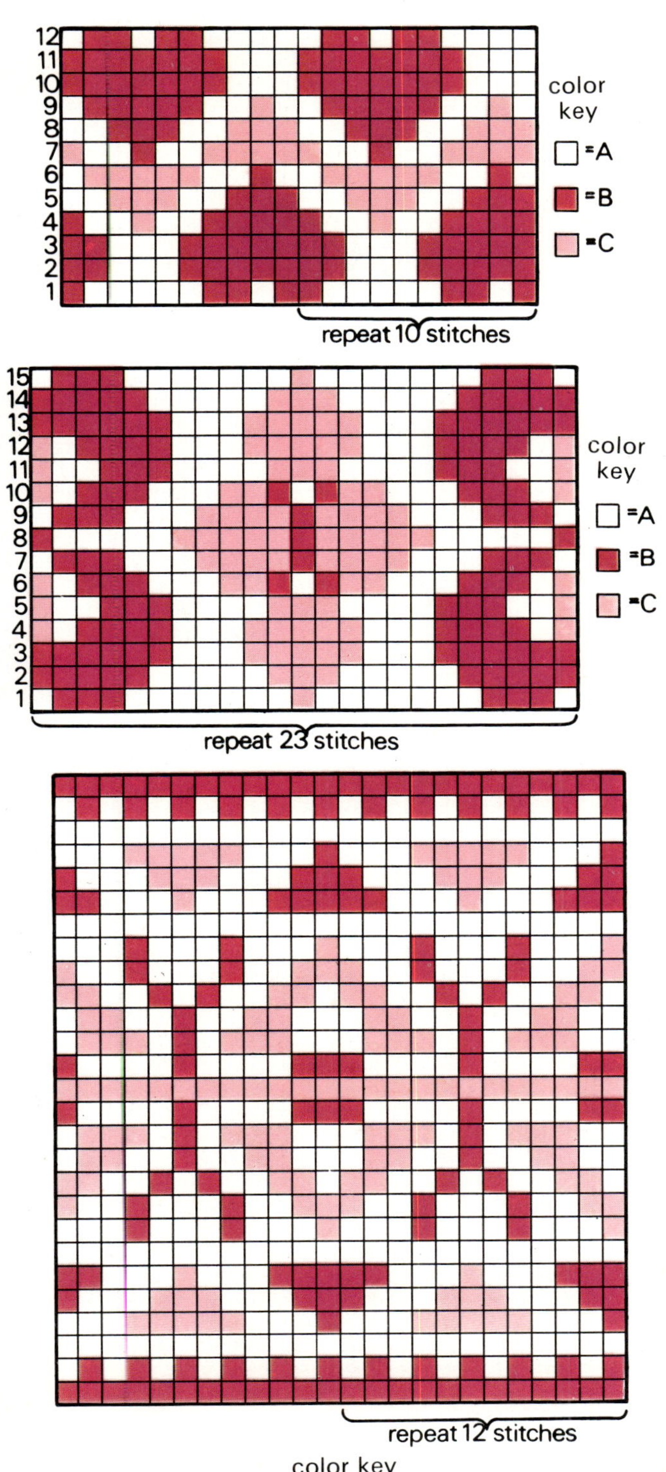

MOTIFS AND COLLAGE

As explained in the previous chapter, jacquard and bobbin knitting provide tremendous scope for interesting all-over patterned fabrics or as a single motif incorporated into an otherwise plain background. Individual motifs can be used very effectively as patch pockets or as decorative panels set into clothes or linens.

The examples shown here should be worked with small, separate balls of yarn, twisting the yarns at the back of the work whenever you change colors.

Motifs

Almost any shape or design can be used as a separate jacquard motif, but if you are working out your own pattern it must be charted out on graph paper first, allowing one square for each stitch and one line of squares for each row. Code each different color with a symbol and make a color key of these symbols. If you do not want to make up your own design, use an embroidery chart, such as given for cross stitch embroidery, and adapt this to suit your own color scheme, again coding each different color with a symbol.

Butterfly motif

This motif is worked in five contrasting colors against a plain background, making six colors in all. Each motif requires a total of 28 stitches and 34 rows to complete.

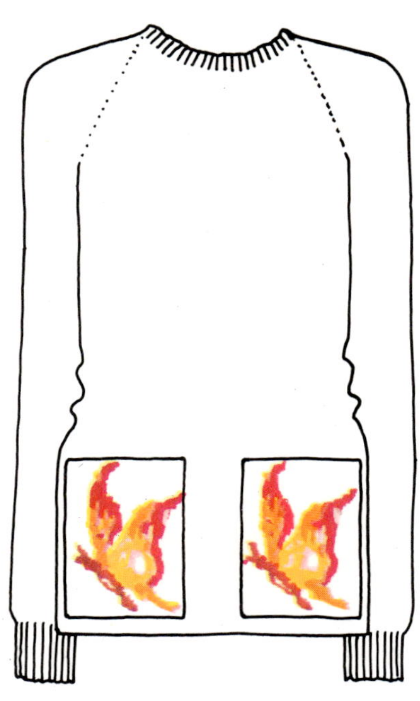

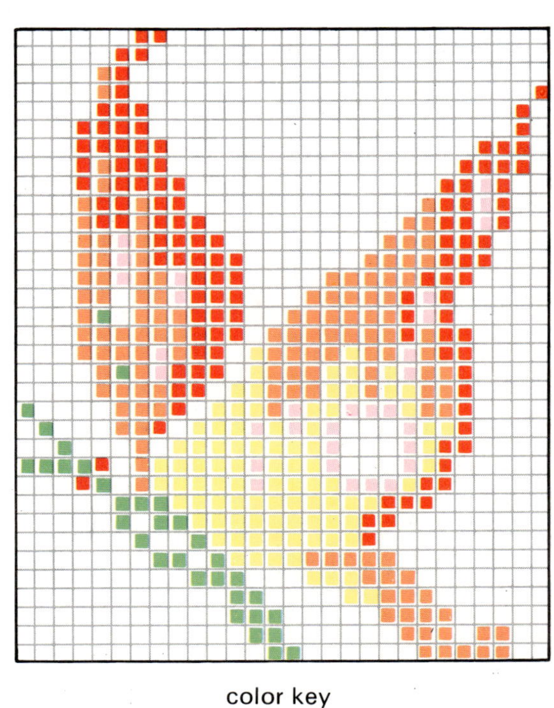

color key

■=B ■=C ■=D ■=E ■=F

Heart motif

Here again, five contrasting colors have been used against a plain background, making a total of six colors. Each motif requires a total of 35 stitches and 32 rows to complete.

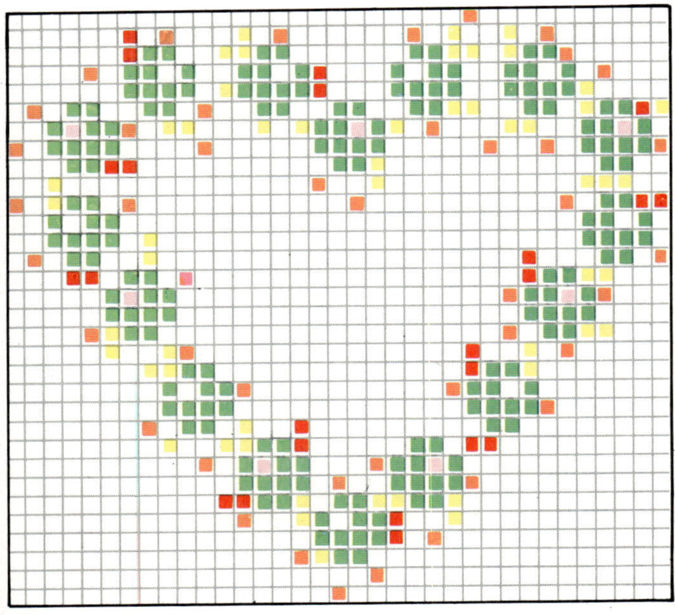

color key

Multi-colored bobbin pattern

This design can be worked with as many colors as you like. You should always vary the sequence to insure

that you do not use the same colors next to each other.

Cast on a number of stitches divisible by 10, using the main color. The sample shown here has been worked on 50 stitches with five colors.

1st row (RS) K10 sts in each of 5 colors.

2nd row Using same colors, P10 sts in each of 5 colors.

Rep 1st and 2nd rows once more.

5th row Varying color sequence as required, K1 with contrast color, K8 with original color, *K2 with next contrast color, K8 with original color, rep from * to last st, K1 with last contrast color.

6th row P2 with same contrast color, *P6 with original color, P4 with same contrast color, rep from * to last 8 sts, P6 with original color, P2 with same contrast color.

7th row K3 with same contrast color, *K4 with original color, K6 with same contrast color, rep from * to last 7 sts, K4 with original color, K3 with same contrast color.

8th row P4 with same contrast color, *P2 with original color, break off original color, P8 with same contrast color, rep from * to last 6 sts, P2 with original color, break off original color, P4 with same contrast color.

9th row K5 with same contrast color, keeping color sequence correct as now set, K10 sts with each color to last 5 sts, K5 sts with same color.

10th row P as 9th row.

Rep 9th and 10th rows 3 times more.

17th row K4 sts with original color as now set, *K2 sts with next contrast color, K8 sts with original color as now set, rep from * to last 6 sts, K2 with next contrast color, K4 with original color as now set.

18th row P3 sts with original color, *P4 with same contrast color, P6 with original color, rep from * to last 7 sts, P4 with same contrast color, P3 with

original color.
19th row K2 with original color, *K6 with same contrast color, K4 with original color, rep from * to last 8 sts, K6 with same contrast color, K2 with original color.
20th row P1 with original color, break off original color, *P8 with same contrast color, P2 with original color, break off original color, rep from * to last 9 sts, P8 with same contrast color, P1 with original color, break off original color.
21st row Keeping color sequence as now set, work as for 1st row.
22nd row As 2nd.
23rd row As 1st.
24th row As 2nd.
These 24 rows form the pattern.

Bobbin baby blanket
Size
22in wide by 32in long

Gauge
18 sts and 22 rows to 4in in stockinette stitch (st st) worked on No.7 needles

Materials
5 × 2oz balls of Sirdar Pullman in main shade, A
1 ball each of 7 contrast colors, B, C, D, E, F, G and H
One pair of No.7 needles

Center
Using No.7 needles and A, cast on 80 sts. Work in multi-colored bobbin pattern until work measures 28in from beg, ending with a 12th patt row.
Bind off.

Border
Using No. 7 needles and A, cast on 100 sts. K 16 rows garter st (g st).
Next row K10 sts, bind off 80 sts, K10 sts.
Complete this side first. Cont in g st until band fits along side edge of cover, ending at inside edge. Break off yarn. Place sts on holder.
With WS of work facing, rejoin yarn to rem 10 sts and complete to correspond to first side, ending at outside edge. Do not break off yarn.
Next row K across first 10 sts, turn and cast on 80 sts, K across rem 10 sts on holder. 100 sts.
K16 rows g st. Bind off loosely.

Finishing
Block center only under a damp cloth with a warm iron. With RS facing, sew border around outer edge of center. Block seams.

PATCHWORK KNITTING

Completely random patchwork fabrics are worked in the same way as bobbin patterns, using separate balls of yarn for each color.
Each patch can be worked on any even number of stitches, and for as many number of rows as desired, and as each patch is completed it is not necessary to bind off, as you simply carry on with the next patch and color sequence. The exciting part of this technique comes in arranging the sequence of patches. Since no two knitters will work either the same color or patch in identical order, each sample has a completely original appearance.
The required number of stitches may be cast on to work two, three, or more patches side by side to give an overall fabric, or single patches can be worked in separate strips to the required length and then sewn together. The latter method means that shaping can be achieved on each side of the strips to achieve a well-fitting skirt, or the delightful patchwork overalls shown here.

Patchwork samples
In all the examples given here the first, or main color, is coded as A, the next color as B, the next as C, and so on and a total of six colors have been used. Once you have decided which colors you would like to use, make a note of the sequence in which you are going to work them so that when you have to pick up contrast color E, for example, you will know immediately to which color this refers.
These samples have been worked over 28 stitches, allowing 30 rows for each patch. Cast on with A.

1st patch
1st row Using A, K to end.
2nd row Using A, P to end.
Rep these 2 rows 14 times more, using each color in turn to form stripes. 30 rows.

2nd patch
1st row K14 B, 14 C.
2nd row P14 C, 14 B.
Rep these 2 rows 6 times more.
15th row Using D, K to end.
16th row Using D, P to end.
17th row K14 E, 14 F.
18th row P14 F, 14 E.
Rep last 2 rows 6 times more. 30 rows.

3rd patch
1st row Using A, K to end.
2nd row Using A, P to end.
Rep these 2 rows 4 times more.
11th row K10 B, 8 C, 10 D.
12th row P10 D, 8 C, 10 B.
Rep last 2 rows 9 times more. 30 rows.

4th patch
1st row Using E, K to end.
2nd row Using E, P to end.
Rep these 2 rows 14 times more. 30 rows.
Each time you work a repeat of this patch, use a different color.

5th patch
1st row K12 F, 4 A, 12 B.
2nd row P12 B, 4 A, 12 F.
Rep these 2 rows 5 times more.
13th row Using C, K to end.
14th row Using C, P to end.
Rep last 2 rows twice more.
19th row K12 D, 4 E, 12 F.
20th row P12 F, 4 E, 12 D.
Rep last 2 rows 5 times more. 30 rows.

Overalls
Size
Length to back waist, 18in
Inside leg, 10in

Gauge
30 sts and 38 rows to 4in in stockinette stitch (st st) worked on No.3 needles

Materials
2 × 2oz balls Bernat Sesame Knitting Worsted in main color, A
1 ball each of 5 contrast colors, B, C, D, E and F
One pair No.3 needles
2 buttons
Waist length of elastic

Right front leg
**Using No.3 needles and A, cast on 28 sts. Beg with a K row work 7 rows st st.
Next row Using A, K all sts tbl to form hemline. Work 1st, 2nd, 3rd, 4th and 5th patches, dec one st at beg of 9th and every foll 4th row 4 times in all, noting that less sts will be worked in first block of color. 24 sts. Cont in patt without shaping until 60th patt row has been completed. **. Maintaining patt, inc one st at beg of next and every foll 4th row 6 times in all, noting that extra sts will be worked in first block of color. 30 sts. Cont without shaping until 82nd patt row has been completed.
Shape crotch
Bind off 2 sts at beg of next row. Work 1 row. Dec one st at beg of next and foll alt rows 4 times in all. 24 sts. Cont without shaping until 142nd patt row has been completed. Using A, work 8 rows K1, P1 rib. Bind off loosely in rib.
Right side leg
Using No.3 needles and A, cast on 32 sts. Work hem as given for right front leg. Work 4th, 5th, 2nd, 1st and 3rd patches, shaping dart on 9th row as foll:
1st dec row Patt 14 sts, K2 tog, sl 1, K1, psso, patt 14 sts. Work 3 rows without shaping.
2nd dec row Patt 13 sts, K2 tog, sl 1, K1, psso, patt 13 sts. Work 3 rows without shaping. Cont dec in this way twice more. 24 sts. Cont in patt without shaping until 143rd row has been completed, ending with a K row.
Shape back
***__Next 2 rows__ Patt to last 8 sts, turn, patt to end.
Next 2 rows Patt to last 16 sts, turn, patt to end.
Next row Patt across all sts.
Using A, work 8 rows K1, P1 rib. Bind off loosely in rib.
***

Right back leg
Work as given for right front leg from ** to **, reversing shaping and working 3rd, 1st, 5th, 2nd and 4th patches in that order. Inc one st at end of next and every alt row, 10 times in all, noting that extra sts will be worked in last block of color. 34 sts. Cont in patt without shaping until 83rd row has been completed, ending with a K row.
Shape crotch
Bind off 2 sts at beg of next row. Work 1 row. Dec one st at beg of next and every alt row 8 times in all. 24 sts. Cont in patt until 149th row has been completed, ending with a K row.
Shape back
Work as given for side from *** to ***, continuing 4th patch.

Left leg
Work 3 pieces as given for right leg, reversing all shaping and sequence of patches, as required.

Bib
Using No.3 needles and A, cast on 44 sts.
1st row Using A, (K1, P1) 4 times, patt 28 sts as 1st row of 5th patch, using separate ball of A, (P1, K1) 4 times.
2nd row Using A, (P1, K1) 4 times, patt 28 sts as given for 2nd row of 5th patch, using A, (K1, P1) 4 times.
Cont in this way until 30th row of patch has been completed. Using A, work 8 rows K1, P1 rib across all sts.
Next row Rib 8, bind off 28 sts, rib to end.
Cont in rib on each set of 8 sts until strap is long enough to reach center back of overalls, making a buttonhole 1in before binding off as foll:
Next row (buttonhole row) Rib 3 sts, yarn in front to make 1, work 2 tog, rib 3 sts.

Finishing
Block each part under a damp cloth with a warm iron. Join 3 right leg sections tog including hem and waistband. Join left leg in same way. Block seams. Join front, back and inner leg seams. Turn hems to WS at lower edge and sew in place. Sew bib in center of front at top of waist ribbing. Sew elastic inside waistband from each side of bib using casing st. Sew on buttons inside back waist.

SIX STITCH PATTERNS

All patterns given here are made up of multiples of six stitches plus two edge stitches. Using the basic pattern which follows, which gives you a gauge of 24 stitches and 32 rows to 4in, you can use any of these stitches providing you make sure you achieve the correct gauge in stockinette stitch.

Cane basket stitch
Cast on a number of stitches divisible by 6+2.
1st row K2, *P4, K2, rep from * to end.
2nd row P2, *K4, P2, rep from * to end.
Rep these 2 rows once more.
5th row P3, *K2, P4, rep from * to last 5 sts, K2, P3.
6th row K3, *P2, K4, rep from * to last 5 sts, P2, K3.
Rep last 2 rows once more. These 8 rows form the pattern.

Trellis stitch
Cast on a number of stitches divisible by 6+2.
1st row P3, *K2, P4, rep from * to last 5 sts, K2, P3.
2nd row K3, *P2, K4, rep from * to last 5 sts, P2, K3.
Rep these 2 rows once more.
5th row P1, *sl next 2 sts on to cable needle and hold at back of work, K1 then P2 from cable needle – called C3B –, sl next st on to cable needle and hold at front of work, P2 then K1 from cable needle – called C3F –, rep from * to last st, P1.
6th row K1, P1, *K4, P2, rep from * to last 6 sts, K4, P1, K1.
7th row P1, K1, *P4, K2, rep from * to last 6 sts, P4, K1, P1.
Rep 6th and 7th rows once more, then 6th row once.
11th row P1, *C3F, C3B, rep from * to last st, P1.
12th row As 2nd.
These 12 rows form the pattern.

Stepped stitch
Cast on a number of stitches divisible by 6+2.
1st row P2, *K4, P2, rep from * to end.
2nd row K2, *P4, K2, rep from * to end.
Rep these 2 rows once more.
5th row P3, *K2, P4, rep from * to last 5 sts, K2, P3.
6th row K3, *P2, K4, rep from * to last 5 sts, P2, K3.
Rep last 2 rows once more.
9th row P to end.
10th row K to end.
These 10 rows form the pattern.

Stepped stitch

Spiral rib
Cast on a number of stitches divisible by 6+2.
1st row P2, *K4, P2, rep from * to end.
2nd and every alt row K2, *P4, K2, rep from * to end.
3rd row P2, *K 2nd st on left hand needle then first st and sl them both off needle tog – called Tw2 –, Tw2, P2, rep from * to end.
5th row P2, *K1, Tw2, K1, P2, rep from * to end.
6th row As 2nd.
The 3rd through 6th rows form the pattern.

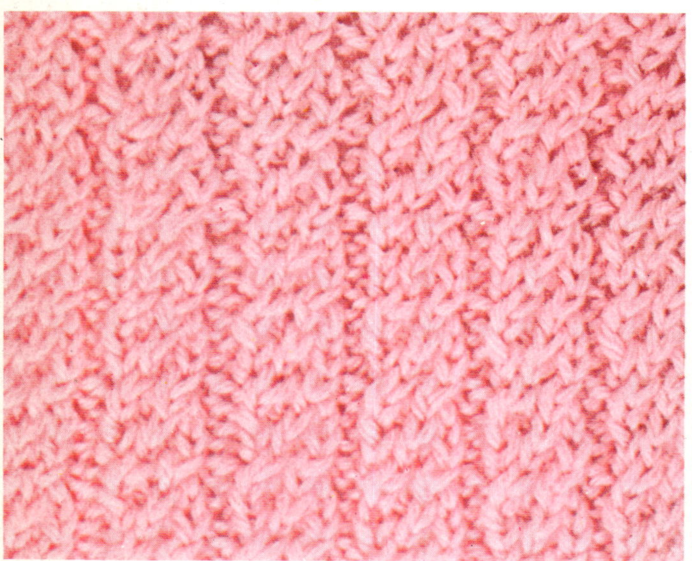

Corded rib
Cast on a number of stitches divisible by 6+2.
1st row P2, *K4, P2, rep from * to end.
2nd row P to end.
3rd row P2, *(sl 1, K1, yfwd, pass slip st over K1 and yfwd) twice, P2, rep from * to end.
4th row As 2nd.
The 3rd and 4th rows form the pattern.

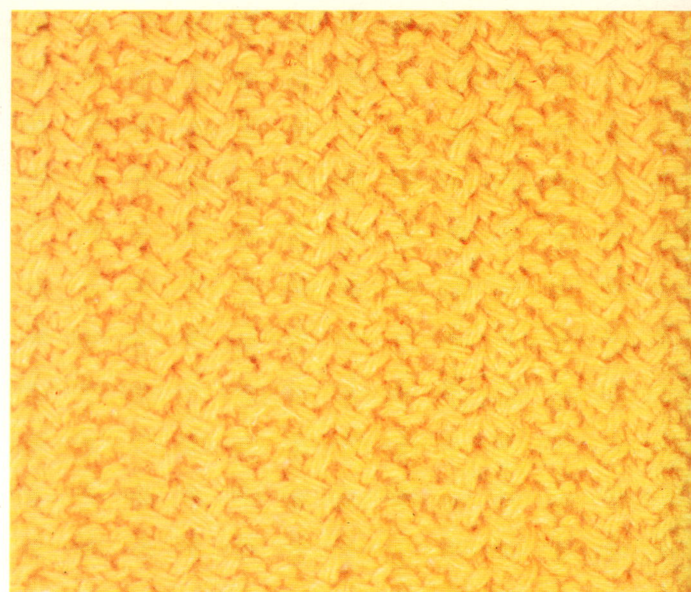
Corded rib

Bobble rib
Cast on a number of stitches divisible by 6+2.
1st row P2, *K1, P2, rep from * to end.
2nd row K2, *P1, K2, rep from * to end.
3rd row P2, *K1, P2, (P1, K1, P1, K1) all into next st – called K4 from 1 –, P2, rep from * to end.
4th row K2, *P4, K2, P1, K2, rep from * to end.
5th row P2, *K1, P2, P4, turn and K4, turn and P4, P2 rep from * to end.
6th row K2, *P4 tog, K2, P1, K2, rep from * to end
Rep 1st and 2nd rows once more.
9th row P2, *K4, from 1, P2, K1, P2, rep from * to end.
10th row K2, *P1, K2, P4, K2, rep from * to end.
11th row P2, *P4, turn and K4, turn and P4, P2, K1, P2 rep from * to end.
12th row K2, *P1, K2, P4 tog, K2, rep from * to end.
These 12 rows form the pattern.

A short-sleeved sweater

The pretty bobble stitch sweater shown on the previous page is a marvelous illustration of the versatility of knitting. It can be made from any of the stitches shown on the previous two pages, provided, of course, that you can correctly work the gauge before you start to work the pattern.

Sizes
Directions are to fit 34in bust. Changes for 36 and 38in bust are in brackets [ ].
Length to shoulder 22[22½:23]in, adjustable
Sleeve seam, 4in

Gauge
24 sts and 32 rows to 4in in stockinette stitch (st st) worked on No.4 needles.

Materials
10[10:11] × 2oz balls Bernat Sesame Knitting Worsted
One pair of No.4 needles
One pair of No.2 needles
Set of 4 No.2 double-pointed needles

Back
Using No.2 needles cast on 109[115:121]sts.
1st row K1, *P1, K1, rep from * to end.
2nd row P1, *K1, P1, rep from * to end.
Rep these 2 rows for 1½in ending with a 2nd row and inc one st in center of last row. 110[116:122]sts. Change to No.4 needles. Work in any desired patt from any of st patts in the previous chapter until piece measures 14½in from beg or desired length to underarm, ending with a WS row.

Shape armholes
Bind off 4 sts at beg of next and every row twice and 2 sts twice. Dec one st at each end of next and foll 5[6:7] alt rows. 86[90:94]sts. Cont without shaping until armholes measure 7½[8:8½]in from beg, ending with a WS row.
Shape neck and shoulders
Next row Bind off 6[7:7]sts, patt 25[25:26]sts, turn and leave rem sts on holder.
Next row Bind off 2 sts, patt to end.
Next row Bind off 6[7:7]sts, patt to end.
Rep last 2 rows once more then the first one once more. Bind off rem 7[5:6] sts.
With RS of work facing, sl first 24[26:28]sts onto holder, rejoin yarn to rem sts and patt to end.
Complete to correspond to first side, reversing shaping.

Front
Work as for back until armhole shaping is completed. Cont without shaping until armholes measure 5½ [6:6½]in from beg, ending with a WS row.

Shape neck
Next row Patt 35[36:37]sts, turn and place rem sts on holder.
Bind off 2 sts at beg of next and foll 2 alt rows, then dec one st at neck edge on foll 4 alt rows.
Cont without shaping until armhole measures same as back to shoulder, ending at armhole edge.

Shape shoulder
Bind off at beg of next and every alt row 6[7:7]sts 3 times and 7[5:6]sts once. With RS of work facing, sl first 16[18:20]sts onto a holder, rejoin yarn to rem sts and patt to end. Complete to correspond to first side, reversing shaping.

Sleeves
Using No.2 needles cast on 73[73:79]sts. Work 1in rib as for back, ending with a 2nd row and inc one st in center of last row. 74[74:80]sts. Change to No.4 needles. Cont in patt as for back, inc one st at each end of 3rd and every foll 8th[6th:6th] row until there are 78[82:86]sts. Cont without shaping until sleeve measures 4in from beg, ending with a WS row.

Shape top
Bind off 4 sts at beg of next 2 rows. Dec one st at each end of next and foll 11[12:13] alt rows, ending with a WS row. Bind off at beg of next and every row 2 sts 8[8:10] times, 3 sts 4 times, 4 sts twice and 10[12:10] sts once.

Neckband
Join shoulder seams. Using set of 4 No.2 needles and with RS of work facing, K 8 sts down right back neck, K across back neck sts inc one st in center, K 8 sts up left back neck and 24 sts down left front neck, K across front neck sts inc one st in center and K 24 sts up right front neck. 106[110:114]sts. Cont in rounds of K1, P1 rib for 2½in.
Bind off loosely in rib.

Finishing
Block each piece under a damp cloth with a warm iron. Set in sleeves. Join side and sleeve seams. Block seams. Fold neckband in half to WS and sew in place.

TEXTURED PATTERNS

These fabric stitches are more complicated than the examples given in the previous chapter and use larger multiples of stitches and rows to form the pattern repeat. Each pattern is formed either by stitches which travel from one position to another in a row or by decreased stitches which are then compensated for by an increased stitch, which gives a lacy effect.

Pyramid pattern
Cast on a number of stitches divisible by 15+1.
1st row K to end.
2nd row P4, *K8, P7, rep from * to last 12 sts, K8, P4.
3rd row K1, *K up 1, K2, sl 1, K1, psso, P6, K2 tog, K2, K up 1, K1, rep from * to end.
4th row P5, *K6, P9, rep from * to last 11 sts, K6, P5.
5th row K2, *K up 1, K2, sl 1, K1, psso, P4, K2 tog, K2, K up 1, K3, rep from * to last 14 sts, K up 1, K2, sl 1, K1, psso, P4, K2 tog, K2, K up 1, K2.
6th row P6, *K4, P11, rep from * to last 10 sts, K4, P6.
7th row K3, *K up 1, K2, sl 1, K1, psso, P2, K2 tog, K2, K up 1, K5, rep from * to last 13 sts, K up 1, K2, sl 1, K1, psso, P4, K2 tog, K2, K up 1, K2.
8th row P7, *K2, P13, rep from * to last 9 sts, K2, P7.
9th row K4, *K up 1, K2, sl 1, K1, psso, K2 tog, K2, K up 1, K7, rep from * to last 12 sts, K up 1, K2, sl 1, K1, psso, K2 tog, K2, K up 1, K4.
10th row P to end.
These 10 rows form the pattern.

Leaf pattern
Cast on a number of stitches divisible by 24+1.
1st row K1, *K up 1, sl 1, K1, psso, K4, K2 tog, K3, K up 1, K1, K up 1, K3, sl 1, K1, psso, K4, K2 tog, K up 1, K1, rep from * to end.
2nd and every alt row P to end.
3rd row K1, *K up 1, K1, sl 1, K1, psso, K2, K2 tog, K4, K up 1, K1, K up 1, K4, sl 1, K1, psso, K2, K2 tog, K1, K up 1, K1, rep from * to end.
5th row K1, *K up 1, K2, sl 1, K1, psso, K2 tog, K5, K up 1, K1, K up 1, K5, sl 1, K1, psso, K2 tog, K2, K up 1, K1, rep from * to end.
7th row K1, *K up 1, K3, sl 1, K1, psso, K4, K2 tog, K up 1, K1, K up 1, sl 1, K1, psso, K4, K2 tog, K3, K up 1, K1, rep from * to end.
9th row K1, *K up 1, K4, sl 1, K1, psso, K2, K2 tog, K1, K up 1, K1, K up 1, K1, sl 1, K1, psso, K2, K2 tog, K4, K up 1, K1, rep from * to end.
11th row K1, *K up 1, K5, sl 1, K1, psso, K2 tog, K2, K up 1, K1, K up 1, K2, sl 1, K1, psso, K2 tog, K5, K up 1, K1, rep from * to end.
12th row P to end.
These 12 rows form the pattern.

Seeded chevron pattern
Cast on a number of stitches divisible by 14+2.
1st row K14, *K second st on left hand needle then K first st and sl both sts off needle tog – called TwR –, K12, rep from * to last 2 sts, K2.
2nd row P1, *sl 1, P12, sl 1, rep from * to last st, P1.
3rd row K1, *put needle behind first st on left hand needle and K into back of second st then K first st and sl both sts off needle tog – called TwL –, K10, TwR, rep from * to last st K1.
4th row P1, K1, *sl 1, P10, sl 1, P1, K1, rep from * to end.
5th row K1, P1, *TwL, K8, TwR, K1, P1, rep from * to end.
6th row P1, K1, *P1, sl 1, P8, sl 1, K1, P1, K1, rep from * to end.
7th row K1, P1, *K1, TwL, K6, TwR, P1, K1, P1, rep from * to end.

8th row *(P1, K1) twice, sl 1, P6, sl 1, P1, K1, rep from * to last 2 sts, P1, K1.
9th row *(K1, P1) twice, TwL, K4, TwR, K1, P1, rep from * to last 2 sts, K1, P1.

10th row P1, *(K1, P1) twice, sl 1, P4, sl 1, (K1, P1) twice, rep from * to last st, K1.
11th row K1, *(P1, K1) twice, TwL, K2, TwR, (P1, K1) twice, rep from * to last st, P1.
12th row *(P1, K1) 3 times, sl 1, P2, sl 1, (P1, K1) twice, rep from * to last 2 sts, P1, K1.
13th row (K1, P1) 3 times, *TwL, TwR, (K1, P1) twice, TwR, (K1, P1) twice, rep from * to last 10 sts, TwL, TwR, (K1, P1) 3 times.
14th row P1, sl 1, *(P1, K1) 3 times, sl 1, K1, (P1, K1) twice, sl 2, rep from * to last 14 sts, (P1, K1) 3 times, sl 1, K1, (P1, K1) twice, sl 1, P1.
15th row K1, *TwL, (P1, K1) twice, TwL, (P1, K1) twice, TwR, rep from * to last st, K1.
16th row P2, *sl 1, (K1, P1) 5 times, sl 1, P2, rep from * to end.
17th row K2, *TwL, (K1, P1) 4 times, TwR, K2, rep from * to end.
18th row P3, *sl 1, (P1, K1) 4 times, sl 1, P4, rep from * to last 13 sts, sl 1, (P1, K1) 4 times, sl 1, P3.
19th row K3, *TwL, (P1, K1) 3 times, TwR, K4, rep from * to last 13 sts, TwL, (P1, K1) 3 times, TwR, K3.
20th row P4, *sl 1, (K1, P1) 3 times, sl 1, P6, rep from * to last 12 sts, sl 1, (K1, P1) 3 times, sl 1, P4.
21st row K4, *TwL, (K1, P1) twice, TwR, K6, rep from * to last 12 sts, TwL, (K1, P1) twice, TwR, K4.
22nd row P5, *sl 1, (P1, K1) twice, sl 1, P8, rep from * to last 11 sts, sl 1, (P1, K1) twice, sl 1, P5.
23rd row K5, *TwL, P1, K1, TwR, K8, rep from * to last 11 sts, TwL, P1, K1, TwR, K5.
24th row P6, *sl 1, K1, P1, sl 1, P10, rep from * to last 10 sts, sl 1, K1, P1, sl 1, P6.
25th row K6, *TwL, TwR, K10, rep from * to last 10 sts, TwL, TwR, K6.
26th row P8, *sl 1, P13, rep from * to last 8 sts, sl 1, P7.
27th row K7, *TwL, K12, rep from * to last 9 sts, TwL, K7.
28th row P to end.
These 28 rows form the pattern.

Travelling rib pattern
Cast on a number of stitches divisible by 12+2.
1st row P6, *K7, P5, rep from * to last 8 sts, K7, P1.
2nd row K1, *P7, K5, rep from * to last st, K1.
3rd row P5, *K second st on left hand needle then K first st and sl both sts off needle tog – called TwR –, K4, TwR, P4, rep from * to last 9 sts, TwR, K4, TwR, P1.
4th row K2, *P7, K5, rep from * to end.
5th row P4, *TwR, K4, TwR, P4, rep from * to last 10 sts, TwR, K4, TwR, P2.
6th row K3, *P7, K5, rep from * to last 11 sts, P7, K4.
7th row P3, *TwR, K4, TwR, P4, rep from * to last 11 sts, TwR, K4, TwR, P3.
8th row K4, *P7, K5, rep from * to last 10 sts, P7, K3.
9th row P2, *TwR, K4, TwR, P4, rep from * to end.
10th row K5, *P7, K5, rep from * to last 9 sts, P7, K2.
11th row P1, *TwR, K4, TwR, P4, rep from * to last st, P1.
12th row K6, *P7, K5, rep from * to last 8 sts, P7, K1.
13th row P1, *put needle behind first st on left hand needle and K into back of second st then K first st and sl both sts off needle tog – called TwL –, K4, TwL, P4, rep from * to last st, P1.
14th row As 10th.
15th row P2, *TwL, K4, TwL, P4, rep from * to end.
16th row As 8th.
17th row P3, *TwL, K4, TwL, P4, rep from * to last 11 sts, TwL, K4, TwL, P3.
18th row As 6th.
19th row P4, *TwL, K4, TwL, P4, rep from * to last 10 sts, TwL, K4, TwL, P2.
20th row As 4th.
21st row P5, *TwL, K4, TwL, P4, rep from * to last 9 sts, TwL, K4, TwL, P1
22nd row As 2nd.
The 3rd through 22nd rows form the pattern.

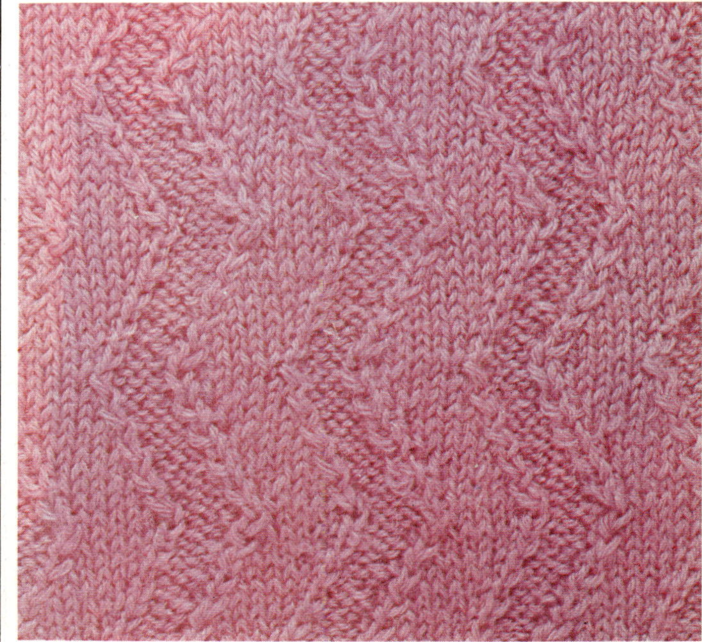

WOVEN FABRIC STITCHES

Just as the yarn can be carried over the needle in a pattern sequence to form additional stitches, or carried across the back of the work to form stripes or multi-colored patterns, it can also be held in front of a sequence of stitches to form a woven fabric. In many instances, the fabric, as with Fair Isle and jacquard patterns, is double the thickness of ordinary knitting and may be used in a variety of ways.

If you use a very fine yarn and any of the all over stitches shown in this chapter you will produce a very warm but light fabric, suitable for baby garments, bedjackets or lingerie, where you may want extra warmth but not extra weight. Using a knitting worsted quality yarn, the fabric will be firm and virtually windproof and most suitable for heavy outdoor garments, such as windbreakers, ski parkas or bulky jackets.

All these stitches are simple to work as the patterns merely require a given sequence of stitches to be slipped from one needle to the other, carrying the yarn in front of these stitches ready to knit the next stitch. They do not have to be worked to produce an all over fabric but can be worked at given intervals, as with the cluster stitch and the woven butterfly stitch, to add texture to an otherwise plain fabric. To keep the sides of the patterns neat and to avoid any 'fluting' effect, it is advisable to knit the first and last stitch on every row to form a firm, garter stitch edge.

Diagonal woven stitch

Cast on a number of stitches divisible by 4+2.

1st row K2, *yfwd, sl 2 P-wise, ybk, K2, rep from * to end.

2nd and every alt row K1, P to last st, K1.

3rd row Yfwd, sl 1 P-wise, ybk, *K2, yfwd, sl 2 P-wise, ybk, rep from * to last st, K1.

5th row Yfwd, sl 2 P-wise, ybk, *K2, yfwd, sl 2 P-wise, ybk, rep from * to end.

7th row K1, yfwd, sl 2 P-wise, ybk, *K2, yfwd, sl 2 P-wise, ybk, rep from * to last 3 sts, K2, yfwd, sl 1 P-wise, ybk.

8th row As 2nd.

These 8 rows form the pattern.

Woven bar stitch

Cast on a number of stitches divisible by 3+1.

1st row (RS) K to end.

2nd row *K1, keeping yarn at back of work sl 2 P-wise, rep from * to last st, K1.

These 2 rows form the pattern.

Woven ladder stitch

Cast on a number of stitches divisible by 8+1.

1st row *K5, yfwd, sl 3 P-wise, ybk, rep from * to last st, K1.

2nd row K1, *ybk, sl 3 P-wise, yfwd, P5, rep from * to end, ending last rep with K1.
3rd row As 1st.
4th row K1, P to last st, K1.
5th row K1, *yfwd, sl 3 P-wise, ybk, K5, rep from * to end.
6th row K1, *P4, ybk, sl 3 P-wise, yfwd, P1, rep from * to end, ending last rep K1.
7th row As 5th.
8th row As 4th.
These 8 rows form the pattern.

Woven chevron stitch
Cast on a number of stitches divisible by 10.
1st row *K1, yfwd, sl 3 P-wise, ybk, K2, yfwd, sl 3 P-wise, ybk, K1, rep from * to end.
2nd row *Ybk, sl 3 P-wise, yfwd, P2, rep from * to end, ending last rep K1.
3rd row Yfwd, *sl 1 P-wise, ybk, K2, yfwd, sl 3 P-wise, ybk, K2, yfwd, sl 2 P-wise, rep from * to end.
4th row Yfwd, *sl 1 P-wise, yfwd, P2, ybk, sl 3 P-wise, yfwd, P2, ybk, sl 2 P-wise, rep from * to end.
5th row *Yfwd, sl 3 P-wise, ybk, K2, rep from * to end.
6th row *P1, ybk, sl 3 P-wise, yfwd, P1, rep from * to end.
7th row As 5th.
8th row As 4th.
9th row As 3rd.

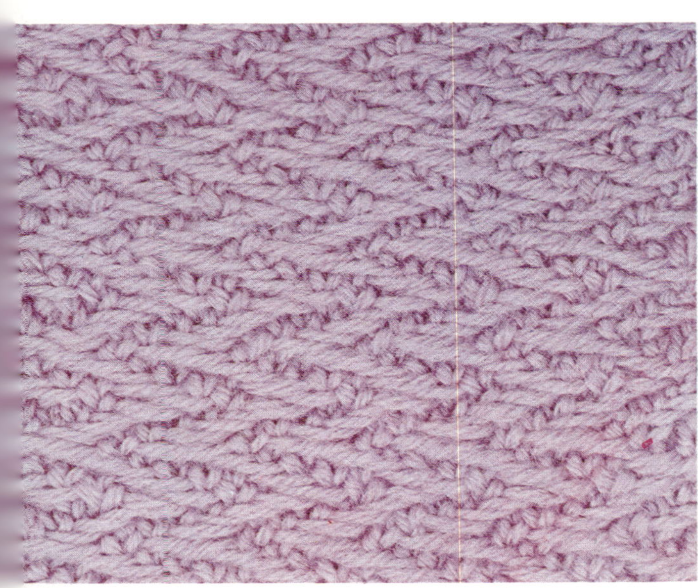

10th row As 2nd.
These 10 rows form the pattern.

Cluster stitch
Cast on a number of stitches divisible by 8+5.
1st row K to end.
2nd row P to end.
3rd row *K5, sl next 3 sts on to cable needle and hold at front of work, pass the yarn across the back of these stitches and right around them 6 times in a counter-clockwise direction then K3 sts from cable needle – called 1CL, –, rep from * to last 5 sts, K5.
4th row P to end.
Rep 1st and 2nd rows once more.
7th row *K1, 1CL, K4, rep from * to last 5 sts, K1, 1CL, K1.
8th row P to end.
These 8 rows form the pattern.

Woven butterfly stitch
Cast on a number of stitches divisible by 10+7.
1st row K6, *yfwd, sl 5 P-wise, ybk, K5, rep from * to last st, K1.
2nd row P to end.
Rep 1st and 2nd rows 3 times more.
9th row K8, *insert right hand needle under the 4 long loops, yarn around the needle and draw through a stitch, then keeping this st on right hand needle K the next st on the left hand needle and pass the first st over the K1 – called B1 –, K9, rep from * to last 9 sts, B1, K8.
10th row As 2nd.
11th row K1, yfwd, sl 5 P-wise, ybk, *K5, yfwd, sl 5 P-wise, ybk, rep from * to last st, K1.
12th row As 2nd.
Rep 11th and 12th rows 3 times more.
19th row K3, B1, *K9, B1, rep from * to last 3 sts, K3.
20th row As 2nd.
These 20 rows form the pattern.

RAISED STITCHES

Bobble and cluster stitches
Although the overall heading refers to a cluster of raised stitches which can be arranged to give an interesting and highly textured fabric, the size of a bobble or cluster can vary considerably.
There are various ways of working bobbles but the basic principle is always the same – working more than once into the stitch where the bobble is required and then decreasing again to the original stitch, either in the same row or several rows later.
Cluster stitches also are worked on this principle but they are not intended to be as dense as bobble stitches and once the cluster is formed, it is decreased more gradually over a number of rows until only the original stitch remains.
Both bobble and cluster stitches may be used very effectively to form an all over pattern but, combined with other stitches such as cables, they produce some of the most beautiful variations of the Aran patterns which are renowned throughout the world.

Bobble patterns
The simplest forms of bobble stitches are small and easy to work. The working methods of the two samples shown here differ slightly, but both produce a small, berry type of stitch. Trinity stitch, which is used in Aran patterns, derives its name from the method of working 'three into one and one into three.'

Blackberry stitch
Cast on a number of stitches divisible by 4.
1st row *(K1, yfwd to make one st, K1) all into next st, P3, rep from * to end.
2nd row *P3 tog, K3, rep from * to end.
3rd row *P3, (K1, yfwd to make one st, K1) all into next st, rep from * to end.
4th row *K3, P3 tog, rep from * to end.
These 4 rows form the pattern.

Trinity stitch
Cast on a number of stitches divisible by 4.
1st row *(K1, P1, K1) all into next st, P3 tog, rep from * to end.
2nd row P to end.
3rd row *P3 tog, (K1, P1, K1) all into next st, rep from * to end.
4th row As 2nd.
These 4 rows form the pattern.

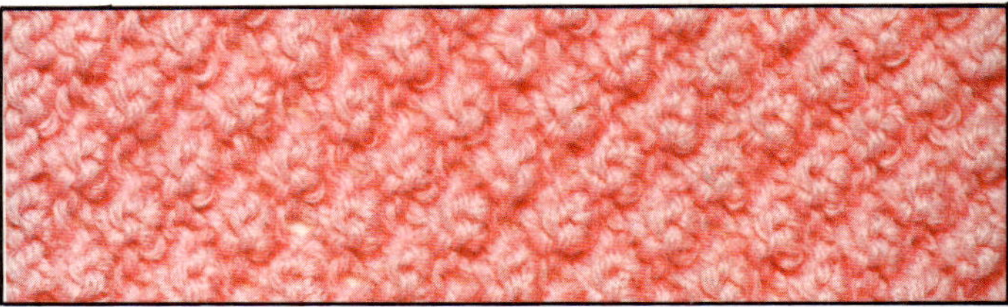

Small bobble stitch
Cast on a number of stitches divisible by 6 plus 5.
1st row (WS) P to end.
2nd row K2, (K1, P1, K1, P1, K1) all into next st then using point of left hand needle lift 2nd, 3rd, 4th and 5th sts over first st and off right hand needle – called B1 –, *K5, B1, rep from * to last 2 sts, K2.
3rd row P to end.
4th row *K5, B1, rep from * to last 5 sts, K5.
These 4 rows form the pattern.

Popcorn stitch
Cast on a number of stitches divisible by 6 plus 5.
1st row (WS) P to end.
2nd row K2, (K1, P1, K1, P1, K1) all into next st, turn and K these 5 sts, turn and P5 then using point of left hand needle lift 2nd, 3rd, 4th and 5th sts over first st and off right hand needle – called B1 –, *K5, B1, rep from * to last 2 sts, K2.
3rd row P to end.
4th row *K5, B1, rep from * to last 5 sts, K5.
These 4 rows form the pattern.

Currant stitch
Cast on a number of stitches divisible by 2 plus 1.
1st row (RS) K to end.
2nd row K1, *(P1, yrn to make one st, P1, yrn, P1) all into next st, K1, rep from * to end.
3rd row P to end.
4th row K1, *sl 2 P-wise keeping yarn at front of work – called sl 2F –, P3 tog, p2sso, K1, rep from * to end.
5th row K to end.
6th row K2, *(P1, yrn, P1, yrn, P1) all into next st, K1, rep from * to last st, K1.
7th row P to end.
8th row K2, *sl 2F, P3 tog, p2sso, K1, rep from * to last st, K1.
These 8 rows form the pattern.

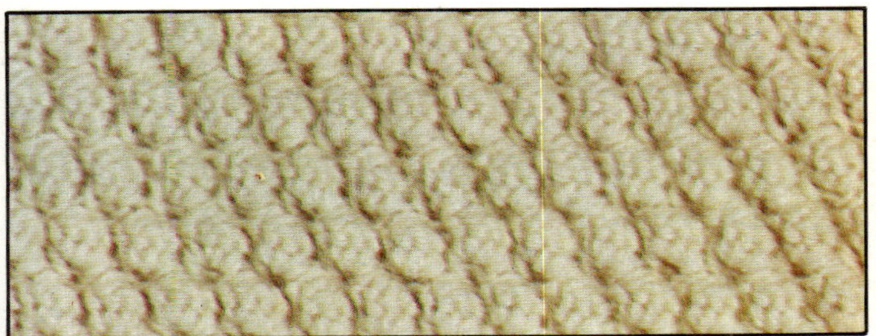

Long bobble stitch
Cast on a number of stitches divisible by 6 plus 3.
1st row (WS) P to end.
2nd row K1, *K3, (K1, yfwd to make one st, K1) all into next st, K1, (turn and P5, turn and K5) twice, K1, rep from * to last 2 sts, K2.
3rd row P1, *P2, P2 tog, P1, P2 tog tbl, P1, rep from * to last 2 sts, P2.
4th row K3, *K4, (K1, yfwd, K1) all into next st, K1, (turn and P5, turn and K5) twice, rep from * to last 6 sts, K6.
5th row P3, *P3, P2 tog, P1, P2 tog tbl, rep from * to last 6sts, P6.
Rows 2 through 5 form the pattern.

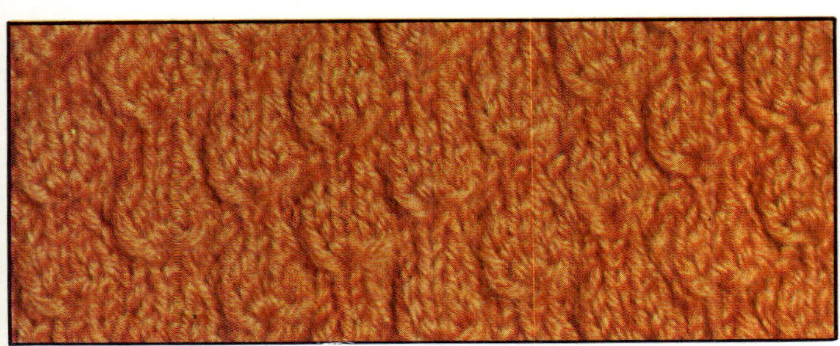

Cluster stitches
These patterns may be worked in two ways – either by increasing and shaping the cluster and working the stitches on either side row by row at the same time, or by working the cluster separately and then continuing to knit the background fabric until it has reached the same height as the cluster.

Bell cluster
Cast on a number of stitches divisible by 4 plus 4.
1st row (WS) K to end.
2nd row P4, *turn and cast on 8 sts – called C1 –, P4, rep from * to end.
3rd row *K4, P8, rep from * to last 4 sts, K4.
4th row P4, *K8, P4, rep from * to end.
5th row As 3rd.
6th row P4, *sl 1, K1, psso, K4, K2 tog, P4, rep from * to end.
7th row *K4, P6, rep from * to last 4 sts, K4.
8th row P4, *sl 1, K1, psso, K2, K2 tog, P4, rep from * to end.
9th row *K4, P4, rep from * to last 4 sts, K4.
10th row P4, *sl 1, K1, psso, K2 tog, P4, rep from * to end.
11th row *K4, P2, rep from * to last 4 sts, K4.
12th row P4, *K2 tog, P4, rep from * to end.
13th row *K4, P1, rep from * to last 4 sts, K4.
14th row P4, *K2 tog, P3, rep from * to end.
These 14 rows form the pattern.

Detached cluster
Cast on a number of stitches divisible by 6 plus 5.
1st row (RS) P to end.
2nd row K to end.
3rd row *P5, (yfwd to make one st, K into next st) 3 times into same st to make 6 out of one, turn and P these 6 sts, turn and sl 1, K5, turn and sl 1, P5, turn and sl 1, K5, turn and (P2 tog) 3 times, turn and sl 1, K2 tog, psso – called C1 –, rep from * to last 5 sts, P5.
4th row K to end.
5th row P to end.
6th row K to end.
7th row P2, *C1, P5, rep from * to last 3 sts, C1, P2.
8th row K to end.
These 8 rows form the pattern.

FUR FABRICS

Knitting patterns which have the appearance of fur fabrics are made by looping strands of yarn onto the main background while the row is being knitted.
The usual method is to loop the yarn around fingers or a strip of cardboard for the required number of times, then to secure the loops to the knitted stitch so that they do not unravel. The fabric produced is warm and light and is very suitable for outer garments, and trimmings such as collars and cuffs, baby blankets and washable throw rugs.
Another method shown here combines a knitted background with lengths of crochet chains forming a fur effect which gives a close, astrakan texture to the fabric. The loops made by using this method will not catch or break as easily as those of the first method and this way is therefore most suitable for babies' and children's garments, where frequent washing or rough-and-tumble use is expected. Although it is not as quick or simple to work as the first method, the effect is so attractive that it is well worth a little time and effort spent in practicing it.

Looped patterns
The density of these patterns may be varied as desired, either by the number of times the yarn is looped around, or by the position of each loop on the background fabric. The samples given here have been worked in a knitting worsted yarn, alternating the position of the loops on every 4th row.

Single loop stitch
Here the loops are formed on a right side row when the work is facing you. Cast on a number of stitches divisible by 2 plus 1.

1st row (RS) K to end.
2nd row P to end.
3rd row *K1, K next st without letting it drop off left hand needle, yfwd, pass yarn over left thumb to make a loop approximately $1\frac{1}{2}$in long, ybk and K st rem on left hand needle letting it drop from the needle, return the 2 sts just worked to the left hand needle and K them tog tbl – called L1 –, rep from * to last st, K1.
4th row P to end.
Rep 1st and 2nd rows once more.
7th row K1, *K1, L1, rep from * to last 2 sts, K2.
8th row P to end.
These 8 rows form the pattern.

Double loop stitch
Here the loops are formed on the right side of the fabric when the wrong side of the work is facing you. Cast on a number of stitches divisible by 2 plus 1.

1st row (RS) K to end.
Rep 1st row twice more.
4th row (WS) K1, *insert right hand needle into next st on left hand needle as if to knit it, wind yarn over right hand needle point and round first and 2nd fingers of left hand twice, then over and around right hand needle point once more, draw all 3 loops through st and sl on to left hand needle, insert right hand needle through back of these 3 loops and through the original st and K tog tbl – called L1 –, K1, rep from * to end.

5th 6th and 7th rows K to end.
8th row K1, *K1, L1, rep from * to last 2 sts, K2.
These 8 rows form the pattern.

Chain loop stitch
Here again, the density of the pattern can be changed by the position of each chain loop on the background fabric and by the number of rows worked between each pattern row. To work the sample given here you will need knitting yarn, a pair of No.5 needles and a Size G crochet hook. Cast on a number of stitches divisible by 2 plus 1.
1st row (RS) K to end.

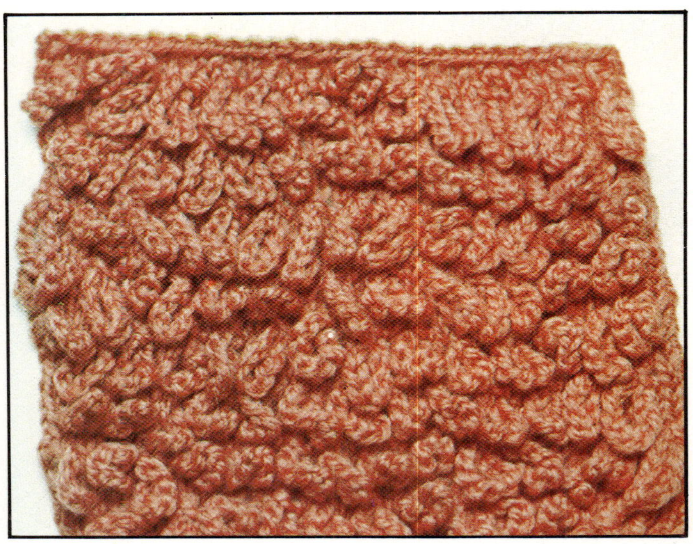

2nd row P to end.
3rd row K1, *K next st without letting it drop off left hand needle, insert crochet hook from front to back through loop on left hand needle, draw a loop through and leave on hook then drop st from left hand needle, wind yarn around left hand and make 12ch in the usual way, then keeping ch at front of work and yarn at back of work sl loop onto right hand needle and remove hook, then lift last K st over loop – called L1 –, K1, rep from * to end.
4th row P to end.
Rep 1st and 2nd rows once more.
7th row K1, *K1, L1, rep from * to last 2 sts, K2.
8th row P to end.
These 8 rows form the pattern.

Tie
7in wide at lower edge by 40in long

Gauge
22 sts and 30 rows to 4in in stockinette stitch (st st) worked on No.5 needles

Materials
4 × 2oz balls of Sports Yarn
One pair No.5 needles

Tie
Using No.5 needles cast on 45 sts. K 3 rows g st. Start patt.
1st row (RS) K2, work in any loop patt over next 41sts, K2.
2nd row K2, patt 41 sts, K2.
Cont in patt, keeping 2 sts at each end in g st throughout, until work measures 5in from beg, ending with a WS row.
Next row K2, sl 1, K1, psso, patt to last 4 sts, K2 tog, K2.
Work 3 rows patt without shaping. Rep last 4 rows 8 times more. 27 sts. Cont without shaping until piece measures 29in from beg, ending with a WS row.
Next row K2, pick up loop lying between sts and K tbl – called inc 1 –, patt to last 2 sts, inc 1, K2.
Work 3 rows patt without shaping. Rep last 4 rows 8 times more. 45 sts. Cont without shaping until work measures $39\frac{3}{4}$in from beg. K 3 rows g st. Bind off.

Loop fastening
Using No.5 needles cast on 6 sts. Work 4in g st.
Bind off.

Finishing
Do not block. Sew loop fastening across back of one end approximately 7in above bottom edge.
Slot other end through loop to secure.

FISHERMAN KNITTING

Fisherman knitting is the name given to the making of seamless pullovers, knitted in a very closely woven fabric similar to a patterned brocade. Because of the fineness of the needles used for this type of knitting, sometimes to as fine a gauge as Ace 1 knitting pins, the textured patterns do not stand out in relief as they do with Aran stitches. The purpose of this knitting is to make a fabric which is virtually windproof and which will stand up to the constant wear and tear of a fisherman's life.

As with many of the folk crafts which have been handed down to us through countless generations, these pullovers were often knitted by the fishermen themselves, but more often they were lovingly knitted by their womenfolk, in traditional patterns which varied from region to region.

The name 'jersey', originated from the island of that name. Another name in regular use is a 'guernsey', or 'gansey', so called after the sister island in the same group, the Channel Islands, which are situated off the coast of France but are politically a dependency of the United Kingdom.

Each port around the coastline of the British Isles has developed its own regional style of fisherman knitting. Some have patterned yokes, others have vertical panels of patterns and some have horizontal bands of patterns, but the original guernseys, which were made purely as hard-wearing working garments, were nearly always made in stockinette stitch with very little decoration and always in the traditional color, navy blue. The more elaborate examples which evolved were kept for Sunday best and in Cornwall they were often referred to as bridal shirts and were knitted by the young women for their betrothed.

A traditional guernsey is knitted entirely without seams, often worked on sets of 5, 6, or even more double-pointed needles. The body is knitted in rounds to the armholes, then instead of dividing the work for the back and front at this point, the work is continued in rounds with the position of the armholes separated

from the main sections of the guernsey by a series of loops wound around the needle on every round. These loops are dropped from the needle on the following round and the process is repeated until the guernsey is the required length. When this section is completed, a series of what look like the rungs of a ladder mark each armhole. These loops are cut in the middle and the ends carefully darned into the main fabric, then the sleeve stitches are picked up round the armholes and the sleeve is knitted in rounds down to the cuff. The shoulder stitches are woven together to finish the garment without a single sewn seam.
The shape of these garments is as distinctive as the patterns. They all feature a dropped shoulder line and crew neckline, with little, if any, shaping. Sometimes buttons and buttonholes would be added to one shoulder for ease in dressing and undressing, a gusset made before the armhole division and carried on into the top of the sleeve, or the neck would be continued to form a small collar, but the simplicity of the basic design has never been bettered, to give the utmost warmth, freedom of movement and protection to the wearer.

Traditional guernsey

Sizes
Directions are to fit 38in chest. Changes for 40, 42 and 44in chest are in brackets [ ].
Length to shoulder, 23[23½:24:24½]in
Sleeve seam, 18in, adjustable

Gauge
28 sts and 36 rows to 4in over stockinette stitch (st st) worked on No.3 needles

Materials
14[15:16:17] × 2oz balls of Sport Yarn
Set of 4 No.3 double-pointed needles or No.3 circular needle
Set of 4 No.1 double-pointed needles or No.1 circular needle

Guernsey body
Using set of 4 No.1 needles cast on 264[276:288:300] sts. Mark beg of round with colored thread. Cont in rounds of K1, P1 rib for 3in. Change to set of 4 No.3 needles. Cont in rounds of st st until work measures 13in from beg. Commence yoke patt.
****1st round** P to end.
2nd round K to end.
Rep these 2 rounds twice more, then 1st round once more. **.
***Work 5 rounds st st.

Divide for armholes
1st round *K132[138:144:150] sts, wind yarn 10 times around right hand needle – called loop 10 –, rep from * once more.
Rep last round once more, dropping extra loops from needle before loop 10.
3rd round *K6[9:0:3], (K6, P1, K11, P1, K5) 5[5:6:6] times, K6[9:0:3], drop extra loops, loop 10, rep from * once more.
4th round *K6[9:0:3], (K4, P1, K1, P1, K9, P1, K1, P1, K5) 5[5:6:6] times, K6[9:0:3], drop extra loops, loop 10, rep from * once more.
5th round *K6[9:0:3], (K4, P1, K3, P1, K7, P1, (K1, P1) twice, K3) 5[5:6:6] times, K6[9:0:3], drop extra loops, loop 10, rep from * once more.
6th round *K6[9:0:3], (K2, P1, (K1, P1) 3 times, (K5, P1) twice, K3) 5[5:6:6] times, K6[9:0:3], drop extra loops, loop 10, rep from * once more.
7th round *K6[9:0:3], (K2, P1, K7, P1, K3, P1, (K1, P1) 4 times, K1) 5[5:6:6] times, K6[9:0:3], drop extra loops, loop 10, rep from * once more.
8th round *K6[9:0:3], (P1, (K1, P1) 6 times, K9, P1, K1) 5 [5:6:6] times, K6[9:0:3], drop extra loops, loop 10, rep from * once more.
9th round *K6[9:0:3], (P1, K11, P12) 5[5:6:6] times, K6[9:0:3], drop extra loops, loop 10, rep from * once more.
10th round *K6[9:0:3], (P11, K1, P1, K9, P1, K1) 5[5:6:6] times, K6[9:0:3], drop extra loops, loop 10, rep from * once more.
11th round *K6[9:0:3], (K2, P1, K7, P1, K13) 5[5:6:6] times, K6[9:0:3], drop extra loops, loop 10, rep from * once more.
12th round *K6[9:0:3], (K14, P1, K5, P1, K3) 5[5:6:6] times, K6[9:0:3], drop extra loops, loop 10, rep from * once more.
13th round *K6[9:0:3], (K4, P1, K3, P1, K15) 5[5:6:6] times, K6[9:0:3], drop extra loops, loop 10, rep from * once more.
14th round *K6[9:0:3], (K16, P1, K1, P1, K5) 5[5:6:6] times, K6[9:0:3]. drop extra loops, loop 10, rep from * once more.
15th and 16th rounds As 1st, dropping extra loops.
Keeping armhole loops correct, work 5 rounds st st, then rep from ** to ** once. ***. Rep from *** to *** once more. Beg with a 2nd row, cont working in patt from ** to ** until work measures 8½[9:9½:10]in from beg of loops, omitting loop 10 at end of last round. Break off yarn.

Divide for shoulders
Maintaining patt, sl first and last 35[37:39:41] sts of back and front sections on to holders, knit across each set of 62[64:66:68] sts of neck separately for 6 rows. Bind off loosely. Weave shoulder sts from holders.

Sleeves
Cut loops of armholes and darn in ends. Using set of 4 No.3 needles and with RS of work facing, K 110 [114:118:122] sts round armhole. K 5 rounds st st, then rep from ** to ** as for body.
Cont in rounds of st st, dec one st at beg and end of next and every foll 6th round until 74[80:84:88] sts rem. Cont without shaping until sleeve measures 16in from beg, or required length less 2in. Change to 4 No.1 needles. Work 2in K1, P1 rib. Bind off in rib.

MAXI KNITTING

Working a fabric on very large knitting needles can be both speedy and fun, as even the most basic stitches take on a completely different appearance. This particular type of knitting is often referred to as 'jiffy knitting' and needles for this special gauge are available in varying sizes.

The most popular needles are made from a special lightweight hollow plastic and are graded upwards from the smallest size 11, on to 13, 15 and to the largest size 19. Extra large jumbo sized needles are also available, and graded as sizes 35 and 50.

Great care must be taken in selecting a suitable yarn for this type of knitting, and often two or more strands are used at the same time, producing a very heavy fabric. Any lightweight yarn, such as mohair, is ideal as this gives sufficient bulk to the fabric without being too heavy.

The stitch chosen also plays an important part, as the texture must be firm enough to prevent the knitting from stretching but not so dense that it produces a thick, harsh fabric. Stockinette stitch does not work too well with this method as it is very difficult to keep the smooth, even tension which is the main characteristic of this stitch. On the other hand, garter stitch, moss stitch and small, repeating lace or fabric patterns, such as are shown here, do produce interesting textures which will hold their shape.

When casting on and binding off, the stitches must be worked very loosely to avoid pulling the fabric out of shape.

Indian pillar stitch

Use two or more strands of yarn, depending upon the size of needle chosen. Cast on a number of stitches divisible by 4 plus 2.

1st row P1, *insert needle purlwise into next 3 sts as if to purl them tog but instead (P1, K1, P1) into these 3 sts, K1, rep from * to last st, P1.

2nd row P to end.

These 2 rows form the pattern.

Waffle stitch

Use two or more strands of yarn, depending upon the size of needle chosen, and cast on a number of stitches divisible by 2.

1st row *K1 tbl, P1, rep from * to end.

2nd row *P1 tbl, K1, rep from * to end.

These 2 rows form the pattern.

Grecian plait stitch

This stitch requires one small and one large needle, the large needle being twice the size of the small needle. Use two strands of yarn and cast on an even number of stitches with the large needle.

1st row Using the small needle, K to end.

2nd row Using the large needle, P to end.

3rd row Using the small needle, lift the 2nd st over the first st and K it then K the first st, lift the 4th st over the 3rd st and K it then K the 3rd st, cont in this way across the row.

4th row Using the large needle, P to end.

These 4 rows form the pattern.

Jiffy-knit scarf

Size

Approximately 9in wide by 66in long, excluding the fringe

Gauge

10 sts to 3in in Indian pillar st worked on No.17 needles

Materials

5 × 2oz balls of Spinnerin Piccadilly in each of 2 contrast colors, A and B
One pair of No.17 needles

Scarf

Using No.17 needles if working in Indian pillar st or waffle st, or one No.11 and one No.17 needle if working in Grecian braid st, and one strand each of A and B, cast on 30 sts loosely. Work in patt as desired until scarf measures 66in from beg.
Bind off very loosely.

Finishing

Do not block. Using 2 strands of A and B tog, make a fringe of desired length along each short end, knotting fringe into every alt st. Trim fringe ends.

TRAVELING STITCHES

Crossed stitches, which have a twisted appearance, are used extensively in Aran patterns and the same methods may be used to create effective miniature and mock cable patterns. Because only two, or at most three, stitches are crossed at any one time, it is not necessary to use a cable needle, therefore these patterns are simple to work.

Crossed stitches should be knitted against a purl background to show to their best advantage, but to produce an even tighter twist on the stitches, it is also necessary to know how to twist them on the wrong side, or on a purl row against a knitted background.

Knitted crossed stitches with back twist

The crossed stitches are worked over two knitted stitches and the twist lies to the left. Pass the right hand needle behind the first stitch on the left hand needle, knit into the back of the next stitch on the left hand needle then knit into the front of the first skipped stitch and slip both stitches off the left hand needle together. The abbreviation for this is 'T2B'.

Mock cable

Cast on a number of stitches divisible by 5 + 3.

1st row P3, *K2, P3, rep from * to end.

2nd row K3, *P2, K3, rep from * to end.

Rep 1st and 2nd rows once more.

5th row P3, *T2B, P3, rep from * to end.

6th row As 2nd.

These 6 rows form the pattern.

Twisted rib

Cast on a number of stitches divisible by 14 + 2.

1st row P2, *T2B, P2, K4, P2, T2B, P2, rep from * to end.

2nd row K2, *P2, K2, P4, K2, P2, K2, rep from * to end.

Rep 1st and 2nd rows once more.

5th row P2, *T2B, P2, into 4th and 3rd sts on left hand needle work T2B leaving sts on needle then work T2B into 2nd and 1st sts and sl all 4 sts off needle tog, P2, T2B, P2, rep from * to end.

6th row As 2nd.

These 6 rows form the pattern.

Knitted crossed stitches with front twist

The crossed stitches are worked over two knitted stitches and the twist lies to the right. Pass the right hand needle in front of the first stitch on the left hand needle, knit into the front of the next stitch on the

left hand needle then knit into the front of the first skipped stitch and slip both stitches off the needle together. The abbreviation for this is 'T2F'.
Three stitches can be crossed in the same way by working into the 3rd stitch, then into the 2nd and then into the first, slipping all 3 stitches off the left hand needle together. The abbreviation for this is 'T3F'.

Twisted panels
Cast on a number of stitches divisible by 8+2.
1st row P2, *(T2F) 3 times, P2, rep from * to end.
2nd row K2, *P6, K2, rep from * to end.
3rd row P2, *(T3F) twice, P2, rep from * to end.
4th row As 2nd.
These 4 rows form the pattern.

Purled crossed stitches with front twist
The crossed stitches are worked over two purled stitches and form a crossed thread lying to the right on the knitted side of the work. Pass the right hand needle in front of the first stitch on the left hand needle and purl the next stitch on the left hand needle, purl the first skipped stitch and slip both stitches off the left hand needle together. The abbreviation for this is 'T2PF'.

Purled crossed stitches with back twist
The crossed stitches are worked over two purled stitches and form a crossed thread lying to the left on the knitted side of the work. Pass the right hand needle behind the first stitch on the left hand needle and purl the next stitch on the left hand needle through the back of the loop, purl the first skipped stitch and slip both stitches off the left hand needle together. The abbreviation for this is 'T2PB'.

Crossing two knitted stitches to the right
Pass the right hand needle in front of the first stitch on the left hand needle and knit into the next stitch on the left hand needle, lift this stitch over the first skipped stitch and off the needle then knit the first skipped stitch. The abbreviation for this is 'C2R'.

Crossing two knitted stitches to the left
Slip the first stitch on to the right hand needle without knitting it, knit the next stitch on the left hand needle and slip it on to the right hand needle, using the left hand needle point pass the first slipped stitch over the knitted stitch, knitting into the slipped stitch at the same time. The abbreviation for this is 'C2L'.

Crossed cable
Cast on a number of stitches divisible by 7+3.
1st row P3, *K4, P3, rep from * to end.
2nd row K3, *P4, K3, rep from * to end.
3rd row P3, *C2R, C2L, P3, rep from * to end.
4th row As 2nd.
These 4 rows form the pattern.

CABLES
Basic stitches

Cable patterns, using variations of stitches, are among the most popular in knitting, since they are easy to work and give an interesting fabric with many uses – they can be thick and bulky for a sports sweater, or fine and lacy for baby garments. Twisting the cables in opposite directions can produce an all-over fabric, or simple panels of cables against the purl side of stockinette stitch can give a special look to the most basic garment. All cable patterns are based on the method of moving a sequence of stitches from one position to another in a row, giving the effect of the twists you see in a rope – the more stitches moved, the thicker the rope.

The previous chapter dealt with the method of crossing two or three stitches to give a twisted effect, but when altering the position of more than two stitches it is easier to do so by means of a third needle, which is used to hold the stitches being moved until they are ready to be worked. For this purpose a special cable needle is the best, although any short, double pointed needle will do. Cable needles are very short and easy to handle and are made in the same sizes as knitting needles. If the cable needle is not the same thickness as the needles being used for the garment, then it should be finer, not thicker. A thicker needle is more difficult to use and, more important, it will stretch the stitches and spoil the appearance of the finished work.

Cable abbreviations

Although working instructions and abbreviations will usually be found in detail in any cable pattern before you begin to knit, it would be as well to study these, as they do vary considerably. As a general guide, the letter 'C' stands for the word 'cable', followed by the number of stitches to be cabled, then the letter 'B' for back, or 'F' for front, indicating the direction in which the stitches are to be moved. In this way a cable twist from right to left over 6 stitches is abbreviated as 'C6F' and a cable twist from left to right over 6 stitches is abbreviated as 'C6B'.

Cable twist from right to left

This is a simple cable worked over 6 knitted stitches against a purl background. To work this sample cast on 24 stitches.

1st row (RS) P9, K6, P9.

2nd row K9, P6, K9.

Rep 1st and 2nd rows twice more.

7th row P9, sl next 3 sts on to cable needle and hold at front of work, K next 3 sts from left hand needle then K3 sts from cable needle – called C6F –, P9.

8th row As 2nd.

These 8 rows form the pattern. Repeat pattern rows twice more. Bind off.

This sample produces a rope-like pattern in the center, consisting of 6 knitted stitches twisted 3 times. Each twist lies in the same direction from the right to the left.

Cable twist from left to right

Cast on and work the first 6 rows as for cable twist from right to left.

7th row P9, sl next 3 sts on to cable needle and hold at back of work, K next 3 sts from left hand needle then K3 sts from cable needle – called C6B –, P9.
8th row As 2nd.
These 8 rows form the pattern. Repeat pattern rows twice more. Bind off.
This sample will be similar to the first, but each twist will lie in the opposite direction from the left to the right.

Cable twist from right to left with row variations
The appearance of each cable twist is altered considerably by the number of rows worked between each twist. Cast on and work the first 4 rows as for cable twist from right to left.
5th row P9, C6F, P9.
6th row As 2nd.
Rep 1st and 2nd rows twice more, then 5th and 6th rows once more.
Rep 1st and 2nd rows 4 times more, then 5th and 6th rows once more.
Rep 1st and 2nd rows 6 times more, then 5th and 6th rows once more.
Rep 1st and 2nd rows once more. Bind off.

This sample shows that the cable twist on every 4th row gives a very close, tight, rope look, whereas twisting on every 8th or 12th row gives a much softer look.

Alternating cables
This combines both the cable twist from right to left and cable twist from left to right, to produce a fabric with a completely different look although the methods used are exactly the same. Cast on and work the first 8 rows as for cable twist from right to left.
9th row As 1st.
10th row As 2nd.
Rep 9th and 10th rows twice more.
15th row P9, C6B, P9.
16th row As 10th.
Rep 9th and 10th rows twice more. Bind off.
This sample shows the same 3 stitches being moved on each twist.

Panels of cable twist from right to left
This pattern is made up of panels of 4 knitted stitches, with one purl stitch between each panel, twisted from right to left on different rows to give a diagonal appearance. Cast on 31 stitches.
1st row P1, *K4, P1, rep from * to end.
2nd row K1, *P4, K1, rep from * to end.
3rd row P1, *K4, P1, sl next 2 sts on to cable needle and hold at front of work, K next 2 sts from left hand needle then K2 sts from cable needle – called C4F –, P1, rep from * to end.
4th row As 2nd.
Rep 1st and 2nd rows once more.
7th row P1, *C4F, P1, K4, P1, rep from * to end.
8th row As 2nd.
These 8 rows form the pattern. Repeat pattern rows 3 times more. Bind off.

More cable stitches

By using combinations of the simple cable twists given in the previous chapter, you can produce numerous patterns. All of the variations given here can be worked as all over patterns or as separate panels against a purl background.
Try incorporating single plaited cable as an all over pattern on a plain sweater design, or use a panel of link cables to highlight the front and center of the sleeves on a basic cardigan. Another simple alternative would be to work two samples of honeycomb cable and use these as patch pockets on a stockinette stitch cardigan, using the reverse side, or purl side, as the right side of the cardigan fabric.

Link cable
The cable pattern is worked on 12 knitted stitches against a purl background. For this sample cast on 24 stitches.
1st row P6, K12, P6.
2nd row K6, P12, K6.
Rep 1st and 2nd rows twice more.
7th row P6, sl next 3 sts on to cable needle and hold at back of work, K next 3 sts from left hand needle then K3 sts from cable needle – called C6B –, sl next 3 sts on to cable needle and hold at front of work, K next 3 sts from left hand needle then K3 sts from cable needle – called C6F –, P6.
8th row As 2nd.
These 8 rows form the pattern. Repeat pattern rows twice more. Bind off.
This pattern gives the appearance of chain links, each link coming up out of the one below.

Inverted link cable
Cast on and work the first 6 rows as for link cable given above.
7th row P6, C6F, C6B, P6.
8th row As 2nd.
These 8 rows form the pattern. Repeat pattern rows twice more. Bind off.
This pattern has the reverse appearance of link cables with each link joining and passing under the link above.

Honeycomb cable
This pattern combines the working methods of link cable and inverted link cable. For this sample cast on 24 stitches.
1st row P6, K12, P6.
2nd row K6, P12, K6.
Rep 1st and 2nd rows once more.

5th row P6, C6B, C6F, P6.
6th row As 2nd.
Rep 1st and 2nd rows twice more.
11th row P6, C6F, C6B, P6.
12th row As 2nd.
These 12 rows form the pattern. Repeat pattern rows twice more. Bind off.
This pattern forms a cable which appears to be superimposed on the fabric beneath.

Single plaited cable

This pattern is achieved by dividing the groups of stitches which are to be cabled into three sections instead of two and cabling each group alternately. For this sample cast on 30 stitches.
1st row P3, *K6, P3, rep from * to end.
2nd row K3, *P6, K3, rep from * to end.
3rd row P3, *sl next 2 sts on to cable needle and hold at back of work, K next 2 sts from left hand needle then K2 from cable needle – called C4B –, K2, P3, rep from * to end.
4th row As 2nd.
5th row P3, *K2, sl next 2 sts on to cable needle and hold at front of work, K next 2 sts from left hand needle then K2 from cable needle – called C4F –, P3, rep from * to end.
6th row As 2nd.
The 3rd through 6th rows from the pattern. Repeat pattern rows 6 times more. Bind off.

Double plaited cable

This pattern is even more textured than single plaited cable and is worked over 18 knitted stitches against a purl background. For this sample cast on 30 stitches.
1st row P6, K18, P6.
2nd row K6, P18, K6.
3rd row P6, (C6B) 3 times, P6.
4th row As 2nd.
Rep 1st and 2nd rows once more.
7th row P6, K3, (C6F) twice, K3, P6.
8th row As 2nd.
These 8 rows form the pattern. Repeat pattern rows twice more. Bind off.

Cable waves

Cable patterns have a completely different appearance when the stitches being moved are worked in knitting against a knitted background, instead of a purl fabric. For this sample cast on 24 stitches.
1st row K to end.
2nd and every alt row P to end.
3rd row *C6F, K6, rep from * to end.
5th row K to end.
7th row *K6, C6B, rep from * to end.
9th row K to end.
10th row As 2nd.
Rows 3 through 10 form the pattern. Repeat pattern rows twice more. Bind off.

Cables in rounds

Cable patterns are just as easy to work in rounds as in rows. Unless the pattern states otherwise, the cable twists are worked on the right side of the fabric and as the right side of the work is always facing you when you knit in rounds, it is a simple matter to use either of these techniques.
This jaunty little hat has been specially designed so that the cable panels can be worked in any one of three variations. This will help you master the method of working cable stitches – while you are making yourself a snug, warm, fashionable accessory!

Size
To fit an average head

Gauge
22 sts and 30 rows to 4in in stockinette stitch (st st) worked on No.8 needles

Materials
1 × 4oz skein of any 4 ply Knitting Worsted Yarn
Set of 4 No.6 double-pointed needles
Set of 4 No.8 double-pointed needles
Cable needle

Hat
Using set of 4 No.6 needles cast on 96 sts and divide on 3 needles.
1st round *P2, K2, rep from * to end.
Rep this round for 4in to form turned back cuff. Change to set of 4 No.8 needles. Start patt.

Cable patt 1
1st round *P2, K6, rep from * to end.
2nd round As 1st.
3rd round As 1st.
4th round *P2, sl next 3 sts on to cable needle and hold at front of work, K next 3 sts from left hand needle then K3 from cable needle – called C6F –, rep from * to end.
These 4 rounds form the patt.

Cable patt 2
1st round *P2, K6, rep from * to end.
2nd round As 1st.
3rd round As 1st.
4th round *P2, sl next 3 sts on to cable needle and hold at front of work, K next 3 sts from left hand needle then K3 from cable needle – called C6F –, rep from * to end.
5th round As 1st.
6th round As 1st.
7th round As 1st.
8th round *P2, sl next 3 sts on to cable needle and hold at back of work, K next 3 sts from left hand needle then K3 from cable needle – called C6B –, rep from * to end.
These 8 rounds form the patt.

Cable patt 3
1st round *P2, K6, rep from * to end.
2nd round As 1st.
3rd round As 1st.
4th round *P2, sl next 2 sts on to cable needle and hold at back of work, K next 2 sts from left hand needle then K2 from cable needle – called C4B –, K2, rep from * to end.
5th round As 1st.
6th round As 1st.
7th round As 1st.
8th round *P2, K2, sl next 2 sts on to cable needle and hold at front of work, K next 2 sts from left hand needle then K2 from cable needle – called C4F –, rep from * to end.
These 8 rounds form the patt.
Cont in patt until work measures 8in from beg of patt, ending with a 4th or 8th patt round.

Shape top
Next round (dec round) *P2, sl 1, K1, psso, K2, K2 tog, rep from * to end. 72 sts.
Next round *P2, K4, rep from * to end.
Next round *P2, sl 1, K1, psso, K2 tog, rep from * to end. 48 sts.
Next round *P2, K2, rep from * to end.
Next round *P2 tog, K2 tog, rep from * to end. 24 sts.
Next round *P1, K1, rep from * to end.
Next round *Sl 1, K1, psso, rep from * to end. 12 sts.
Break off yarn, thread through rem sts, draw up and fasten off.

Finishing
Blocking on WS is necessary. Omit the ribbing and take care not to flatten the patt. Turn RS out.
Fold cuff in half to outside, then fold back again to form a double cuff.

Cable panels

Panels of cable stitches are a most effective way of highlighting even the most basic pullover or cardigan design. They can be incorporated as separate bands spaced between panels of purl background stitches to form an all over sweater fabric, or a single panel of cable stitches can be used as a border inside the ribbed front bands of a cardigan. Worked lengthwise, they can be used as separate bands which can be sewn onto the lower edge or sleeves of a sweater, or as a headband on a snug little cap, as shown here.

Seeded cable
Cast on 12 stitches.
1st row (WS) K4, P4, K4.
2nd row P4, K4, P4.
3rd row K4, P1, sl next 2 sts keeping yarn at front of work, P1, K4.
4th row P2, sl next 3 sts on to cable needle and hold at back of work, K1 then K1, P1, K1 from cable needle, sl next st on to cable needle and hold at front of work, K1, P1, K1 then K1 from cable needle, P2.
5th row K2, (P1, K1) 3 times, P2, K2.
6th row P2, (K1, P1) 3 times, K2, P2.
Rep 5th and 6th rows twice more.
11th row K2, yfwd, sl 1 keeping yarn at front of work, ybk, (K1, P1) 3 times, sl 1 keeping yarn at front of work, ybk, K2.
12th row P2, sl next st on to cable needle and hold at front of work, P2, K1 then K1 from cable needle, sl next 3 sts on to cable needle and hold at back of work, K1, then K1, P2 from cable needle, P2.
Rep 1st and 2nd rows twice more.
These 16 rows form the pattern.

Round linked cable
Cast on 12 sts.
1st row (WS) K2, yfwd, sl 1 keeping yarn at front of work, P6, sl 1 keeping yarn at front of work, ybk, K2.
2nd row P2, sl next st on to cable needle and hold at front of work, P3 then K1 from cable needle, sl next 3 sts on to cable needle and hold at back of work, K1 then P3 from cable needle, P2.
3rd row K5, P2, K5.
4th row P2, sl next 3 sts on to cable needle and hold at back of work, K1 then K3 from cable needle, sl next st on to cable needle and hold at front of work, K3 then K1 from cable needle, P2.
5th row K2, P8, K2.
6th row P2, K8, P2.
Rep 5th and 6th rows twice more.
These 10 rows form the pattern.

Wishbone cable
Cast on 12 sts.
1st row (RS) P2, sl next 3 sts on to cable needle and hold at back of work, K1 then P1, K1, P1 from cable needle, sl next st on to cable needle and hold at front of work, K1, P1, K1 then K1 from cable needle, P2.
2nd row K2, (P1, K1) 3 times, P2, K2.
3rd row P2, (K1, P1) 3 times, K2, P2.
Rep 2nd and 3rd rows once more.
6th row As 2nd.
7th row P2, K1, P1, K3, P1, K2, P2.
8th row K2, P1, K1, P3, K1, P2, K2.
These 8 rows form the pattern.

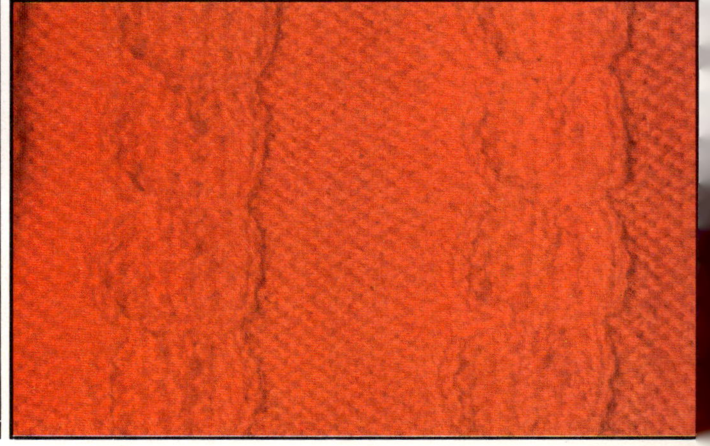

Cross cable
Cast on 12 sts.
1st row (RS) P3, K6, P3.
2nd row K3, P6, K3.
Rep 1st and 2nd rows twice more.
7th row P3, sl next 3 sts on to cable needle and hold at back of work, K3 then K3 from cable needle, P3.
8th row As 2nd.
9th row As 1st.
Rep 8th and 9th rows once more, then 8th row once more.
13th row P5, K2, P5.
14th row K5, P2, K5.
Rep 13th and 14th rows 3 times more.
These 20 rows form the pattern.

Diagonal link cable
Cast on 12 sts.
1st and every alt row (WS) K2, P8, K2.
2nd row P2, K2, sl next 2 sts on to cable needle and hold at front of work, K2 then K2 from cable needle, K2, P2.
4th row P2, K8, P2.
6th row As 2nd.
8th row As 4th.
10th row As 6th.
12th row P2, K2, K2 tog, sl 1, K1, psso, K2, P2.
13th row (WS) K2, P6, K2.
14th row P2, K1, sl 1, K1, psso, K2 tog, K1, K2.
15th row K2, P4, K2.
16th row P2, sl next 2 sts on to cable needle and hold at back of work, K2 then K2 from cable needle, P2.
17th row As 15th.
18th row P2, K1, pick up loop lying between needles and K tbl – called M1 –, K2, M1, K1, P2.
19th row As 13th.
20th row P2, (K2, M1) twice, K2, P2.
These 20 rows form the pattern.

Pull-on cap
Size
To fit an average adult head

Gauge
24 sts and 32 rows to 4in in stockinette st (st st) worked on No.5 needles

Materials
1 × 4oz ball of any Knitting Worsted
One pair No.5 needles
Cable needle

Cap
Using No.5 needles cast on 96 sts. Beg with a P row work in reverse st st until piece measures $4\frac{1}{2}$in from beg, ending with a P row.
Shape top
Next row *K2 tog, K6, rep from * to end. 84 sts.
Next row P to end.
Next row *K2 tog, K5, rep from * to end. 72 sts.
Next row P to end.
Cont dec 12 sts in this way on next and every alt row until 12 sts rem. Break off yarn, thread through rem sts, draw up and fasten off.

Headband
Using No.5 needles cast on 24 sts. Work any cable patt as desired.
1st row Patt 12 sts, K12.
2nd row P12, patt 12 sts.
Rep last 2 rows until band fits round lower edge of cap. Bind off.

Finishing
Block. With RS tog, sew patt edge of head-band to lower edge of cap. Join center back seam. Fold st st edge of headband in half to WS and sew in place.

Experiments with cable stitch

More about cable patterns! There are so many variations of cable stitches and the fabric formed is so effective that it is well worth experimenting to see how they can best be included as, for instance, part of a basic pullover or cardigan design.

As already suggested in the preceding chapters, the cable patterns do not need to be worked as an all-over fabric, but panels can be incorporated in many interesting ways. The patterns shown here required a given number of stitches to form one panel, but if you wish to work more than one panel side by side, intersperse each panel with a few extra stitches, to outline each pattern.

Diamond rope cable

This panel is worked on 18 stitches.

1st row (WS) K7, P4, K7.

2nd row P6, sl next st on to cable needle and hold at back of work, K2, then K1 from cable needle – called Cb3 –, sl next 2 sts on to cable needle and hold at front of work, K1, then K2 from cable needle – called Cf3 –, P6.

3rd and every alt row K all K sts and P all P sts.

4th row P5, Cb3, K2, Cf3, P5.

6th row P4, sl next st on to cable needle and hold at back of work, K2 then P1 from cable needle – called Bc3 –, sl next 2 sts on to cable needle and hold at back of work, K2 then K2 from cable needle – called Cb4 –, sl next 2 sts on to cable needle and hold at front of work, P1 then K2 from cable needle – called Fc3 –, P4.

8th row P3, Bc3, P1, K4, P1, Fc3, P3.
10th row P2, Bc3, P2, Cb4, P2, Fc3, P2.
12th row P1, Bc3, P3, K4, P3, Fc3, P1.
14th row P1, K2, P4, Cb4, P4, K2, P1.
16th row P1, Fc3, P3, K4, P3, Bc3, P1.
18th row P2, Fc3, P2, Cb4, P2, Bc3, P2.
20th row P3, Fc3, P1, K4, P1, Bc3, P3.
22nd row P4, Fc3, Cb4, Bc3, P4.
24th row P5, Fc3, K2, Bc3, P5.
26th row P6, Fc3, Bc3, P6.
28th row P7, sl next 2 sts on to cable needle and hold at front of work, K2 then K2 from cable needle, P7.
These 28 rows form the pattern.

Plaited braid cable
This panel is worked on 16 stitches.

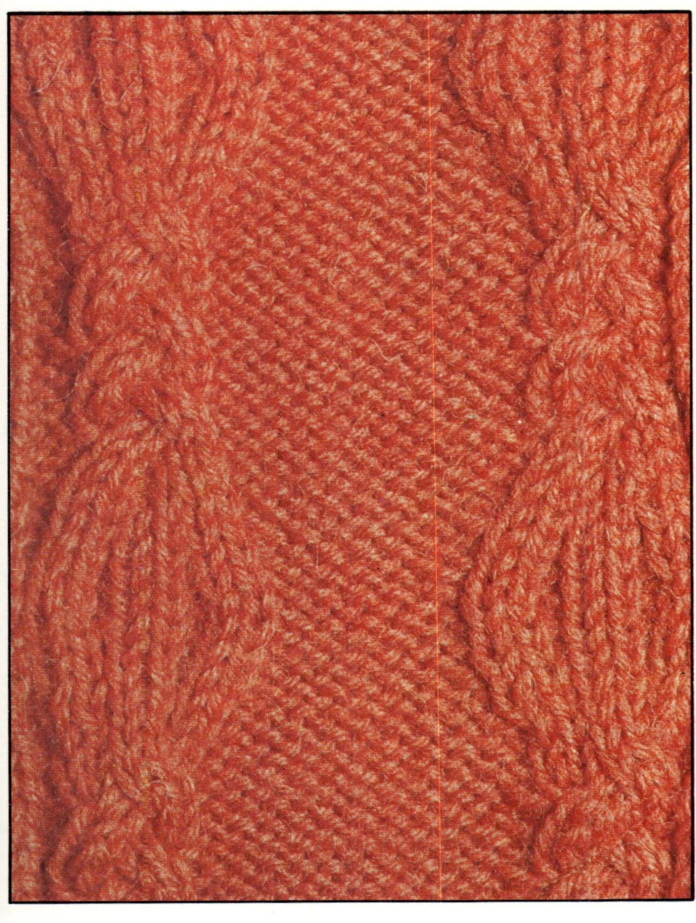

1st row (WS) K5, P6, K5.
2nd row P5, K2, sl next 2 sts on to cable needle and hold at back of work, K2 then K2 from cable needle – called Cb4 –, P5.
3rd and every alt row K all K sts and P all P sts.
4th row P5, sl next 2 sts on to cable needle and hold at front of work, K2 then K2 from cable needle – called Cf4 –, K2, P5.
6th row As 2nd.
8th row As 4th.
10th row As 2nd.
12th row As 4th.
14th row P4, sl next st on to cable needle and hold at back of work, K2 then P1 from cable needle – called Bc3 –, K2, sl next 2 sts on to cable needle and hold at front of work, P1 then K2 from cable needle – called Fc3 –, P4.
16th row P3, Bc3, P1, K2, P1, Fc3, P3.
18th row P2, Bc3, P2, K2, P2, Fc3, P2.
20th row P2, Fc3, P2, K2, P2, Bc3, P2.
22nd row P3, Fc3, P1, K2, P1, Bc3, P3.
24th row P4, Fc3, K2, Bc3, P4.
These 24 rows form the pattern.

Outlined cable
This panel is worked on 18 stitches.

1st row (WS) K5, P8, K5.
2nd row P4, sl next st on to cable needle and hold at back of work, K1 tbl then P1 from cable needle – called Cb2 –, K6, sl next st on to cable needle and hold at front of work, P1 then K1 tbl from cable needle – called Cf2 –, P4.
3rd and every alt row K all K sts and P all P sts.
4th row P3, Cb2, P1, K6, P1, Cf2, P3.
6th row P2, Cb2, P2, sl next 3 sts on to cable needle and hold at front of work, K3 then K3 from cable needle – called Cf6 –, P2, Cf2, P2.
8th row P1, Cb2, P3, K6, P3, Cf2, P1.
10th row P1, Cf2, P3, K6, P3, Cb2, P1.
12th row P2, Cf2, P2, Cf6, P2, Cb2, P2.
14th row P3, Cf2, P1, K6, P1, Cb2, P3.
16th row P4, Cf2, K6, Cb2, P4.
These 16 rows form the pattern.

ARAN KNITTING
Basic stitches

The skilful and imaginative use of such patterns as cables, bobbles and crossed stitches form the basis for a range of intricate and thickly textured fabrics referred to as 'Aran' patterns. Most of the traditional stitches, with their highly evocative names, were originated in the remote Aran islands and derived their inspiration from the daily life of the islanders. The rocks are depicted by chunky bobble stitches, the cliff paths by zig-zag patterns, while the fishermen's ropes inspire a vast number of cable variations. The wealth of the sea around the islands and religious symbols and the ups and downs of married life all play a part in the formation of a rich tapestry of patterns unique in knitting.

The Irish name for the thick, homespun yarn used for Aran knitting is 'bainin', which literally means 'natural'. The traditional stitches are shown to their best advantage in this light-colored natural yarn, although many vivid colors are now used with them, to make fashion garments.

Practice the samples given here, using a knitting worsted yarn and No.5 needles to form separate squares or panels, which can then be joined together to form throw pillows, afghans or even bedspreads.

Ladder of life

This simple design depicts man's eternal desire to climb upwards, the purl ridges forming the rungs of the ladder. Cast on a number of stitches divisible by 6 plus 1.

1st row (RS) P1, *K5, P1, rep from * to end.
2nd row K1, *P5, K1, rep from * to end.
3rd row P to end.
4th row As 2nd.
These 4 rows form the pattern.

Lobster claw stitch

This represents the bounty of the sea. Cast on a number of stitches divisible by 9.

1st row (RS) *P1, K7, P1, rep from * to end.
2nd row *K1, P7, K1, rep from * to end.
3rd row *P1, sl next 2 sts on to cable needle and hold at back of work, K1 from left hand needle then K2 from cable needle, K1 from left hand needle, sl next st on to cable needle and hold at front of work, K2 from left hand needle, then K1 from cable needle, P1, rep from * to end.
4th row As 2nd.
These 4 rows form the pattern.

Tree of life

Narrow lines of traveling stitches branching out from a central stem form the basis for this traditional pattern. Cast on a number of stitches divisible by 15.

1st row (RS) *P7, K1, P7, rep from * to end.
2nd row *K7, P1, K7, rep from * to end.
3rd row *P5, sl next st on to cable needle and hold at back of work, K1 from left hand needle then P1 from cable needle – called C2B –, K1 from left hand needle, sl next st on to cable needle and hold at front of work, P1 from left hand needle, then K1 from cable needle – called C2F –, P5, rep from * to end.
4th row *K5, sl 1 P-wise keeping yarn at front of work, K1, P1, K1, sl 1, K5, rep from * to end.
5th row *P4, C2B, P1, K1, P1, C2F, P4, rep from * to end.
6th row *K4, sl 1, K2, P1, K2, sl 1, K4, rep from * to end.
7th row *P3, C2B, P2, K1, P2, C2F, P3, rep from * to end.
8th row *K3, sl 1, K3, P1, K3, sl 1, K3, rep from * to end.

9th row *P2, C2B, P3, K1, P3, C2F, P2, rep from * to end.
10th row *K2, sl 1, K4, P1, K4, sl 1, K2, rep from * to end.
These 10 rows form the pattern.

Aran plaited cable
This simple cable depicts the interweaving of family life. Cast on a number of stitches divisible by 12.
1st row (WS) *K2, P8, K2, rep from * to end.
2nd row *P2, (sl next 2 sts on to cable needle and hold at back of work, K2 from left hand needle then K2 from cable needle) twice, P2, rep from * to end.
3rd row As 1st.
4th row *P2, K2, sl next 2 sts on to cable needle and hold at front of work, K2 from left hand needle then K2 from cable needle, K2, P2, rep from * to end.
These 4 rows form the pattern.

Aran diamond and bobble cable
The small diamond outlined with knitted stitches represents the small walled fields of Ireland and the bobble depicts the stony nature of the ground. Cast on a number of stitches divisible by 17.
1st row (WS) *K6, P2, K1, P2, K6, rep from * to end.
2nd row *P6, sl next 3 sts on to cable needle and hold at back of work, K2 from left hand needle, sl P1 from end of cable needle back on to left hand needle and P1 then K2 from cable needle, P6, rep from * to end.
3rd row As 1st.
4th row *P5, sl next st on to cable needle and hold at back of work, K2 from left hand needle then P1 from cable needle – called C3B –, K1, sl next 2 sts on to cable needle and hold at front of work, P1 from left hand needle then K2 from cable needle – called C3F –, P5, rep from * to end.
5th and every alt row K all K sts and P all P sts.
6th row *P4, C3B, K1, P1, K1, C3F, P4, rep from * to end.

8th row *P3, C3B, (K1, P1) twice, K1, C3F, P3, rep from * to end.
10th row *P2, C3B, (K1, P1) 3 times, K1, C3F, P2, rep from * to end.
12th row *P2, C3F, (P1, K1) 3 times, P1, C3B, P2, rep from * to end.
14th row *P3, C3F, (P1, K1) twice, P1, C3B, P3, rep from * to end.
16th row *P4, C3F, P1, K1, P1, C3B, P4, rep from * to end.
18th row *P5, C3F, P1, C3B, P5, rep from * to end.
20th row As 2nd.
22nd row *P5, C3B, P1, C3F, P5, rep from * to end.
24th row *P4, C3B, P3, C3F, P4, rep from * to end.
26th row *P4, K2, P2, (K1, yfwd to make one st, K1, yfwd, K1) all into next st, turn and P5, turn and K5, turn and P2 tog, P1, P2 tog, turn and sl 1, K2 tog, psso – called B1 –, P2, K2, P4, rep from * to end.
28th row *P4, C3F, P3, C3B, P4, rep from * to end.
30th row As 18th.
These 30 rows form the pattern.

Shoulder bag
Size
12in wide by 12in deep

Gauge
24 sts and 32 rows to 4in in stockinette stitch (st st) worked on No.5 needles

Materials
2 × 4oz balls of any Knitting Worsted
One pair of No.5 needles

Bag
Using No.5 needles cast on 85 sts. Work in Aran diamond and bobble cable patt. Rep 30 patt rows 6 times in all, then first 20 rows once more. Bind off.

Finishing
Fold work in half with RS facing. Join side seams and turns RS out. Turn under $\frac{1}{2}$in hem around top edge and sew in place. Make a braid approx 60in long, leaving a tassel at each end. Sew braid to side seams above tassels, leaving remainder of braid free for strap.

Aran patterns

Aran panels
The variety and complexity of Aran stitches which may be formed give such scope for textured patterns that it is sometimes difficult to know where to begin a design and how best to combine these stitches to produce the most effective fabric. If each stitch is run on into the next, all definition will be lost and none of the stitches will show to their best advantage. Because these stitches nearly always have a raised texture, their beauty is enhanced if they are worked against a purled background. Similarly, if each panel of stitches is enclosed with a rope of twisted stitches and alternated with panels of either purl or moss stitches, each separate Aran panel stands out without detracting in any way from the next panel. The poncho design given here uses these techniques to full effect. It is made from two simple pieces and the size can easily be adjusted by changing the number of stitches in each purl panel.

Poncho
Size
Approx 35in square, without fringe

Gauge
18 sts and 24 rows to 4in in stockinette stitch (st st) worked on No.6 needles

Materials
17 × 2oz balls Bernat Blarney-Spun
One pair No.6 needles
One pair No.5 needles
Set of 4 No.4 double-pointed needles
One No.6 circular needle
One No.5 circular needle
One cable needle

First piece
Using No.5 circular needle cast on 146 sts. K4 rows garter st.
Next row (inc row) K3, pick up loop lying between needles and P tbl – called M1 –, K2, M1, *(K2, M1) twice, (K2, K into front and back of next st – called Kfb –) twice, K3, (M1, K2) twice, *, **(M1, K2) twice, (P1, M1, P1, P into front and back of next st – called Pfb –, P1, M1, P1, K2) twice, M1, K2, M1, **, ***K2, Pfb, K2, Kfb, K3, Pfb, K1, Pfb, K2, Kfb, K3, Pfb, K2, ***, rep from ** to **, then from *** to ***, then from ** to ** again, then rep from * to * once more, M1, K2, M1, K3. 204 sts.
Change to No.6 circular needle. Commence patt.
1st row K2, P1, K1 tbl, P2, K1 tbl, *P2, sl next st on to cable needle and hold at front of work, P1, then K1 tbl from cable needle – called T2L –, P1, T2L, P9, sl next st on to cable needle and hold at back of work, K1 tbl, then P1 from cable needle – called T2R –, P1, T2R, P2, *, K1 tbl, P2, K1 tbl, **(P2, K8) twice, P2, K1 tbl, P2, K1 tbl, P2, K2, P3, into next st (K1, (yfwd, K1) twice, turn, P these 5 sts, turn, K5, turn, P5, turn, sl 2nd, 3rd and 4th sts over first st, then K first and last st tog tbl – called MB –) P3, sl next 3 sts on to cable needle and hold at back of work, K2, sl P st from cable needle onto left hand needle and hold cable needle at front of work, P1 from left hand needle, then K2 from cable needle – called Cr5 –, P3, MB, P3, K2, P2, K1 tbl, P2, K1 tbl, **, rep from ** to ** once more, (P2, K8) twice, P2, K1 tbl, P2, K1 tbl, rep from * to * once more, K1 tbl, P2, K1 tbl, P1, K2.
2nd row K3, *P1 tbl, K2, P1 tbl, K3, P1 tbl, K2, P1 tbl, K9, P1 tbl, K2, P1 tbl, K3, *, P1 tbl, K2, P1 tbl, ** (K2, P8) twice, K2, P1 tbl, K2, P1 tbl, K2, (P2, K7, P2, K1) twice, K1, P1 tbl, K2, P1 tbl, **, rep from ** to ** once more, (K2, P8) twice, K2, rep from * to * once more, P1 tbl, K2, P1 tbl, K3.
3rd row K2, P1, *K1 tbl, P2, K1 tbl, P3, T2L, P1, T2L, P7, T2R, P1, T2R, P3, *, K1 tbl, P2, K1 tbl, **(P2, sl next 2 sts on to cable needle and hold at back of work, K2, then K2 from cable needle – called C4B –, sl next 2 sts on to cable needle and hold at front of work, K2, then K2 from cable needle – called C4F –) twice, P2, K1 tbl, P2, K1 tbl, P2, (sl next 2 sts on to cable needle and hold at front of work, P1, then K2 from cable needle – called C3L –, P5, sl next st on to cable needle and hold at back of work, K2, then P1 from cable needle – called C3R –, P1) twice, P1, K1 tbl, P2, K1 tbl, **, rep from ** to ** once more, (P2, C4B, C4F) twice, P2, rep from * to * once more, K1 tbl, P2, K1 tbl, P1, K2.
4th row K3, P1 tbl, K2, *P1 tbl, K4, P1 tbl, K2, P1 tbl, K7, P1 tbl, K2, P1 tbl, K4, *, P1 tbl, K2, P1 tbl, **(K2, P8) twice, K2, P1 tbl, K2, P1 tbl, (K3, P2, K5, P2) twice, K3, P1 tbl, K2, P1 tbl, **, rep from ** to ** once more, (K2, P8) twice, K2, P1 tbl, K2, rep from * to * once more, P1 tbl, K2, P1 tbl, K3.
5th row K2, P1, K1 tbl, *P2, K1 tbl, P4, T2L, P1, T2L, P5, T2R, P1, T2R, P4, *, K1 tbl, P2, K1 tbl, **(P2, K8) twice, P2, K1 tbl, P2, K1 tbl, (P3, C3L, P3, C3R) twice, P3, K1 tbl, P2, K1 tbl, **, rep from ** to ** once more, (P2, K8) twice, P2, K1 tbl, rep from * to * once more, K1 tbl, P2, K1 tbl, P1, K2.
6th row K3, P1 tbl, *K2, P1 tbl, (K5, P1 tbl, K2, P1 tbl) twice, K5, *, P1 tbl, K2, P1 tbl, **(K2, P8) twice, K2, P1 tbl, K2, P1 tbl, K4, P2, K3, P2, K5, P2, K3, P2, K4, P1 tbl, K2, P1 tbl, **, rep from ** to ** once more, (K2, P8) twice, K2, P1 tbl, rep from * to * once more, P1 tbl, K2, P1 tbl, K3.

7th row K2, P1, K1 tbl, *P2, K1 tbl, P5, T2L, P1, T2L, P3, T2R, P1, T2R, P5, *, K1 tbl, P2, K1 tbl, **(P2, C4B, C4F) twice, P2, K1 tbl, P2, K1 tbl, P4, C3L, P1, C3R, P5, C3L, P1, C3R, P4, K1 tbl, P2, K1 tbl, **, rep from ** to ** once more, (P2, C4B, C4F) twice, P2, K1 tbl, rep from * to * once more, K1 tbl, P2, K1 tbl, P1, K2.
8th row K3, P1 tbl, *K2, P1 tbl, K6, P1 tbl, K2, P1 tbl, K3, P1 tbl, K2, P1 tbl, K6, *, P1 tbl, K2, P1 tbl, **(K2, P8) twice, K2, P1 tbl, K2, P1 tbl, K5, P2, K1, P2, K7, P2, K1, P2, K5, P1 tbl, K2, P1 tbl, **, rep from ** to ** once more, (K2, P8) twice, K2, P1 tbl, rep from * to * once more, P1 tbl, K2, P1 tbl, K3.
9th row K2, P1, K1 tbl, *P2, K1 tbl, P5, T2R, P1, T2R, P3, T2L, P1, T2L, P5, *, K1 tbl, P2, K1 tbl, **(P2, K8) twice, P2, K1 tbl, P2, K1 tbl, P5, Cr5, P3, MB, P3, Cr5, P5, K1 tbl, P2, K1 tbl, **, rep from ** to ** once more, (P2, K8) twice, P2, K1 tbl, rep from * to * once more, K1 tbl, P2, K1 tbl, P1, K2.
10th row K3, P1 tbl, *K2, P1 tbl, (K5, P1 tbl, K2, P1 tbl) twice, K5, *, P1 tbl, K2, P1 tbl, **(K2, P8) twice, K2, P1 tbl, K2, P1 tbl. K5, P2, K1, P2, K7, P2, K1, P2, K5, P1 tbl, K2, P1 tbl, **, rep from ** to ** once more, (K2, P8) twice, K2, P1 tbl, rep from * to * once more, P1 tbl, K2, P1 tbl, K3.
11th row K2, P1, K1 tbl, *P2, K1 tbl, P4, T2R, P1, T2R, P5, T2L, P1, T2L, P4, *, K1 tbl, P2, K1 tbl, **(P2, C4F, C4B) twice, P2, K1 tbl, P2, K1 tbl, P4, C3R, P1, C3L, P5, C3R, P1, C3L, P4, K1 tbl, P2, K1 tbl, **, rep from ** to ** once more, (P2. C4F, C4B) twice, P2, K1 tbl, rep from * to * once more, K1 tbl, P2, K1 tbl, P1, K2.
12th row K3, P1 tbl, *K2, P1 tbl, K4, P1 tbl, K2, P1 tbl, K7, P1 tbl, K2, P1 tbl, K4, *, P1 tbl, K2, P1 tbl, **(K2, P8) twice, K2, P1 tbl, K2, P1 tbl, K4, P2, K3, P2, K5, P2, K3, P2, K4, P1 tbl, K2, P1 tbl, **, rep from ** to ** once more, (K2, P8) twice, K2, P1 tbl, rep from * to * once more, P1 tbl, K2, P1 tbl, K3.
13th row K2, P1, K1 tbl, *P2, K1 tbl, P3, T2R, P1, T2R, P7, T2L, P1, T2L, P3, *, K1 tbl, P2, K1 tbl, **(P2, K8) twice, P2, K1 tbl, P2, K1 tbl, (P3, C3R, P3, C3L) twice, P3, K1 tbl, P2, K1 tbl, **, rep from ** to ** once more, (P2, K8) twice, P2, K1 tbl, rep from * to * once more, K1 tbl, P2, K1 tbl, P1, K2.
14th row K3, P1 tbl, *K2, P1 tbl, K3, P1 tbl, K2, P1 tbl, K9, P1 tbl, K2, P1 tbl, K3, *, P1 tbl, K2, P1 tbl, ** (K2, P8) twice, K2, P1 tbl, K2, P1 tbl, (K3, P2, K5) twice, K3, P1 tbl, K2, P1 tbl, **, rep from ** to ** once more, (K2, P8) twice, K2, P1 tbl, rep from * to * once more, P1 tbl, K2, P1 tbl, K3.
15th row K2, P1, K1 tbl, *P2, K1 tbl, P2, T2R, P1, T2R, P9, T2L, P1, T2L, P2, *, K1 tbl, P2, K1 tbl, **(P2, C4F, C4B) twice, P2, K1 tbl, P2, K1 tbl, P2, (C3R, P5, C3L, P1) twice, P1, K1 tbl, P2, K1 tbl, **, rep from ** to ** once more, (P2, C4F, C4B) twice, P2, K1 tbl, rep from * to * once more, K1 tbl, P2, K1 tbl, P1, K2.
16th row K3, P1 tbl, *K2, P1 tbl, (K2, P1 tbl) twice, K11, (P1 tbl, K2) twice, *, P1 tbl, K2, P1 tbl, **(K2, P8) twice, K2, P1 tbl, K2, P1 tbl, K2, (P2, K7, P2, K1) twice, K1, P1 tbl, K2, P1 tbl, **, rep from ** to ** once more, (K2, P8) twice, K2, P1 tbl, rep from * to * once more, P1 tbl, K2, P1 tbl, K3.
These 16 rows form the patt. Cont in patt until 8th row of 6th patt has been completed.

Shape neck
Next row Patt 93 sts, *(K2 tog, K1) twice, K2 tog, P2, (K2 tog, K1) twice, K2 tog, *, (P1, K2 tog) twice, ** P5, K2 tog, P1, K2 tog, (P1, P2 tog) twice, (P1, K2 tog) twice, P5, **, (K2 tog tbl, P1) twice, rep from * to * once more, (P1, K2 tog) twice, P2, P2 tog, (P1, K2 tog) twice, P3, (K2 tog tbl, P1) twice, P2 tog, P2, K2 tog tbl, P1, K2 tog tbl, K2. 172 sts.
Next row Eind off 79 sts, patt to end. 93 sts.

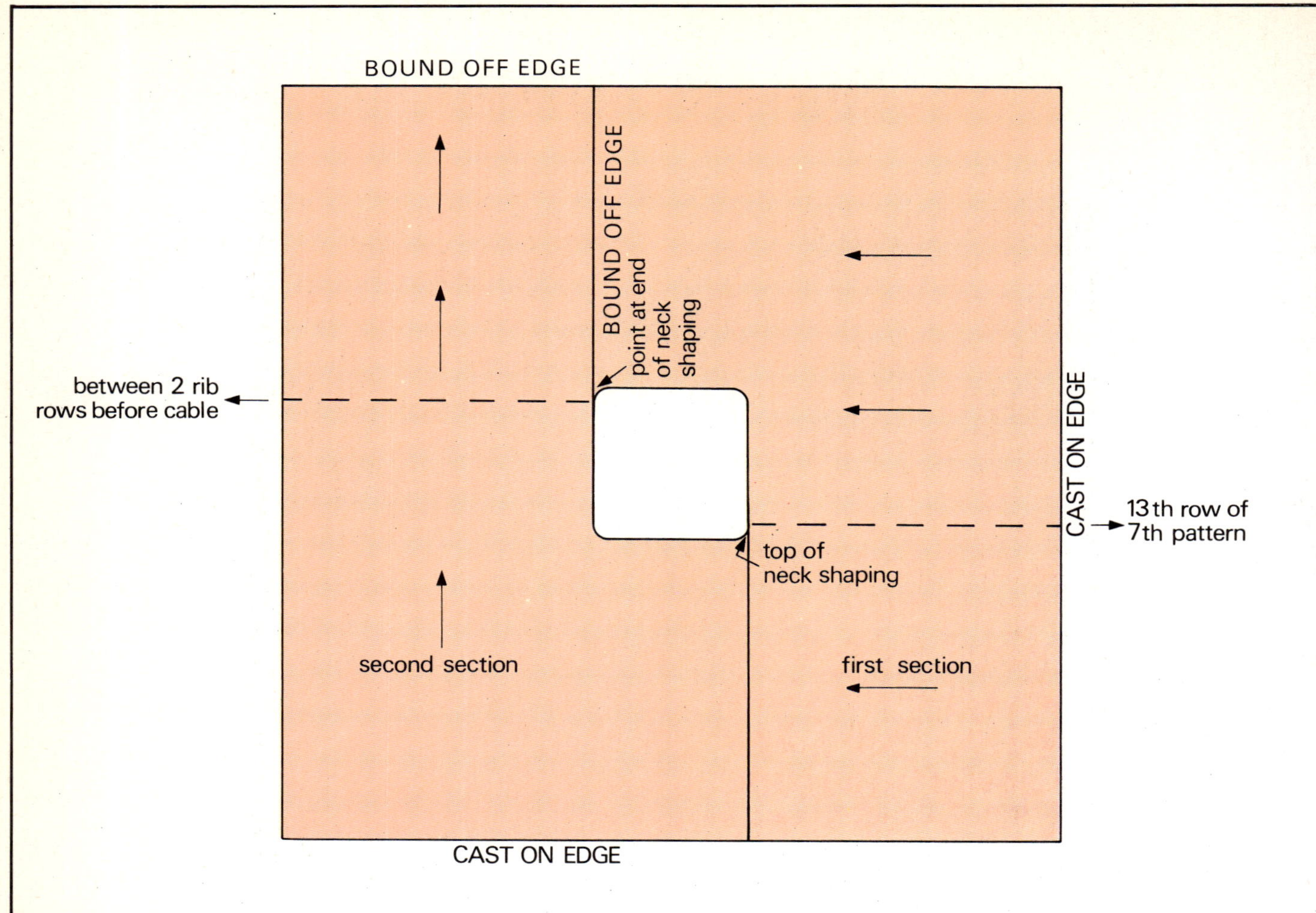

Next row Patt to last 2 sts, P2 tog.
Maintaining patt, cont dec one st at beg of next and every foll alt row 5 times in all. Work 8 rows without shaping. Inc one st at end of next and every alt row 6 times in all. 93 sts.
Next row K2, K2 tog, P1, K2 tog, P2, P2 tog, (P1, K2 tog tbl) twice, P3 (K2 tog, P1) twice, P2 tog, P2, (K2 tog tbl, P1) twice, rep from * to * of 1st shaping row, (P1, K2 tog) twice, rep from ** to ** of 1st shaping row, patt to end. 69 sts.
Bind off loosely.

Second piece
Using No.5 needles cast on 83 sts. K 4 rows g st.
Next row (inc row) K3, M1, K2, M1, rep from * to * of inc row in first section, then from ** to ** in same row, then from *** to *** in same row, then from ** to ** again, omitting M1 at end of Row. 116 sts.
Change to No.6 needles. Start patt.
1st row K1, P1, K1 tbl, (P2, K8) twice, P2, K1 tbl, P2, K1 tbl, P2, K2, P3, MB, P3, Cr5, P3, MB, P3, K2, P2, K1 tbl, P2, K1 tbl, (P2, K8) twice, P2, K1 tbl, P2, K1 tbl, P2, T2L, P1, T2L, P9, T2R, P1, T2R, P2, K1 tbl, P2, K1 tbl, P1, K2.
2nd row K3, P1 tbl, K2, P1 tbl, patt as now set to last 3 sts, P1 tbl, K2.
Cont in patt as now set until 8th row of 6th patt has been completed.

Shape neck
1st row K1, P1, K1 tbl, P2, (K2 tog, K1) twice, K2 tog, P2, (K2 tog, K1) twice, K2 tog, patt to end.
2nd row Patt 93 sts and leave these sts on a holder, bind off 12 sts, patt to end. 5 sts.
Dec one st at neck edge on foll 3 alt rows. Bind off.
With RS of work facing, rejoin yarn to rem sts at neck edge, cont in patt dec one st at neck edge on foll 3 alt rows. 90 sts. Cont without shaping until 13th patt rep has been completed. Change to No.5 needles.
Next row K2, (K2 tog, K2, K2 tog, K1) 12 times, K2 tog, K2. 65 sts.
K 3 rows g st. Bind off.

Finishing
Join both sections as shown in diagram, noting positions of top of neck shaping on second section and point at end of neck shaping on first section. Block seams on wrong side under a damp cloth with a warm iron.
Neckband Using set of 4 No.4 needles, pick up and K 104 sts all around neck edge. Work 5 rounds K1, P1 rib. Bind off in rib, working K2 tog at each corner.
Fringe Cut yarn into lengths of 10in. Using 3 strands folded in half, draw center of threads through edge of poncho and knot. Rep at $\frac{1}{2}$in intervals around entire outer edge.

Aran shaping

Aran shaping
Where each Aran panel is combined with alternate panels of purl or moss stitches, it is simple to make provision for any shaping.
Because Aran stitches are rather complex, it is not advisable to try to combine them with any increasing or decreasing and most designs take this into account. The number of stitches required, for example, for a raglan armhole and sleeve top shaping are carefully calculated to insure that the correct number of stitches are decreased in a plain panel, without interfering with the Aran panels.
The variety of Aran designs available is sometimes restricted by this problem of shaping. This can be overcome, however, by the skillful use of shaping in each alternate plain panel and by the careful choice of a basic stitch, such as garter stitch or ribbing, to complete the shaped sections. The lightweight camisole shell top shown here perfectly illustrates these techniques.

Camisole shell top
Sizes
Directions are to fit 32in bust. Changes for 34 and 36in bust are in brackets [].
Length to shoulder, 18[19$\frac{1}{4}$:20]in

Gauge
32 sts and 40 rows in 4in over reverse stockinette stitch (rev st st) worked on No.2 needles

Materials
3 × 2oz balls Brunswick Pomfret Sport Yarn
One pair No.2 needles
One No.2 circular needle
One No.1 circular needle
7 buttons

Camisole shell fronts and back
Using No.1 circular needle cast on 237[253:269] sts and work in one piece, beg at lower edge.
1st row K1, *P1, K1, rep from * to end.
2nd row P1, *K1, P1, rep from * to end.
Rep last 2 rows 3 times more, then 1st row once more.
Next row P to end.
Next row P to end to form hemline.
Base row Cast on 7 sts for right front band, turn, K8, *P2, K15, P2, K8[10:12], P2, K3, P1, K2, P1, K8, P2, K8 [10:12], rep from * 3 times more, P2, K15, P2, K1, turn and cast on 7 sts for left front band. 251[267:283] sts.
Change to No.2 circular needle. Start patt.
1st row (RS) K7, P1, *K 2nd st on left hand needle, then first st – called T2 –, P7, K1, P7, T2, P8[10:12], T2, P7, K 2nd st on left hand needle, then P first st – called C2R –, P1, C2R, P3, T2, P8[10:12], T2, P2, K2, P7, K2, P2, T2, P8[10:12], T2, P7, C2R, P1, C2R, P3, T2, P8[10:12], rep from * once more, T2, P7, K1, P7, T2, P1, K7.
2nd row K8, *P2, K7, P1, K7, P2, K8[10:12], P2, K4, P1, K2, P1, K7, P2, K8[10:12], P2, K2, P3, K5, P3, K2, P2, K8[10:12], P2, K4, P1, K2, P1, K7, P2, K8[10:12], rep from * once more, P2, K7, P1, K7, P2, K8.
3rd row K7, P1, *T2, P6, K1, P1, K1, P6, T2, P8[10:12], T2, P6, C2R, P1, C2R, P4, T2, P8[10:12], T2, (P3, K3) twice, P3, T2, P8[10:12], T2, P6, C2R, P1, C2R, P4, T2, P8[10:12], rep from * once more, T2, P6, K1, P1, K1, P6, T2, P1, K7.
4th row K8, *P2, K6, P1, K1, P1, K6, P2, K8[10:12], P2, K5, P1, K2, P1, K6, P2, K8[10:12], P2, K4, P3, K1, P3, K4, P2, K8[10:12], P2, K5, P1, K2, P1, K6, P2, K8[10:12], rep from * once more, P2, K6, P1, K1, P1, K6, P2, K8.
5th row (buttonhole row) K2, K2 tog, (yrn) twice, sl 1, K1, psso, K1, P1, *T2, P5, (K1, P1) twice, K1, P5, T2, P8[10:12], T2, P5, C2R, P1, C2R, P5, T2, P8[10:12], T2, P5, K5, P5, T2, P8[10:12], T2, P5, C2R, P1, C2R, P5, T2, P8[10:12], rep from * once more, T2, P5, (K1, P1) twice, K1, P5, T2, P1, K7.
6th row K8, *P2, K5, (P1, K1) twice, P1, K5, P2, K8[10:12], P2, K6, P1, K2, P1, K5, P2, K8[10:12], P2, K6, P3, K6, P2, K8[10:12], P2, K6, P1, K2, P1, K5, P2, K8[10:12], rep from * once more, P2, K5, (P1, K1) twice, P1, K5, P2, K3, drop one loop of double loop to make long st and work K1, P1 into same st, K3.
Work 5 more buttonholes in same way with 18[20:22] rows between each buttonhole.
7th row K7, P1, *T2, P4, (K1, P1) 3 times, K1, P4, T2, P8[10:12], T2, P4, C2R, P1, C2R, P6, T2, P8[10:12], T2, P5, K5, P5, T2, P8[10:12], T2, P4, C2R, P1, C2R, P6, T2, P8[10:12], rep from * once more, T2, P4, (K1, P1) 3 times, K1, P4, T2, P1, K7.
8th row K8, *P2, K4, (P1, K1) 3 times, P1, K4, P2, K8[10:12], P2, K7, P1, K2, P1, K4, P2, K8[10:12], P2, K4, P3, K1, P3, K4, P2, K8[10:12], P2, K7, P1, K2, P1, K4, P2, K8[10:12], rep from * once more, P2, K4, (P1, K1) 3 times, P1, K4, P2, K8.
9th row K7, P1, *T2, P3, (K1, P1) 4 times, K1, P3, T2, P8[10:12], T2, P3, C2R, P1, C2R, P7, T2, P8[10:12], T2, (P3, K3) twice, P3, T2, P8[10:12], T2, P3, C2R, P1, C2R, P7, T2, P8[10:12], rep from * once more, T2, P3, (K1, P1) 4 times, K1, P3, T2, P1, K7.
10th row K8, *P2, K3, (P1, K1) 4 times, P1, K3, P2, K8 [10:12], P2, K8, P1, K2, P1, K3, P2, K8[10:12], P2, K2, P3, K5, P3, K2, P2, K8[10:12], P2, K8, P1, K2, P1, K3, P2, K8[10:12], rep from * once more, P2, K3, (P1, K1) 4 times, P1, K3, P2, K8.
11th row K7, P1, *T2, P2, (K1, P1) 5 times, K1, P2, T2, P8[10:12], T2, P3, K1, P2, K1, P8, T2, P8[10:12], T2, P2, K2, P7, K2, P2, T2, P8[10:12], T2, P3, K1, P2, K1, P8, T2, P8[10:12], rep from * once more, T2, P2, (K1, P1) 5 times, K1, P2, T2, P1, K7.
12th row K8, *P2, K2, (P1, K1) 5 times, P1, K2, P2, K8 [10:12], P2, K8, P1, K2, P1, K3, P2, K8[10:12], P2, K15, P2, K8[10:12], P2, K8, P1, K2, P1, K3, P2, K8[10:12], rep from * once more, P2, K2, (P1, K1) 5 times, P1, K2, P2, K8.
13th row K7, P1, *T2, P3, (K1, P1) 4 times, K1, P3, T2, P8[10:12], T2, P3, P 2nd st on left hand needle, then K first st – called C2L –, P1, C2L, P7, T2, P8[10:12], T2, P6, K3, P6, T2, P8[10:12], T2, P3, C2L, P1, C2L, P7, T2, P8 [10:12], rep from * once more, T2, P3, (K1, P1) 4 times, K1, P3, T2, P1, K7.

Shape waist
14th row K8, *P2, K3, (P1, K1) 4 times, P1, K3, P2, sl 1, K1, psso, K4[6:8], K2 tog, P2, K7, P1, K2, P1, K4, P2, sl 1, K1, psso, K4[6:8], K2 tog, P2, K5, P5, K5, P2, sl 1, K1, psso, K4[6:8], K2 tog, P2, K7, P1, K2, P1, K4, P2, sl 1, K1, psso, K4[6:8], K2 tog, rep from * once more, P2, K3, (P1, K1) 4 times, P1, K3, P2, K8, 235[251:267] sts.
15th row K7, P1, *T2, P4, (K1, P1) 3 times, K1, P4, T2, P6[8:10], T2, P4, C2L, P1, C2L, P6, T2, P6[8:10], T2, P4, K3, P1, K3, P4, T2, P6[8:10], T2, P4, C2L, P1, C2L, P6, T2, P6[8:10], rep from * once more, T2, P4, (K1, P1) 3 times, K1, P4, T2, P1, K7.
16th row K8, *P2, K4, (P1, K1) 3 times, P1, K4, P2, K6[8:10], P2, K6, P1, K2, P1, K5, P2, K6[8:10], P2, (K3, P3) twice, K3, P2, K6[8:10], P2, K6, P1, K2, P1, K5, P2, K6[8:10], rep from * once more, P2, K4, (P1, K1) 3 times, P1, K4, P2, K8.
17th row K7, P1, *T2, P5, (K1, P1) twice, K1, P5, T2, P6 [8:10], T2, P5, C2L, P1, C2L, P5, T2, P6[8:10], T2, P2, K3, P5, K3, P2, T2, P6[8:10], T2, P5, C2L, P1, C2L, P5, T2, P6[8:10], rep from * once more, T2, P5, (K1, P1) twice, K1, P5, T2, P1, K7.
18th row K8, *P2, K5, (P1, K1) twice, P1, K5, P2, K6[8:10], P2, K5, P1, K2, P1, K6, P2, K6[8:10], P2, K2, P2, K7, P2, K2, P2, K6[8:10], P2, K5, P1, K2, P1, K6, P2, K6[8:10], rep from * once more, P2, K5, (P1, K1) twice, P1, K5, P2, K8.

19th row K7, P1, *T2, P6, K1, P1, K1, P6, T2, P6[8:10], T2, P6, C2L, P1, C2L, P4, T2, P6[8:10], T2, P2, K3, P5, K3, P2, T2, P6[8:10], T2, P6, C2L, P1, C2L, P4, T2, P6[8:10], rep from * once more, T2, P6, K1, P1, K1, P6, T2, P1, K7.
20th row K8, *P2, K6, P1, K1, P1, K6, P2, sl 1, K1, psso, K2[4:6], K2 tog, P2, K4, P1, K2, P1, K7, P2, sl 1, K1, psso, K2[4:6], K2 tog, P2, (K3, P3) twice, K3, P2, sl 1, K1, psso, K2[4:6], K2 tog, P2, K4, P1, K2, P1, K7, P2, sl 1, K1, psso, K2[4:6], K2 tog, rep from * once more, P2, K6, P1, K1, P1, K6, P2, K8. 219[235:251] sts.
21st row K7, P1, *T2, P7, K1, P7, T2, P4[6:8], T2, P7, C2L, P1, C2L, P3, T2, P4[6:8], T2, P4, K3, P1, K3, P4, T2, P4[6:8], T2, P7, C2L, P1, C2L, P3, T2, P4[6:8], rep from * once

more, T2, P7, K1, P7, T2, P1, K7.
22nd row K8, *P2, K7, P1, K7, P2, K4[6:8], P2, K3, P1, K2, P1, K8, P2, K4[6:8], P2, K5, P5, K5, P2, K4[6:8], P2, K3, P1, K2, P1, K8, P2, K4[6:8], rep from * once more, P2, K7, P1, K7, P2, K8.
23rd row K7, P1, *T2, P15, T2, P4[6:8], T2, P8, K1, P2, K1, P3, T2, P4[6:8], T2, P6, K3, P6, T2, P4[6:8], T2, P8, K1, P2, K1, P3, T2, P4[6:8], rep from * once more, T2, P15, T2, P1, K7.
24th row K8, *P2, K15, P2, K4[6:8], P2, K3, P1, K2, P1, K8, P2, K4[6:8], P2, K15, P2, K4[6:8], P2, K3, P1, K2, P1, K8, P2, K4[6:8], rep from * once more, P2, K15, P2, K8.
These 24 rows set patt for Aran panels with rev st st between each one. Maintaining patt as now set, dec 2 sts as before within each rev st st panel on foll alt row. 203[219:235] sts. Cont in patt until work measures $4\frac{1}{2}[4\frac{3}{4}:5]$in from hemline, ending with a RS row.
Next row K8, *P2, patt 15, P2, pick up loop lying between needles and K tbl – called M1 –, K2[4:6], M1, rep from * 7 times more, P2, patt 15, P2, K8.
Maintaining patt, inc 2 sts as before within each rev st st panel on foll 20th row twice more. 251[267:283] sts. Maintain patt without shaping until piece measures $11[11\frac{1}{2}:12\frac{1}{2}]$in from hemline, ending with a WS row.

Shape yoke
Next row K8, *K2 tog, K6, K2 tog, K7, K2 tog, K8[10:12], rep from * 7 times more, K2 tog, K6, K2 tog, K7, K2 tog, K8. 224[240:256] sts.
Beg with a K row, cont in g st until work measures $12[12\frac{1}{2}:13]$in from hemline, ending with a WS row.
Divide for armholes
Change to No.2 straight needles.
Next row K55[58:61], turn and place rem sts on holder. Complete right front first.
Shape armhole
Bind off at beg of next and every foll alt row 2 sts 3 times and one st 3[4:5] times, *at the same time* work 7th buttonhole 18[20:22] rows above previous buttonhole. K 2 rows, ending at front edge.
Shape neck
Bind off at beg of next and every foll alt row 23[24:25] sts once, 4 sts once, 2 sts 3 times and one st 3 times. 10[11:12] sts. Cont without shaping until piece measures $18[19\frac{1}{4}:20]$in from hemline. Bind off.
With RS of work facing, rejoin yarn to back sts, bind off first 8[10:12] sts, K until there are 98[104:110] sts on right hand needle, turn and place rem sts on holder for left front. Complete back first.
Shape armholes
Bind off 2 sts at beg of next 5 rows.
Shape back neck
Next row Bind off 2, K until there are 26[28:30] sts on right hand needle, bind off 34[36:38] sts for neck, K to end.
Dec one st at armhole edge on every alt row 3[4:5] times in all, *at the same time* bind off at neck edge on every alt row 4 sts once, 2 sts 3 times and one st 3 times. 10[11:12] sts. Cont without shaping until piece measures $18[19\frac{1}{4}:20]$in from hemline. Bind off.
With WS of work facing, rejoin yarn to rem back sts and complete as for first side, reversing shaping. With RS of work facing, rejoin yarn to rem left front sts. Bind off 8[10:12] sts, K to end. 55[58:61] sts. Finish to correspond to right front, reversing shaping and omitting buttonhole.

Finishing
Block under a damp cloth with a warm iron. Join shoulder seams. Turn hem to WS at lower edge and sew in place. Block seams. Sew on buttons.

LACE STITCHES
Simple lace

Knitted lace stitches do not need to be complicated in order to produce openwork fabrics. Some of the most effective traditional patterns require only a few stitches and as little as two rows to form the pattern repeat.
The principle used for almost all lace stitches is that of decreasing one or more stitches at a given point in a row and compensating for these decreased stitches, either in the same row or a following row by working more than once into a stitch, or making one or more stitches by taking the yarn over or around the right hand needle the required number of times, as shown on page 25. Use a 3 ply yarn and No.3 needles to practice these simple lace stitches.

Laburnum stitch
Cast on a number of stitches divisible by 5+2.
1st row P2, *K3, P2, rep from * to end.
2nd row K2, *P3, K2, rep from * to end.
3rd row P2, *keeping yarn at front of work, sl 1, ybk, K2 tog, psso, bring yarn over top of needle from back to front then around needle again, P2, rep from * to end.
4th row K2, *P into the back of the first made st then into the front of the second made st, P1, K2, rep from * to end.
These 4 rows form the pattern.

Indian pillar stitch
Cast on a number of stitches divisible by 4+3.
1st row (RS) P to end.
2nd row K2, *insert needle P-wise into the next 3 sts as if to P3 tog but instead work (P1, K1, P1) into these 3 sts, K1, rep from * to last st, K1.
These 2 rows form the pattern.

Indian pillar stitch

Faggoting rib
Cast on a number of stitches divisible by 5+1.
1st row P1, *K2, yfwd, sl 1, K1, psso, P1, rep from * to end.
2nd row K1, *P2, yrn, P2 tog, K1, rep from * to end.
These 2 rows form the pattern.

Lace rib
Cast on a number of stitches divisible by 5+2.
1st row P2, *K1, yfwd, sl 1, K1, psso, P2, rep from * to end.
2nd row K2, *P3, K2, rep from * to end.
3rd row P2, *K2 tog, yfwd, K1, P2, rep from * to end.
4th row As 2nd.
These 4 rows form the pattern.

Eyelet cable rib

Cast on a number of stitches divisible by 5+2.
1st row P2, *K3, P2, rep from * to end.
2nd row K2, *P3, K2, rep from * to end.
3rd row P2, *sl 1, K2, psso the K2, P2, rep from * to end.
4th row K2, *P1, yrn, P1, K2, rep from * to end.
These 4 rows form the pattern.

Cat's eye pattern

Cast on a number of stitches divisible by 4.
1st row K4, *yfwd over and round the needle again to make 2 sts, K4, rep from * to end.
2nd row P2, *P2 tog, P the first made st and K the second made st, P2 tog, rep from * to last 2 sts, P2.
3rd row K2, yfwd, *K4, yfwd over and around the needle again, rep from * to last 6sts, K4, yfwd, K2.
4th row P3, *(P2 tog) twice, P the first made st and K the second made st, rep from * to last 7 sts, (P2 tog) twice, P3.
These 4 rows form the pattern.

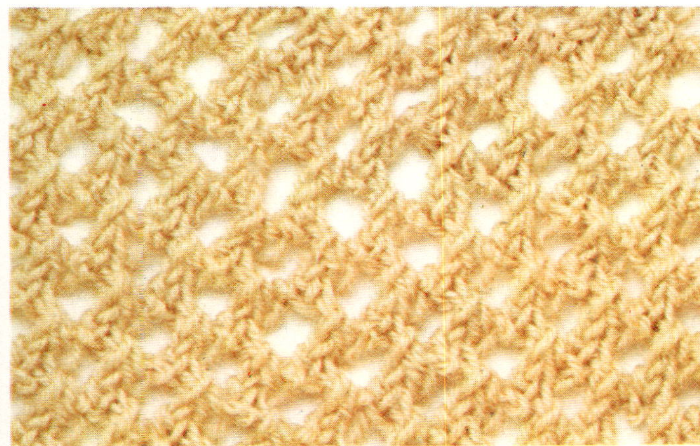

Open star stitch

Cast on a number of stitches divisible by 3.
1st row K2, *yfwd, K3 then pass the first of these 3 sts over the other 2 and off the right hand needle, rep from * to last st, K1.
2nd row P to end.
3rd row K1, *K3 then pass the first of these 3 sts over the other 2, yfwd, rep from * to last 2 sts, K2.
4th row P to end.
These 4 rows form the pattern.

Open star stitch

Hyacinth stitch

Cast on a number of stitches divisible by 6+3.
1st, 3rd and 5th rows P to end.
2nd row K1, *(K1, P1, K1, P1, K1) all into next st, K5 tog, rep from * to last 2 sts, (K1, P1, K1, P1, K1) into next st, K1.
4th row K1, *K5 tog, (K1, P1, K1, P1, K1) all into next st, rep from * to last 6 sts, K5 tog, K1.
6th row K to end winding yarn 3 times round right hand needle for each stitch.
7th row P to end dropping the extra loops.
Rows 2 through 7 form the pattern.

Diagonal openwork stitch

Cast on a number of stitches divisible by 2+1.
1st row K1, *yfwd, K2 tog, rep from * to end.
2nd row P to end.
3rd row K2, *yfwd, K2 tog, rep from * to last st, K1.
4th row P to end.
These 4 rows form the pattern.

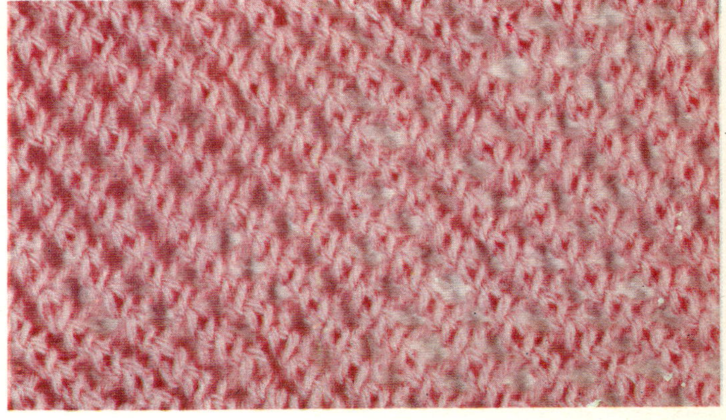

More simple lace

This chapter gives more simple lace patterns which are easy to work and produce most effective fabrics. Use a 3 ply yarn and No.2 or No.3 needles to practice these stitches.

Lace diamond pattern
Cast on a number of stitches divisible by 6+1.
1st row P1, *K5, P1, rep from * to end.
2nd row K1, *P5, K1, rep from * to end.
3rd row P1, *yon, sl 1, K1, psso, K1, K2 tog, yrn, P1, rep from * to end.
4th row K1, *K into back of next st – called K1B –, P3, K1B, K1, rep from * to end.
5th row P2, *yon, sl 1, K2, psso the 2 sts, yrn, P3, rep from * to last 5 sts, yon, sl 1, K2, psso the 2 sts, yrn, P2.
6th row K2, *K1B, P2, K1B, K3, rep from * to last 6 sts, K1B, P2, K1B, K2.
7th row P2, *K2 tog, yfwd, sl 1, K1, psso, P3, rep from * to last 6 sts, K2 tog, yfwd, sl 1, K1, psso, P2.
8th row K1, *P2 tog tbl, yrn, P1, yrn, P2 tog, K1, rep from * to end.
These 8 rows form the pattern.

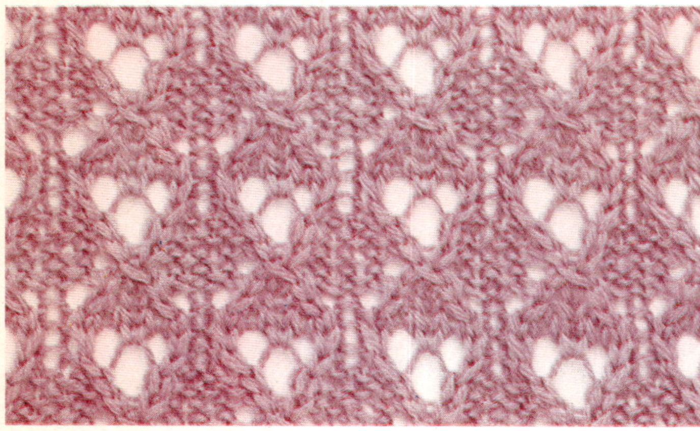

Embossed leaf pattern
Cast on a number of stitches divisible by 7.
1st row P to end.
2nd row K to end.
3rd row P3, *yon, K1, yrn, P6, rep from * to last 4 sts, yon, K1, yrn, P3.
4th row K3, *P3, K6, rep from * to last 6 sts, P3, K3.
5th row P3, *K1, (yfwd, K1) twice, P6, rep from * to last 6 sts, K1, (yfwd, K1) twice, P3.
6th row K3, *P5, K6, rep from * to last 8 sts, P5, K3.
7th row P3, *K2, yfwd, K1, yfwd, K2, P6, rep from * to last 8 sts, K2, yfwd, K1, yfwd, K2, P3.
8th row K3, *P7, K6, rep from * to last 10 sts, P7, K3.
9th row P3, *K3, yfwd, K1, yfwd, K3, P6, rep from * to last 10 sts, K3, yfwd, K1, yfwd, K3, P3.
10th row K3, *P9, K6, rep from * to last 12 sts, P9, K3.
11th row P3, *sl 1, K1, psso, K5, K2 tog, P6, rep from * to last 12 sts, sl 1, K1, psso, K5, K2 tog, P3.
12th row As 8th.
13th row P3, *sl 1, K1, psso, K3, K2 tog, P6, rep from * to last 10 sts, sl 1, K1, psso, K3, K2 tog, P3.
14th row As 6th.
15th row P3, *sl 1, K1, psso, K1, K2 tog, P6, rep from * to last 8 sts, sl 1, K1, psso, K1, K2 tog, P3.
16th row As 4th.
17th row P3, *sl 1, K2 tog, psso, P6, rep from * to last 6 sts, sl 1, K2 tog, psso, P3.
18th row As 2nd.
19th row As 1st.
20th row As 2nd.
These 20 rows form the pattern.

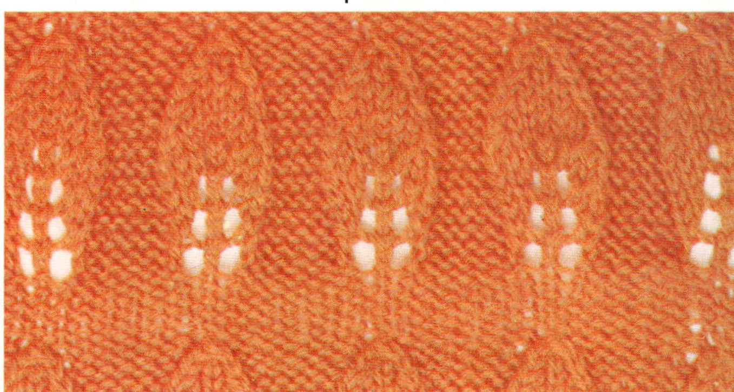

Snowdrop lace pattern
Cast on a number of stitches divisible by 8+3.
1st row K1, K2 tog, yfwd, *K5, yfwd, sl 1, K2 tog, psso, yfwd, rep from * to last 8 sts, K5, yfwd, sl 1, K1, psso, K1.
2nd and every alt row P to end.
3rd row As 1st.
5th row K3, *yfwd, sl 1, K1, psso, K1, K2 tog, yfwd, K3, rep from * to end.
7th row K1, K2 tog, yfwd, *K1, yfwd, sl 1, K2 tog, psso, yfwd, rep from * to last 4 sts, K1, yfwd, sl 1, K1, psso, K1.
8th row As 2nd.
These 8 rows form the pattern.

Falling leaf pattern

Cast on a number of stitches divisible by 10 + 1.

1st row K1, *yfwd, K3, sl 1, K2 tog, psso, K3, yfwd, K1, rep from * to end.

2nd and every alt row P to end.

3rd row K1, *K1, yfwd, K2, sl 1, K2 tog, psso, K2, yfwd, K2, rep from * to end.

5th row K1, *K2, yfwd, K1, sl 1, K2 tog, psso, K1, yfwd, K3, rep from * to end.

7th row K1, *K3, yfwd, sl 1, K2 tog, psso, yfwd, K4, rep from * to end.

9th row K2 tog, *K3, yfwd, K1, yfwd, K3, sl 1, K2 tog, psso, rep from * to last 9 sts, K3, yfwd, K1, yfwd, K3, sl 1, K1, psso.

11th row K2 tog, *K2, yfwd, K3, yfwd, K2, sl 1, K2 tog, psso, rep from * to last 9 sts, K2, yfwd, K3, yfwd, K2, sl 1, K1, psso.

13th row K2 tog, *K1, yfwd, K5, yfwd, K1, sl 1, K2 tog, psso, rep from * to last 9 sts, K1, yfwd, K5, yfwd, K1, sl 1, K1, psso.

15th row K2 tog, *yfwd, K7, yfwd, sl 1, K2 tog, psso, rep from * to last 9 sts, yfwd, K7, yfwd, sl 1, K1, psso.

16th row As 2nd.

These 16 rows form the pattern.

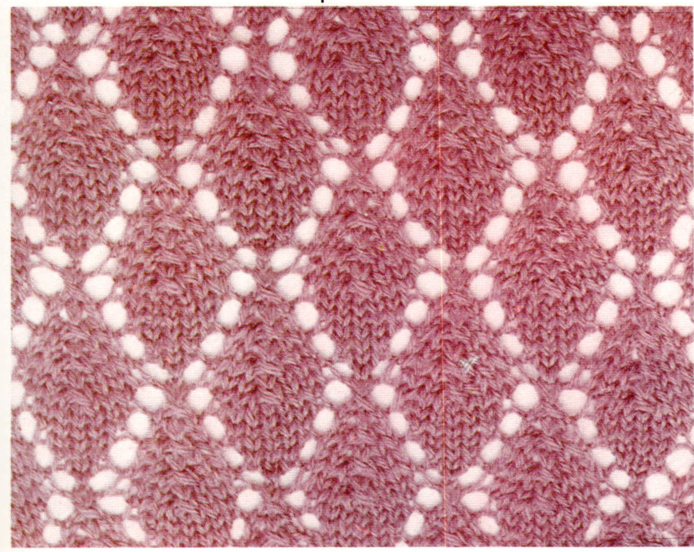

Cat's paw pattern

Cast on a number of stitches divisible by 12 + 1.

1st row K5, *yfwd, sl 1, K2 tog, psso, yfwd, K9, rep from * to last 8 sts, yfwd, sl 1, K2 tog, psso, yfwd, K5.

2nd and every alt row P to end.

3rd row K3, *K2 tog, yfwd, K3, yfwd, sl 1, K1, psso, K5, rep from * to last 10 sts, K2 tog, yfwd, K3, yfwd, sl 1, K1, psso, K3.

5th row As 1st.

7th row K to end.

9th row K2 tog, *yfwd, K9, yfwd, sl 1, K2 tog, psso, rep from * to last 11 sts, yfwd, K9, yfwd, sl 1, K1, psso.

11th row K2, *yfwd, sl 1, K1, psso, K5, K2 tog, yfwd, K3, rep from * to last 11 sts, yfwd, sl 1, K1, psso, K5, K2 tog, yfwd, K2.

13th row As 9th.

15th row As 7th.

16th row As 2nd.

These 16 rows form the pattern.

Gothic Pattern

Cast on a number of stitches divisible by 10 + 1.

1st row K1, *yfwd, sl 1, K1, psso, K5, K2 tog, yfwd, K1, rep from * to end.

2nd and every alt row P to end.

3rd row K2, *yfwd, sl 1, K1, psso, K3, K2 tog, yfwd, K3, rep from * to last 9 sts, yfwd, sl 1, K1, psso, K3, K2 tog, yfwd, K2.

5th row K3, *yfwd, sl 1, K1, psso, K1, K2 tog, yfwd, K5, rep from * to last 8 sts, yfwd, sl 1, K1, psso, K1, K2 tog, yfwd, K3.

7th row K4, *yfwd, sl 1, K2 tog, psso, yfwd, K7, rep from * to last 7 sts, yfwd, sl 1, K2 tog, psso, yfwd, K4.

9th row K1, *yfwd, sl 1, K1, psso, K2 tog, yfwd, K1, rep from * to end.

10th row As 2nd.

11th-18th rows Rep the 9th and 10th rows 4 times more.

19th row K2, *yfwd, sl 1, K1, psso, K3, K2 tog, yfwd, K3, rep from * to last 9 sts, yfwd, sl 1, K1, psso, K3, K2 tog, yfwd, K2.

21st row K3, *yfwd, sl 1, K1, psso, K1, K2 tog, yfwd, K5, rep from * to last 8 sts, yfwd, sl 1, K1, psso, K1, K2 tog, yfwd, K3.

23rd row K4, *yfwd, sl 1, K2 tog, psso, yfwd, K7, rep from * to last 7 sts, yfwd, sl 1, K2 tog, psso, yfwd, K4.

24th row As 2nd.

These 24 rows form the pattern.

Traditional lace patterns

The history of lace stitches spans several centuries; many of the stitches, like those described in this chapter, have traditional names which are both beautiful and descriptive.

Shell and shower
Cast on a number of stitches divisible by 12 + 3.
1st row K2, *yfwd, K4, sl 1, K2 tog, psso, K4, yfwd, K1, rep from * to last st, K1.
2nd and every alt row P to end.
3rd row K3, *yfwd, K3, sl 1, K2 tog, psso, K3, yfwd, K3, rep from * to end.
5th row K1, K2 tog, *yfwd, K1, yfwd, K2, sl 1, K2 tog, psso, K2, yfwd, K1, yfwd, sl 1, K2 tog, psso, rep from * to last 12 sts, yfwd, K1, yfwd, K2, sl 1, K2 tog, psso, K2, yfwd, K1, yfwd, sl 1, K1, psso, K1.
7th row K1, *yfwd, sl 1, K1, psso, K2, yfwd, K1, sl 1, K2 tog, psso, K1, yfwd, K3, rep from * to last 2 sts, yfwd, K2 tog.
9th row K2, *yfwd, sl 1, K2 tog, psso, yfwd, K1, rep from * to last st, K1.
10th row As 2nd
These 10 rows form the pattern.

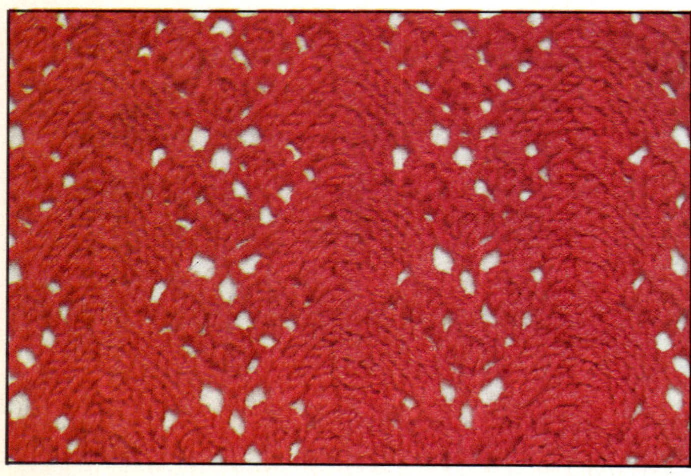

Ogee lace
Cast on a number of stitches divisible by 24 + 1.
1st row *K2, yfwd, K2 tog, K1, K2 tog, K3, yfwd, sl 1, K1, psso, yrn, P1, yon, K2, yfwd, sl 1, K1, psso, K1, sl 1, K1, psso, K1, sl 1, K1, psso, yfwd, K1, rep from * to last st, K1.
2nd row P1, *P7, yrn, P2 tog, P5, yrn, P2 tog, P8, rep from * to end.
3rd row *K1, yfwd, K2 tog, K1, K2 tog, K3, yfwd, sl 1, K1, psso, K1, yfwd, K1, yfwd, K3, yfwd, sl 1, K1, psso, K1, sl 1, K1, psso, K1, sl 1, K1, psso, yfwd, rep from * to last st, K1.
4th row P1, *P6, yrn, P2 tog, P7, yrn, P2 tog, P7, rep from * to end.
5th row *K3, K2 tog, K3, yfwd, sl 1, K1, psso, K1, yfwd, K3, yfwd, K3, yfwd, sl 1, K1, psso, K1, sl 1, K1, psso, K2, rep from * to last st, K1.
6th row P1, *P5, yrn, P2 tog, P9, yrn, P2 tog, P6, rep from * to end.
7th row *K2, K2 tog, K3, yfwd, sl 1, K1, psso, K3, yfwd, K1, yfwd, K5, yfwd, sl 1, K1, psso, K1, sl 1, K1, psso, K1, rep from * to last st, K1.
8th row P1, *P4, yrn, P2 tog, P11, yrn, P2 tog, P5, rep from * to end.
9th row *K1, K2 tog, K3, yfwd, sl 1, K1, psso, K3, yfwd, K3, yfwd, K5, yfwd, sl 1, K1, psso, K1, sl 1, K1, psso, rep from * to last st, K1.
10th row P1, *P3, yrn, P2 tog, P13, yrn, P2 tog, P4, rep from * to end.
11th row Sl 1, K1, psso, *K3, yfwd, sl 1, K1, psso, K1, sl 1, K1, psso, yfwd, K2, yfwd, K1, yfwd, K2, yfwd, K2 tog, K3, yfwd, sl 1, K1, psso, K1, sl 1, K2 tog, psso, rep from * to last 23 sts, K3, yfwd, sl 1, K1, psso, K1, sl 1, K1, psso, yfwd, K2, yfwd, K1, yfwd, K2, yfwd, K2 tog, K3, yfwd, sl 1, K1, psso, K1, sl 1, K1, psso.
12th row P1, *P2, yrn, P2 tog, P15, yrn, P2 tog, P3, rep from * to end.
13th row Sl 1, K1, psso, *K2, yfwd, sl 1, K1, psso, K5, yfwd, K3, yfwd, K7, yfwd, sl 1, K1, psso, sl 1, K2 tog, psso, rep from * to last 23 sts, K2, yfwd, sl 1, K1, psso, K5, yfwd, K3, yfwd, K7, yfwd, sl 1, K1, psso, sl 1, K1, psso.
14th row K1, *P1, yrn, P2 tog, P17, yrn, P2 tog, P1, K1, rep from * to end.
15th row *P1, yon, K2, yfwd, sl 1, K1, psso, K1, sl 1, K1, psso, K1, sl 1, K1, psso, yfwd, K3, yfwd, K2 tog, K1, K2 tog, K3, yfwd, sl 1, K1, psso, yrn, rep from * to last st, P1.
16th row As 12th.
17th row *K1, yfwd, K3, yfwd, sl 1, K1, psso, K1, sl 1, K1, psso, K1, sl 1, K1, psso, yfwd, K1, yfwd, K2 tog, K1, K2 tog, K3, yfwd, sl 1, K1, psso, K1, yfwd, rep from * to last st, K1.
18th row As 10th.
19th row *K2, yfwd, K3, yfwd, sl 1, K1, psso, K1, sl 1, K1, psso, K5, K2 tog, K3, yfwd, sl 1, K1, psso, K1, yfwd, K1, rep from * to last st, K1.
20th row As 8th.
21st row *K1, yfwd, K5, yfwd, sl 1, K1, psso, K1, sl 1, K1, psso, K3, K2 tog, K3, yfwd, sl 1, K1, psso, K3, yfwd, rep from * to last st, K1.
22nd row As 6th.
23rd row *K2, yfwd, K5, yfwd, sl 1, K1, psso, K1, sl 1, K1, psso, K1, K2 tog, K3, yfwd, sl 1, K1, psso, K3, yfwd, K1, rep from * to last st, K1.

24th row As 4th.
25th row *K1, yfwd, K2, yfwd, K2 tog, K3, yfwd, sl 1, K1, psso. K1, sl 1, K2 tog, psso, K3, yfwd, sl 1, K1, psso, K1, sl 1, K1, psso, yfwd, K2, yfwd, rep from * to last st, K1.
26th row As 2nd.
27th row *K2, yfwd, K7, yfwd, sl 1, K1, psso, sl 1, K2 tog, psso, K2. yfwd, sl 1, K1, psso, K5, yfwd, K1, rep from * to last st, K1.
28th row P1, *P8, yrn, P2 tog, P1, K1, P1, yrn, P2 tog, P9, rep from * to end.
These 28 rows form the pattern.

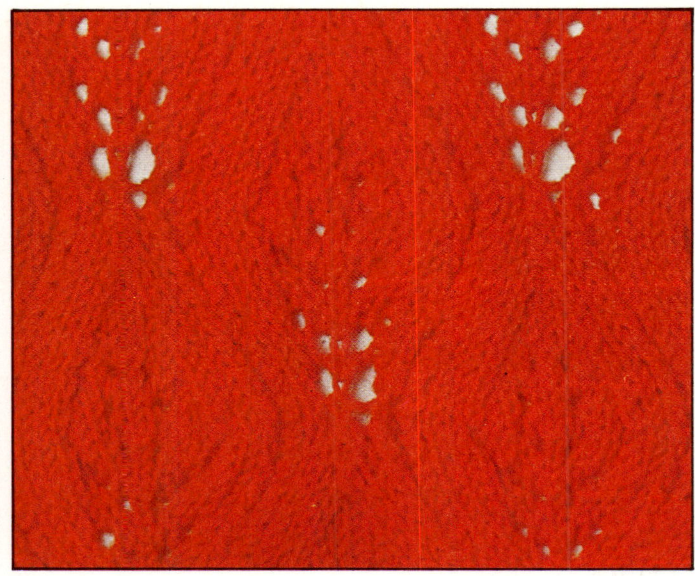

Spanish lace

Cast on a number of stitches divisible by 34+4.
1st row K2, *K3, K2 tog, K4, yrn, P2, (K2, yfwd, sl 1, K1, psso) 3 times, P2, yon, K4, sl 1, K1, psso, K3, rep from * to last 2 sts, K2.
2nd row P4, *P2 tog tbl, P4, yrn, P1, K2, (P2, yrn, P2 tog) 3 times, K2, P1, yrn, P4, P2 tog, P4, rep from * to end.
3rd row K3, *K2 tog, K4, yfwd, K2, P2, (K2, yfwd, sl 1, K1, psso) 3 times, P2, K2, yfwd, K4, sl 1, K1, psso, K2, rep from * to last st, K1.
4th row P2, *P2 tog tbl, P4, yrn, P3, K2, (P2, yrn, P2 tog) 3 times, K2, P3, yrn, P4, P2 tog, rep from * to last 2 sts, P2.
Rep the 1st through 4th rows twice more.
13th row *(K2, yfwd, sl 1, K1, psso) twice, P2, yon, K4, sl 1, K1, psso, K6, K2 tog, K4, yrn, P2, K2, yfwd, sl 1, K1, psso, rep from * to last 4 sts, K2, yfwd, sl 1, K1, psso.
14th row *(P2, yrn, P2 tog) twice, K2, P1, yrn, P4, P2 tog, P4, P2 tog tbl, P4, yrn, P1, K2, P2, yrn, P2 tog, rep from * to last 4 sts, P2, yrn, P2 tog.
15th row *(K2, yfwd, sl 1, K1, psso) twice, P2, K2, yfwd, K4, sl 1, K1, psso, K2, K2 tog, K4, yfwd, K2, P2, K2, yfwd, sl 1, K1, psso, rep from * to last 4 sts, K2, yfwd, sl 1, K1, psso.
16th row *(P2, yrn, P2 tog) twice, K2, P3, yrn, P4, P2 tog, P2 tog tbl, P4, yrn, P3, K2, P2, yrn, P2 tog, rep from * to last 4 sts, P2, yrn, P2 tog.
Rep the 13th through 16th rows twice more.
These 24 rows form the pattern.

Candlelight lace

Cast on a number of stitches divisible by 12+1.
1st row K1, *yfwd, sl 1, K1, psso, K7, K2 tog, yfwd, K1, rep from * to end.
2nd and every alt row P to end.
3rd row K1, *yfwd, K1, sl 1, K1, psso, K5, K2 tog, K1, yfwd, K1, rep from * to end.
5th row K1, * yfwd, K2, sl 1, K1, psso, K3, K2 tog, K2, yfwd, K1, rep from * to end.
7th row K1, *yfwd, K3, sl 1, K1, psso, K1, K2 tog, K3, yfwd, K1, rep from * to end.
9th row K1, *yfwd, K4, sl 1, K2 tog, psso, K4, yfwd, K1, rep from * to end.
11th row *K4, K2 tog, yfwd, K1, yfwd, sl 1, K1, psso, K3, rep from * to last st, K1.
13th row *K3, K2 tog, K1, (yfwd, K1) twice, sl 1, K1, psso, K2, rep from * to last st, K1.
15th row *K2, K2 tog, K2, yfwd, K1, yfwd, K2, sl 1, K1, psso, K1, rep from * to last st, K1.
17th row *K1, K2 tog, K3, yfwd, K1, yfwd, K3, sl 1, K1, psso, rep from * to last st, K1.
19th row K2 tog, *K4, yfwd, K1, yfwd, K4, sl 1, K2 tog, psso, rep from * to last 11 sts, K4, yfwd, K1, yfwd, K4, sl 1, K1, psso.
20th row As 2nd.
These 20 rows form the pattern.

Larger lace patterns

The traditional lace stitches described here vary in complexity but each of them can be used to form a fabric of delicate beauty.

Wheat ear pattern
Cast on a number of stitches divisible by 11.
1st row (RS) *K1, (K1, yfwd to make a st, K1, yfwd, K1) all into same st, turn and K5, turn and P5, turn and K1, sl 1, K2 tog, psso, K1, turn and P3 tog – called B1 –, K2, yfwd, K1, yfwd, K4, K2 tog, rep from * to end, noting that one extra st is inc in each rep on this and every RS row.
2nd, 4th, 6th, 8th and 10th rows *P2 tog, P10, rep from * to end.
3rd row *K5, yfwd, K1, yfwd, K3, K2 tog, rep from * to end.
5th row *K6, yfwd, K1, yfwd, K2, K2 tog, rep from * to end.
7th row *K7, (yfwd, K1) twice, K2 tog, rep from * to end.
9th row *K8, yfwd, K1, yfwd, K2 tog, rep from * to end.
11th row *Sl 1, K1, psso, K4, yfwd, K1, yfwd, K2, B1, K1, rep from * to end.
12th, 14th, 16th and 18th rows *P10, P2 tog tbl, rep from * to end.
13th row *Sl 1, K1, psso, K3, yfwd, K1, yfwd, K5, rep from * to end.
15th row *Sl 1, K1, psso, K2, yfwd, K1, yfwd, K6, rep from * to end.
17th row *Sl 1, K1, psso, (K1, yfwd) twice, K7, rep from * to end.
19th row *Sl 1, K1, psso, yfwd, K1, yfwd, K8, rep from * to end.
20th row As 12th.
These 20 rows form the pattern.

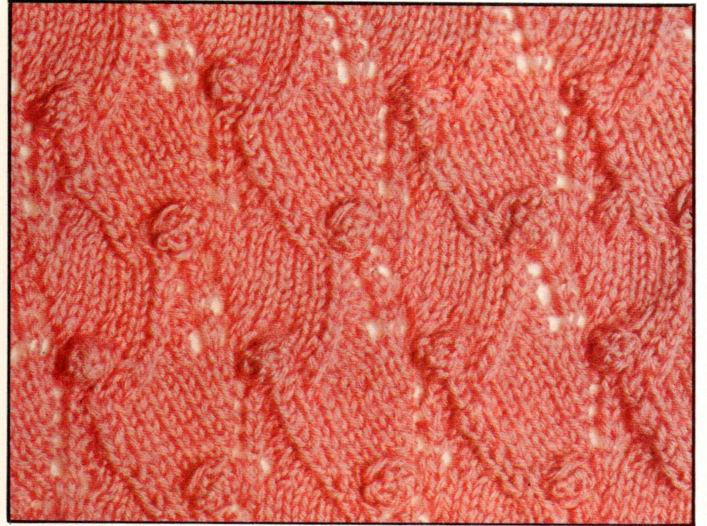

Fountain pattern
Cast on a number of stitches divisible by 16 plus 1.
1st row (WS) P to end.
2nd row Sl 1, K1, psso, *yfwd, K2, K2 tog, yfwd, K1, yfwd, sl 1, K2 tog, psso, yfwd, K1, yfwd, sl 1, K1, psso, K2, yfwd, sl 1, K2 tog, psso, rep from * ending last rep K2 tog instead of sl 1, K2 tog, psso.
3rd and every alt row P to end.
4th row Sl 1, K1, psso, *K3, yfwd, K2 tog, yfwd, K3, yfwd, sl 1, K1, psso, yfwd, K3, sl 1, K2 tog, psso, rep from * ending last rep as 2nd row.
6th row Sl 1, K1, psso, *(K2, yfwd) twice, K2 tog, K1, sl 1, K1, psso, (yfwd, K2) twice, sl 1, K2 tog, psso, rep from * ending last rep as 2nd row.
8th row Sl 1, K1, psso, *K1, yfwd, K3, yfwd, K2 tog, K1, sl 1, K1, psso, yfwd, K3, yfwd, K1, sl 1, K2 tog, psso, rep from * ending last rep as 2nd row.
These 8 rows form the pattern.

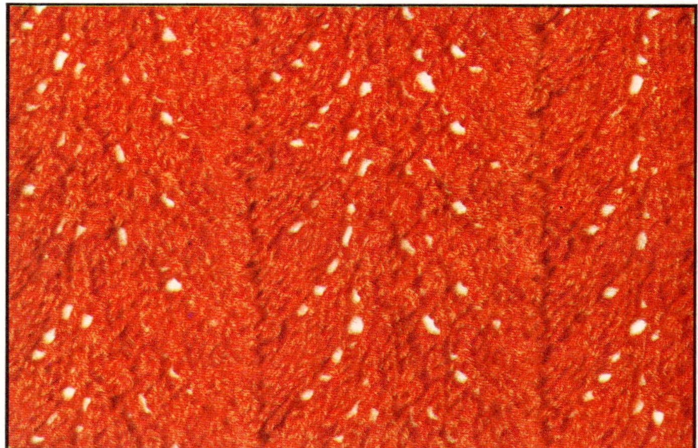

Oriel pattern
Cast on a number of stitches divisible by 12 plus 1.
1st row (RS) P1, *sl 1, K1, psso, K3, yrn, P1, yon, K3, K2 tog, P1, rep from * to end.
2nd row K1, *P5, K1, rep from * to end.
Rep 1st and 2nd rows twice more.
7th row P1, *yon, K3, K2 tog, P1, sl 1, K1, psso, K3, yrn, P1, rep from * to end.
8th row As 2nd.
9th row P2, *yon, K2, K2 tog, P1, sl 1, K1, psso, K2, yrn, P3, rep from * ending last rep P2 instead of P3.
10th row K2, *P4, K1, P4, K3, rep from * ending last rep K2 instead of K3.
11th row P3, *yon, K1, K2 tog, P1, sl 1, K1, psso, K1, yrn, P5, rep from * ending last rep P3 instead of P5.
12th row K3, *P3, K1, P3, K5, rep from * ending last rep K3 instead of K5.
13th row P4, *yon, K2 tog, P1, sl 1, K1, psso, yrn, P7, rep

from * ending last rep P4 instead of P7.
14th row K4, *P2, K1, P2, K7, rep from * ending last rep K4 instead of K7.
15th row As 7th.
16th row As 2nd.
Rep 15th and 16th rows twice more.
21st row As 1st.
22nd row As 2nd.
23rd row P1, *sl 1, K1, psso, K2, yrn, P3, yon, K2, K2 tog, P1, rep from * to end.
24th row K1, *P4, K3, P4, K1, rep from * to end.
25th row P1, *sl 1, K1, psso, K1, yrn, P5, yon, K1, K2 tog, P1, rep from * to end.
26th row K1, *P3, K5, P3, K1, rep from * to end.
27th row P1, *sl 1, K1, psso, yrn, P7, yon, K2 tog, P1, rep from * to end.
28th row K1, *P2, K7, P2, K1, rep from * to end.
These 28 rows form the pattern.

Bell pattern
Cast on a number of stitches divisible by 18 plus 1, noting that the number of stitches do not remain the same on every row but will revert to the original number on the 12th, 14th, 26th and 28th rows.
1st row (RS) K1, *(P2, K1) twice, yfwd, K2 tog, yfwd, K1, yfwd, sl 1, K1, psso, yfwd, (K1, P2) twice, K1, rep from * to end.
2nd row *(P1, K2) twice, P9, K2, P1, K2, rep from * to last st, P1.
3rd row K1, *(P2, K1) twice, yfwd, K2 tog, yfwd, K3, yfwd, sl 1, K1, psso, yfwd, (K1, P2) twice, K1, rep from * to end.
4th row *(P1, K2) twice, P11, K2, P1, K2, rep from * to last st, P1.
5th row K1, *(P2 tog, K1) twice, yfwd, K2 tog, yfwd, sl 1, K1, psso, K1, K2 tog, yfwd, sl 1, K1, psso, yfwd, (K1, P2 tog) twice, K1, rep from * to end.
6th row *(P1, K1) twice, P11, K1, P1, K1, rep from * to last st, P1.
7th row K1, *(P1, K1) twice, yfwd, K2 tog, yfwd, K1 tbl, yfwd, sl 1, K2 tog, psso, yfwd, K1, tbl, yfwd, sl 1, K1, psso, yfwd, (K1, P1) twice, K1, rep from * to end.
8th row *(P1, K1) twice, P13, K1, P1, K1, rep from * to last st, P1.
9th row K1, *(K2 tog) twice, yfwd, K2 tog, yfwd, K3, yfwd, K1 yfwd, K3, yfwd, sl 1, K1, psso, yfwd, (sl 1, K1, psso) twice, K1, rep from * to end.
10th, 12th and 14th rows P to end.
11th row K1, *(K2 tog, yfwd) twice, sl 1, K1, psso, K1, K2 tog, yfwd, K1, yfwd, sl 1, K1, psso, K1, K2 tog, (yfwd, sl 1, K1, psso) twice, K1, rep from * to end.
13th row K2 tog, *yfwd, K2 tog, yfwd, K1 tbl, yfwd, sl 1, K2 tog, psso, yfwd, K3, yfwd, sl 1, K2 tog, psso, yfwd, K1 tbl, yfwd, sl 1, K1, psso, yfwd, sl 1, K2 tog, psso, rep from * ending last rep sl 1, K1, psso, instead of sl 1, K2 tog, pssc.
15th row K1, *yfwd, sl 1, K1, psso, yfwd, (K1, P2) 4 times, K1, yfwd, K2 tog, yfwd, K1, rep from * to end.
16th row P5, *(K2, P1) 3 times, K2, P9, rep from * ending last rep P5 instead of P9.
17th row K2, *yfwd, sl 1, K1, psso, yfwd, (K1, P2) 4 times, K1, yfwd, K2 tog, yfwd, K3, rep from * ending last rep K2 instead of K3.
18th row P6, *(K2, P1) 3 times, K2, P11, rep from * ending last rep P6 instead of P11.
19th row K1, *K2 tog, yfwd, sl 1, K1, psso, yfwd, (K1, P2 tog) 4 times, K1, yfwd, K2 tog, yfwd, sl 1, K1, psso, K1, rep from * to end.
20th row P6, *(K1, P1) 3 times, K1, P11, rep from * ending last rep P6 instead of P11.
21st row K2 tog, *yfwd, K1 tbl, yfwd, sl 1, K1, psso, yfwd, (K1, P1) 4 times, K1, yfwd, K2 tog, yfwd, K1 tbl, yfwd, sl 1, K2 tog, psso, rep from * ending last rep sl 1, K1, psso, instead of sl 1, K2 tog, psso.
22nd row P7, *(K1, P1) 3 times, K1, P13, rep from * ending last rep P7 instead of P13.
23rd row K1, *yfwd, K3, yfwd, sl 1, K1, psso, yfwd, (sl 1, K1, psso) twice, K1, (K2 tog) twice, yfwd, K2 tog, yfwd, K3, yfwd, K1, rep from * to end.
24th and 26th rows P to end.
25th row K1, *yfwd, sl 1, K1, psso, K1, K2 tog, (yfwd, sl 1, K1, psso) twice, K1, (K2 tog, yfwd) twice, sl 1, K1, psso, K1, K2 tog, yfwd, K1, rep from * to end.
27th row K2, *yfwd, sl 1, K2 tog, psso, yfwd, K1 tbl, yfwd, sl 1, K1, psso, yfwd, sl 1, K2 tog, psso, yfwd, K2 tog, yfwd, K1 tbl, yfwd, sl 1, K2 tog, psso, yfwd, K3, rep from * ending last rep K2 instead of K3.
28th row P to end.
These 28 rows form the pattern.

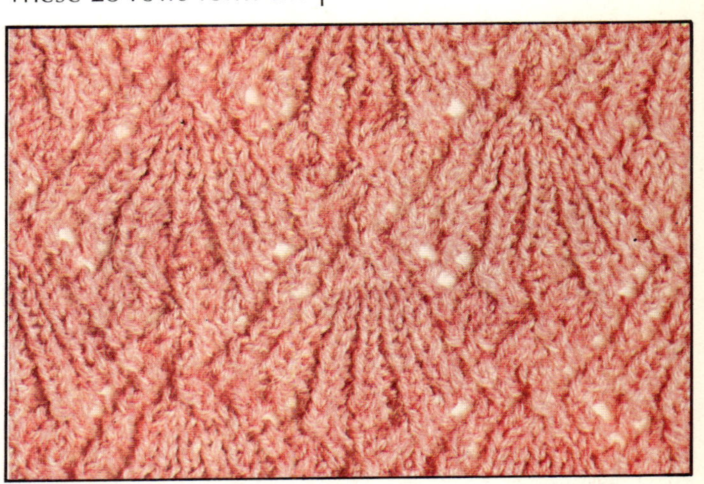

PATTERN SHAPES AND PICTURES

Patterned shapes and pictures can be achieved in knitting by means of different textures and stitches, using a single, overall color. This technique can be incorporated into any plain, basic garment most effectively, either as a repeating border such as the fir trees and tulip stitches shown here, or as a single motif, such as the house pattern, in the middle or placed on the front of a sweater.

Before you begin to knit, work out the position for the border or motif, making sure that you have the correct multiple of stitches for the design repeat or that a single motif is correctly placed.

Fir tree border

This pattern requires a multiple of 12 stitches plus 1 and is worked against a reverse stockinette stitch backround.

1st row (RS) K1, *P1, K1, rep from * to end.
2nd row P1, *K1, P1, rep from * to end.
3rd row P6, *K1, P11, rep from * to last 7 sts, K1, P6.
4th row K6, *P1, K11, rep from * to last 7 sts, P1, K6.
Rep last 2 rows 3 times more.
11th row P2, *K1, P3, rep from * to last 3 sts, K1, P2.
12th row K2, *P1, K3, rep from * to last 3 sts, P1, K2.
13th row P2, *K2, P2, K1, P2, K2, P3, rep from * to last 11 sts, K2, P2, K1, P2, K2, P2.
14th row K2, *P2, K2, P1, K2, P2, K3, rep from * to last 11 sts, P2, K2, P1, K2, P2, K2.
15th row P2, *K3, P3, rep from * to last 5 sts, K3, P2.
16th row K2, *P3, K3, rep from * to last 5 sts, P3, K2.
17th row P2, *K4, P1, K4, P3, rep from * to last 11 sts, K4, P1, K4, P2.
18th row K2, *P4, K1, P4, K3, rep from * to last 11 sts, P4, K1, P4, K2.
19th row P3, *K7, P5, rep from * to last 10 sts, K7, P3.
20th row K3, *P7, K5, rep from * to last 10 sts, P7, K3.
21st row P4, *K5, P7, rep from * to last 9 sts, K5, P4.
22nd row K4, *P5, K7, rep from * to last 9 sts, P5, K4.
23rd row P5, *K3, P9, rep from * to last 8 sts, K3, P5.
24th row K5, *P3, K9, rep from * to last 8 sts, P3, K5.
25th row P6, *K1, P11, rep from * to last 7 sts, K1, P6.
26th row K6, *P1, K11, rep from * to last 7 sts, P1, K6.
These 26 rows complete the border pattern.

Tulip bed border

This pattern requires a multiple of 20 stitches plus 1 and is worked against a stockinette stitch background.

1st row (RS) K5, *K2 tog, yfwd, K1, yfwd, K2 tog, P1, sl 1, K1, psso, yfwd, K1, yfwd, sl 1, K1, psso, K9, rep from * ending last rep K5 instead of K9.

2nd and every alt row P to end.
3rd row K4, *K2 tog, yfwd, K2, yfwd, K2 tog, P1, sl 1, K1, psso, yfwd, K2, yfwd, sl 1, K1, psso, K7, rep from * ending last rep K4.
5th row K3, *K2 tog, yfwd, K3, yfwd, K2 tog, P1, sl 1, K1, psso, yfwd, K3, yfwd, sl 1, K1, psso, K5, rep from * ending last rep K3.
7th row K2, *K2 tog, yfwd, K4, yfwd, K2 tog, P1, sl 1, K1, psso, yfwd, K4, yfwd, sl 1, K1, psso, K3, rep from * ending last rep K2.
9th row K1, *K2 tog, yfwd, K5, yfwd, K2 tog, P1, sl 1, K1, psso, yfwd, K5, yfwd, sl 1, K1, psso, K1, rep from * to end.
11th row K2, *yfwd, K2 tog, K2, (K2 tog, yfwd) twice, K1, (yfwd, sl 1, K1, psso) twice, K2, sl 1, K1, psso, yfwd, K3, rep from * ending last rep K2.
13th row K2, *yfwd, K2 tog, K1, (K2 tog, yfwd) twice, K3, (yfwd, sl 1, K1, psso) twice, K1, sl 1, K1, psso, yfwd, K3, rep from * ending last rep K2.
15th row K2, *yfwd, (K2 tog) twice, yfwd, K2 tog, yfwd, K5, yfwd, sl 1, K1, psso, yfwd, (sl 1, K1, psso) twice, yfwd, K3, rep from * ending last rep K2.
17th row K2, *yfwd, sl 2, K1, p2sso, yfwd, K2 tog, yfwd, K7, yfwd, sl 1, K1, psso, yfwd, sl 2, K1, p2sso, yfwd, K3, rep from * ending last rep K2.
19th row K2, *K2 tog, yfwd, K2, yfwd, K2 tog, K5, sl 1, K1, psso, yfwd, K2, yfwd, sl 1, K1, psso, K3, rep from * ending last rep K2.
21st row K6, *yfwd, K2 tog, K5, sl 1, K1, psso, yfwd, K11, rep from * ending last rep K6.
23rd row K6, *yfwd, (K2 tog) twice, yfwd, K1, yfwd, (sl 1, K1, psso) twice, yfwd, K11, rep from * ending last rep K6.
25th row K6, *yfwd, sl 2, K1, p2sso, yfwd, K3, yfwd, sl 2, K1, p2sso, yfwd, K11, rep from * ending last rep K6.
26th row As 2nd.
These 26 rows complete the border pattern.

House motif
This pattern is worked on 28 stitches in all against a reverse stockinette stitch background.
1st row (RS) P2, K7, K into front of 2nd st on left hand needle then into front of first st – called T2R –, P6, K into back of 2nd st on left hand needle then into front of first st – called T2L –, K7, P2.
2nd row K2, P9, K6, P9, K2.
Rep 1st and 2nd rows once more.
5th row P2, K2, (K2, yfwd, K2 tog for window), K1, T2R, P6, T2L, K1, (K2, yfwd, K2 tog), K2, P2.
6th row K2, P2, (P2, yrn, P2 tog), P3, K6, P3, (P2, yrn, P2 tog) P2, K2.
Rep 5th and 6th rows twice more.
11th row P2, K2, (K2, yfwd, K2 tog), K1, T2R, P1, (P1, K1, P1) all into next st, turn and K3, turn and P3 then lift 2nd and 3rd sts over first st to form door knob, P4, T2L, K1, (K2, yfwd, K2 tog), K2, P2.
12th row As 6th.
Rep 5th and 6th rows twice more.
17th row As 1st.
18th row As 2nd.
19th row P2, K8, T2R, P4, T2L, K8, P2.
20th row K2, P10, K4, P10, K2.
21st row P2, K9, T2R, P2, T2L, K9, P2.
22nd row K2, P11, K2, P11, K2.
23rd row P2, K10, T2R, T2L, K10, P2.
24th row K2, P24, K2.
25th row P2, K24, P2.
26th row As 24th.
27th row P2, K2, (K2, yfwd, K2 tog for window), K4, (K2, yfwd, K2 tog), K4, (K2, yfwd, K2 tog), K2, P2.
28th row K2, P2, (P2, yrn, P2 tog), P4, (P2, yrn, P2 tog), P4, (P2, yrn, P2 tog), P2, K2.
Rep 27th and 28th rows twice more, then 25th and 26th rows twice more.
37th row K to end.
38th row K to end.
39th row P1, K26, P1.
40th row K to end.
41st row P2, K24, P2.
42nd row K to end.
43rd row P3, K22, P3.
44th row K to end.
45th row P4, K20, P4.
46th row K to end.
47th row P5, K18, P5.
48th row K to end.
49th row P10, (K1, P1) twice, K1, P13.
50th row K13, (P1, K1) twice, P1, K10.
Rep 49th and 50th rows 3 times more.
These 56 rows complete the motif.

A simple patterned pullover

Here is a simple pullover pattern which incorporates the house motif given in the previous chapter on patterned shapes and motifs. The motifs are positioned in rows across front and back of the sweater, and a single motif has been incorporated into each of the short set-in sleeves.

Pullover

Sizes

Directions are to fit 34in bust. Changes for 36 and 38in bust are in brackets [ ].

Length to shoulder, 23[23$\frac{1}{4}$:23$\frac{1}{2}$]in

Sleeve seam, 7in

Gauge
28 sts and 36 rows to 4in in stockinette stitch (st st) worked on No.3 needles

Materials
12[13:14] × 1oz balls 3 ply fingering yarn
One pair No.3 needles
One pair No.2 needles

Back
Using No.2 needles cast on 120[124:128] sts. Work 2in K1, P1 rib. Change to No.3 needles. Beg with a P row work 4 rows reverse st st.
Next row P2, (patt 28 sts as for 1st row of house motif, P16 [18:20] sts) twice, patt 28 sts as shown for 1st row of house motif, P2.
Next row K2, (patt 28 sts as for 2nd row of house motif, K16 [18:20] sts) twice, patt 28 sts as for 2nd row of house motif, K2.
Cont in patt as now set until 56 patt rows have been completed. Beg with a P row work 4 rows reverse st st.
Next row P24 [25:26] sts, patt 28 sts as for 1st row of house motif, P16 [18:20] sts, patt 28 sts as for 1st row of house motif, P24 [25:26].
Next row K24 [25:26] sts, patt 28 sts as for 2nd row of house motif, K16 [18:20] sts, patt 28 sts as for 2nd row of house motif, K24 [25:26].
Cont in patt as now set until second 56 patt rows have been completed. Beg with a P row work 4 rows reverse st st.
Next row P46 [48:50] sts, patt 28 sts as for 1st row of house motif, P46 [48:50].
Next row K46 [48:50] sts, patt 28 sts as for 2nd row of house motif, K46 [48:50].
Cont in patt as now set until work measures 16in from beg, ending with a K row.
Shape armholes
Maintaining patt until third 56 patt rows have been completed, then cont in reverse st st across all sts, bind off at beg of next and every row 5 sts twice and 2 sts 4 times. Dec one st at each end of next and foll 5 alt rows 90[94:98] sts. Cont without shaping until armholes measure 7[7¼:7½]in from beg, ending with a K row.
Shape shoulders
Bind off at beg of next and every row 7 sts 4 times and 11[12:13] sts twice. Place rem 40[42:44] sts on holder for center back neck.

Front
Work as for back until armhole shaping is completed and third 56 patt rows have been worked. Cont without shaping in reverse st st until armholes measure 5[5¼:5½]in from beg, ending with a K row.
Shape neck
Next row P35[36:37] sts, bind off 20[22:24] sts, P to end. Complete this side first. K 1 row. Bind off at beg of next and every alt row 2 sts 3 times, then dec one st at neck edge on every alt row 4 times. 25[26:27] sts.

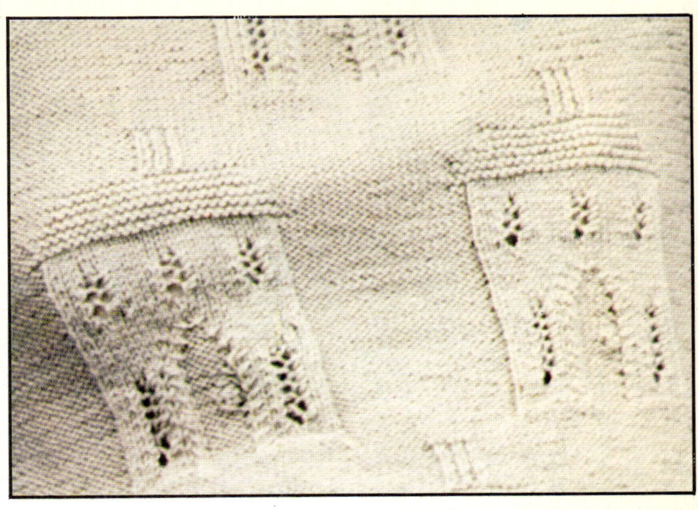

Cont without shaping until armhole measures same as back to shoulder, ending at armhole edge.
Shape shoulder
Bind off at beg of next and every alt row 7 sts twice and 11[12:13] sts once.
With WS of work facing, rejoin yarn to rem sts and complete to correspond to first side, reversing shaping.

Sleeves
Using No.2 needles cast on 76[78:80] sts. Work 1in K1, P1 rib. Change to No.3 needles. Beg with a P row work 4 rows reverse st st.
Next row P2, patt 28 sts as given for 1st row of house motif, P16[18:20] sts, patt 28 sts as for 1st row of house motif, P2.
Next row K2, patt 28 sts as for 2nd row of house motif, K16[18:20] sts, patt 28 sts as given for 2nd row of house motif, K2.
Cont in patt as now set, inc one st at each end of next and every foll 6th row until there are 86[90:94] sts, working extra sts in reverse st st, until 56 patt rows have been completed. Cont in reverse st st across all sts.
Shape top
Bind off 5 sts at beg of next 2 rows. Dec one st at each end of next and foll 10[11:12] alt rows, ending with a K row. Bind off at beg of next and every row 2 sts 6 times, 3 sts 6 times and 4 sts 4 times. Bind off rem 8[10:12] sts.

Neckband
Join right shoulder seam. Using No.2 needles and with RS of work facing, K 20[21:22] sts down left front neck, K 20[22:24] sts across front neck, K 20[21:22] sts up right front neck and K across 40[42:44] back neck sts on holder. 100[106:112] sts. Work 2in K1, P1 rib. Bind off in rib.

Finishing
Block as suggested on label. Join rem shoulder and neckband seam. Set in sleeves. Join side and sleeve seams. Fold neckbands in half to WS and sew in place. Block seams.

SHETLAND LACE

Of all the traditional knitting techniques which have flourished in Britain, such as Aran and Fair Isle patterns, typical Shetland Isle lace stitches are among the most beautiful.

The finest examples come from Unst, the most northerly of all the Shetland Islands, where a few skilled knitters have carried on the tradition for many generations.

The stitches are few in number, only ten being truly native, and were inspired by examples of fine Spanish lace brought to the Shetland Isles as part of an exhibition in the early nineteenth century. Each stitch has been adapted to represent the natural beauty of the islands and they carry such evocative names as 'Ears o' Grain', 'Print o' the Wave' and 'Fir Cones'.

Even today, the yarn used for the superb examples of this craft is hand spun to a single ply of such delicate fineness that few knitters would be able to work with it. However, a 3 ply yarn worked on No.1 needles can produce a reasonable facsimile of this most beautiful and rewarding method of knitting.

Casting on and binding off for lace knitting

Thick, harsh lines caused by casting on and binding off, or seaming, must be avoided or they will immediately detract from the delicate appearance of the lace.

Use the 2 needle method of casting on but instead of inserting the right hand needle between the last

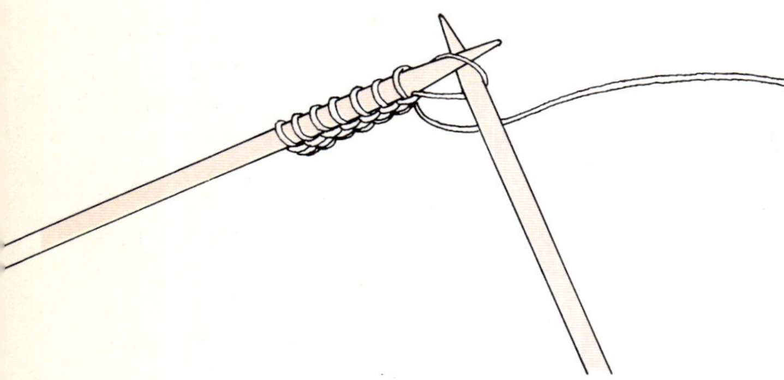

2 stitches on the left hand needle, insert it from front to back into the last stitch on the left hand needle and then draw a loop through to form the next stitch, transferring this to the left hand needle. This forms a loose, open edge.

Binding off should be worked in the usual way, using a needle 2 times larger to work the binding off than the size used for the main fabric.

Where the fabric has to be joined, it is best to use a spare length of yarn for casting on which can later be withdrawn, to allow the first and last rows to be woven together for an invisible join.

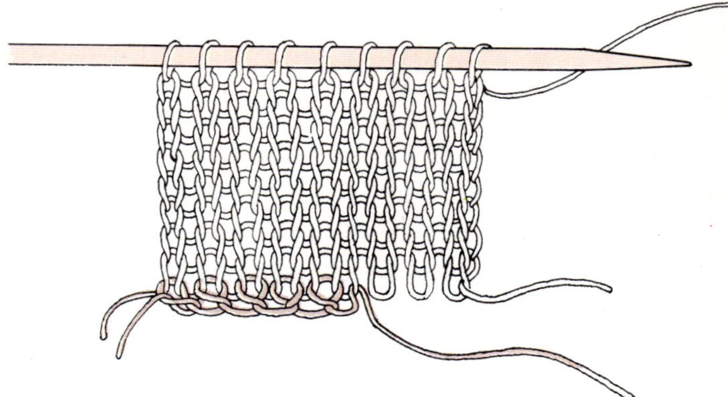

Crown of Glory pattern

This stitch is also known by the descriptive name of 'Cat's paw'. Cast on a number of stitches divisible by 14 plus 5.

1st row (RS) K3, *sl 1, K1, psso, K9, K2 tog, K1, rep from * to last 2 sts, K2.
2nd row P2, *P1, P2 tog, P7, P2 tog tbl, rep from * to last 3 sts, P3.
3rd row K3, *sl 1, K1, psso, K2, yrn 3 times, K3, K2 tog, K1, rep from * to last 2 sts, K2.
4th row P2, *P1, P2 tog, P2, (K1, P1, K1, P1, K1) all into yrn 3 times making 5 sts, P1, P2 tog tbl, rep from * to last 3 sts, P3.
5th row K3, *sl 1, K1, psso, K6, K2 tog, K1, rep from * to last 2 sts, K2.
6th row P2, *P1, P2 tog, P6, rep from * ending last rep P3.
7th row K3, *K1, (yfwd, K1) 6 times, K1, rep from * to last 2 sts, K2.
8th row P to end.
9th and 10th rows K to end.
11th row P to end.

12th row K to end.
These 12 rows form the pattern.

Razor shell pattern
This stitch takes its name from the shells on the beach. It can be worked in multiples of 4, 6, 8, 10 or 12 stitches. For the sample shown here, cast on a number of stitches divisible by 6 plus 1.

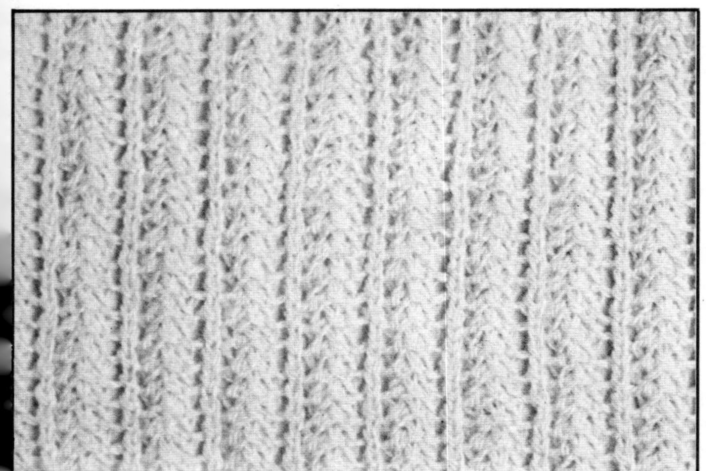

1st row (WS) P to end.
2nd row K1, *yfwd, K1, sl 1, K2 tog, psso, K1, yfwd, K1, rep from * to end.
These 2 rows form the pattern.

Horseshoe print pattern
Derived from the imprint of horseshoes on wet sand, this sample requires a number of stitches divisible by 10 plus 1.

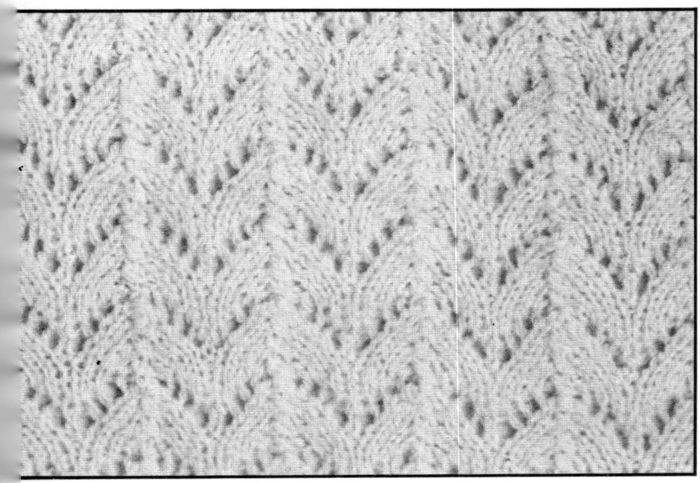

1st row (WS) P to end.
2nd row K1, *yfwd, K3, sl 1, K2 tog, psso, K3, yfwd, K1, rep from * to end.
3rd row As 1st.
4th row P1, *K1, yfwd, K2, sl 1, K2 tog, psso, K2, yfwd, K1, P1, rep from * to end.
5th row K1, *P9, K1, rep from * to end.
6th row P1, *K2, yfwd, K1, sl 1, K2 tog, psso, K1, yfwd, K2, P1, rep from * to end.
7th row As 5th.
8th row P1. *K3, yfwd, sl 1, K2 tog, psso, yfwd, K3, P1, rep from * to end.
These 8 rows form the pattern.

Fern pattern
This stitch is often used as a shawl border since the shape of the motif allows for easy corner shaping. The size of the lace motif can vary but the working method remains the same. For the sample shown here, cast on a number of stitches divisible by 15.

1st row (RS) *K7, yfwd, sl 1 K-wise, K1, psso, K6, rep from * to end.
2nd row P to end.
3rd row *K5, K2 tog, yfwd, K1, yfwd, sl 1 K-wise, K1, psso, K5, rep from * to end.
4th row P to end.
5th row *K4, K2 tog, yfwd, K3, yfwd, sl 1 K-wise, K1, psso, K4, rep from * to end.
6th row P to end.
7th row *K4, yfwd, sl 1 K-wise, K1, psso, yfwd, sl 1, K2 tog, psso yfwd, K2 tog, yfwd, K4, and rep from * to end.
8th row P to end.
9th row *K2, K2 tog, yfwd, K1, yfwd, sl 1 K-wise, K1, psso, K1, K2 tog, yfwd, K1, yfwd, sl 1 K-wise, K1, psso, K2, rep from * to end.
10th row P to end.
11th row *K2, (yfwd, sl 1 K-wise, K1, psso) twice, K3, (K2 tog, yfwd) twice, K2, rep from * to end.
12th row *P3, (yrn, P2 tog) twice, P1, (P2 tog tbl, yrn) twice, P3, rep from * to end.
13th row *K4, yfwd, sl 1 K-wise, K1, psso, yfwd, sl 1, K2 tog, psso, yfwd, K2 tog, yfwd, K4, and rep from * to end.
14th row *P5, yrn, P2 tog, P1, P2 tog tbl, yrn, P5, rep from * to end.
15th row *K6, yfwd, sl 1, K2 tog, psso, yfwd, K6, rep from * to end.
16th row P to end.
These 16 rows form the pattern.

A Shetland lace shawl

The gossamer Shetland lace shawl shown here is a superb example of what is known as a 'wedding ring' shawl. It is so fine that it can easily be pulled through a wedding ring, hence its name, and it can be likened to a spider's web, having no beginning and no end.

This particular shawl is reproduced by kind permission of Highland Home Industries of Edinburgh, who still employ a few highly skilled Shetland Islanders to make these garments in their own homes. Traditionally this would be made as a christening shawl, but it could also be used as a beautiful winter wedding veil. As you can imagine, these shawls are in great demand but take so long to knit that they are literally worth their weight in gold. The yarn used has been homespun and is so fine that two strands together have been used to knit this shawl. It has been spun from the fine, soft wool which grows around the sheep's neck.

The needles used to knit this shawl are still called by their traditional name of 'wires' and, in all probability the pattern has been passed from one generation tc another by word of mouth and the instructions have never been written down.

Once a shawl of this delicacy has been completed it will be washed and then 'dressed' or stretched intc shape. To dress the shawl in the traditional manner special wooden frames as large as a bed are needed The shawl is tied to this frame with lacing through every point along the edges of the border and left to dry naturally. In this way it is kept taut and square and each point or scallop of the borde is stretched out to its correct shape.

In this chapter we give two other traditional lac stitches to inspire you to experiment with this mos beautiful craft.

Fir cone pattern
As its name implies, this pattern represents the cones of fir trees and the number of times the pattern rows are repeated can be varied. For the sample shown here cast on a number of stitches divisible by 10 plus 1.
1st row (RS) K1, *yfwd, K3, sl 1, K2 tog, psso, K3, yfwd, K1, rep from * to end.
2nd row P to end.
Rep these 2 rows 3 times more.
9th row K2 tog, *K3, yfwd, K1, yfwd, K3, sl 1, K2 tog, psso, rep from * to last 9 sts, K3, yfwd, K1, yfwd, K3, sl 1, K1, psso.
10th row P to end.
Rep 9th and 10th rows 3 times more.
These 16 rows form the pattern.

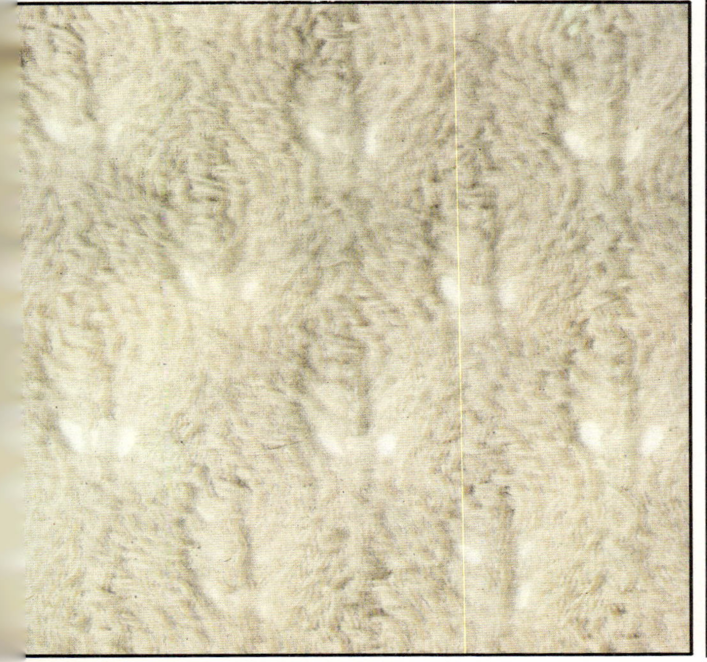

Point o' the wave pattern
This beautiful undulating pattern is a reminder that the sea is a constant part of life in the islands. To work this sample, cast on a number of stitches divisible by 22 plus 3 *very* loosely.
1st row (RS) K4, *K2 tog, K3, (yfwd, K2 tog) twice, yfwd, K13, rep from * to end, ending last rep with K12 instead of K13.
2nd and every alt row P to end.
3rd row K3, *K2 tog, K3, yfwd, K1, yfwd, (sl 1, K1, psso, yfwd) twice, K3, sl 1, K1, psso, K7, rep from * to end.
5th row K2, *K2 tog, (K3, yfwd) twice, (sl 1, K1, psso, yfwd) twice, K3, sl 1, K1, psso, K5, rep from * to last st, K1.
7th row K1, *K2 tog, K3, yfwd, K5, yfwd, (sl 1, K1, psso, yfwd) twice, K3, sl 1, K1, psso, K3, rep from * to last 2 sts, K2.
9th row *K12, yfwd, (sl 1, K1, psso, yfwd) twice, K3, sl 1, K1, psso, K1, rep from * to last 3 sts, K3.
11th row *K7, K2 tog, K3, (yfwd, K2 tog) twice, yfwd, K1, yfwd, K3, sl 1, K1, psso, rep from * to last 3 sts, K3.
13th row K6, *K2 tog, K3, (yfwd, K2 tog) twice, (yfwd, K3) twice, sl 1, K1, psso, K5, rep from * to end, ending last rep with K2 instead of K5.
15th row K5, *K2 tog, K3, (yfwd, K2 tog) twice, yfwd, K5, yfwd, K3, sl 1, K1, psso, K3, rep from * to end, ending last rep with K1 instead of K3.
16th row As 2nd.
These 16 rows form the pattern.

PICOT KNITTING

Picot knitting is an unusual technique which imitates Irish crochet, worked with a pair of knitting needles instead of a crochet hook. It looks its best when it is worked in a very fine cotton, such as No.20, and on fine needles.

It has many applications and can be used as edgings, insertions, motifs or as an all-over background fabric. The dainty baby bonnet shown here is an example of how the various methods can be combined to form a garment.

To make a picot point

Make a slip loop in the usual way and place this on the left hand needle, *cast on 2 stitches, making 3 in all. Knit and bind off 2 of these 3 stitches, leaving one stitch on the needle. This forms one picot point. Transfer the remaining stitch to the left hand needle and repeat from * until the required length of picot points is completed. Fasten off.

The size of these picot points may be varied by casting on and binding off 3 stitches, 4 stitches or as many as required. This strip forms the basis of picot work and can be used to join motifs such as flower centers, or as a simple edging.

It can also be used to form a dainty bound off edge on a garment as follows:

Binding off row Insert the needle through the first st of the row to be bound off, *cast on 2 sts, knit and bind off 2 sts, knit the next st of the row, knit and bind off one st, transfer the rem st to the left hand needle, rep from * to end of row.

Fasten off.

Picot point crown

This method is worked across a number of stitches to give the width of edging required. Once this first section has been completed, it forms the basis for what is termed a 'lacis', or openwork fabric, and is referred to as a 'strip' and not a row. To continue working strips to build up a lacis, the last stitch is not fastened off.

Cast on a number of stitches divisible by 5 plus one.

1st row K to end.

2nd row Insert needle into the first st, *cast on 2 sts, bind off 2 sts, transfer rem st to left hand needle, *, rep from * to * 3 times more, (4 picot points formed), knit and bind off next 5 sts, transfer rem st to left hand needle, rep from * to end.

This completes first strip.

Next strip *Transfer rem st to left hand needle, make 4 picot points as in 2nd row of first strip, join to center of next picot crown in first strip by picking up and knitting a st between the 2 center picot points, bind off one st, rep from * to end of strip.

Cont in this way until lacis is required depth. Fasten off.

Picot point motif

This simple motif can be used separately or to form the center of a flower. Each separate motif can be stitched from the top of one point to the corresponding point of the next motif to form a daisy edging, and a number of rows can be joined in the same way to form delicate shawls, or interesting table linen, such as place mats and coasters.

However you wish to use these motifs, you can make as many picot points as you like, varying the size of each picot point as already explained. The example shown here has 6 picot points, using 3 stitches instead of 2 for each point.

Make a slip loop and place on left hand needle, *cast on 3 sts, making 4 in all, bind off 3 of these sts, transfer rem sts to left hand needle, rep from * 5 times more. To join into a circle, insert needle into the first loop and draw up a st, bind off one st. Fasten off.

To continue making a flower motif, do not fasten off but transfer remaining stitch to left hand needle, ready to begin the first petal.

Picot point flower

Make a motif as above. Cast on one st, making 2 stitches on left hand needle.

1st row K1, K into front then into back of next st – called M1. 3 sts.

2nd and 4th rows K to end.

3rd row K2, M1.

5th row K3, M1. 5sts.

K4 rows g st.

10th row Bind off one st, K to end. 4sts.

11th row K to end.

Rep last 2 rows twice more.

16th row Cast off one st, pick up and knit a loop between next 2 picot points, cast off one st, transfer rem st to left hand needle.

Cont in this way making 6 petals in all, or desired number, joining last petal to same place as first petal, as shown for picot point.

Picot flower and lacis motif

Make a picot point flower and fasten off. Rejoin yarn to center of any petal tip.

1st round Make 4 picot points casting on and binding off sts for each point, K up one st at tip of next petal, bind off one st, transfer rem st to left hand needle, rep from * all around flower.

2nd round Make 4 picot points and join between 2nd and 3rd picots of 1st round, make another 4 picot points and skip 2 picot points of 1st round, join between next 2 picot points of 1st round, cont in this way to end of round joining last stitch to same place as first stitch. Fasten off.

3rd round Rejoin yarn between 2nd and 3rd of any picot points, *make 4 picot points and join between 2nd and 3rd of next 4 picot points, rep from * to end of round, joining as before. 12 loops. Fasten off.

4th round Rejoin yarn between 2nd and 3rd of any picot points, *make 3 picot points and join into same place to form a picot crest, make 4 picot points and join between 2nd and 3rd of next 4 picot points, rep from * to end of round, joining as before. Fasten off. Make as many more motifs as required, joining picot crests of each motif where they touch to form a row.

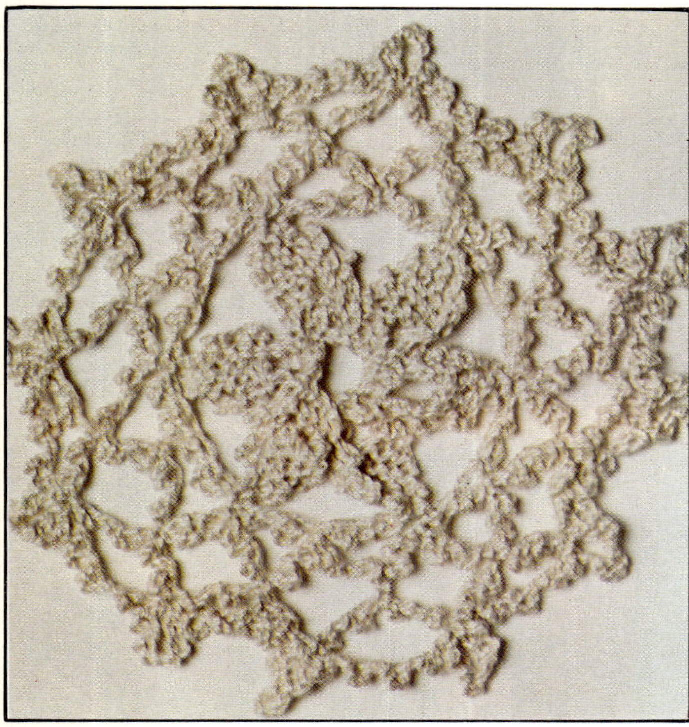

Baby bonnet
Size
To fit newborn to 3 months.

Gauge
32sts and 60 rows to 3·9 inches over garter stitch (g st) worked on No.1 needles.

Materials
1 1oz ball 3 ply baby yarn
One pair No.1 needles
1 yard ribbon for ties

Bonnet
Make one flower and lacis motif, omitting 4th round, to form center of crown.
Make 11 picot point motifs and join into a row, joining the center picots on each side and leaving 2 free at top and bottom. Sew around edge of center motif, joining 2 free points of each motif to the center 2 picots of each loop and leaving one loop free for bottom edge of bonnet.
Make a strip of 42 picots, mark the last picot with contrast thread and turn.
Next row Make 4 picots, join between 3rd and 4th picots after marker, *make 4 picots, skip 4 picots, join between 4th and 5th picots, rep from * to last 3 picots, make 4 picots, join to end of strip after last picot. Fasten off and turn.

Next row Rejoin yarn between 2nd and 3rd picots c first loop, make 4 picots, join between 2nd and 3r picots of next loop, rep from * to end., Do not faste off but turn.
Next row Make 4 picots, join between 2nd and 3r picots of first loop, *make 4 picots, join between 2n and 3rd picots of next loop, rep from * to end, mak 4 picots, join to beg of previous row where yarn wa rejoined.
Rep last 2 rows once more. Fasten off.
Join the cast on edge of this strip to the center piec joining the first 2 picots to the 2 picots of first moti *skip 2 picots, join next 2 picots to 2 points of ne motif, rep from * to end.

Finishing
Pin out and block under a damp cloth with a war iron. Sew ribbon to each corner to tie at front.

FILET KNITTING

The word 'filet' means 'net', and this type of square nesh fabric can be produced in both knitting and crochet. Just as with crochet, patterns can be introduced into the knitted mesh background, consisting of solid parts of the pattern, which are referred to as 'blocks', and open parts of the pattern which are called 'spaces'. The stitch used to produce filet lace abric is garter stitch throughout, so it is a very simple nethod to work.
This fabric looks best when it is worked in a fine cotton on small size needles to give a lace effect. It as many uses but is better used for insertions and edgings, rather than as an all over fabric.

To knit filet lace

Working a block: These comprise solid sections of garter stitch and each block consists of three knitted titches in width and four rows in depth. Whether vorking an insertion or an edging, a number of extra titches are required at the beginning and end of he rows and these are knitted throughout in the usual way.

Vorking a space: These are the open sections of a lesign and each space is worked on three stitches. The third stitch of each space is knitted in the usual vay and is either used as an edge stitch, or as a bridging stitch between spaces or between spaces nd blocks. Each space is worked over two rows in depth.
After completing a block of three knitted stitches or he edge stitches, as the case may be, bring the yarn orward between the needles, take it over the right and needle and to the front again – called y2rn. Over the next three stitches, slip the first stitch knitvise, then slip the 2nd stitch knitwise, using the point of the left hand needle lift the first stitch over he 2nd stitch and off the right hand needle.
Slip the 3rd stitch knitwise, using the point of the left hand needle lift the 2nd stitch over the 3rd stitch and ff the right hand needle, return the 3rd stitch to the eft hand needle and knit this in the usual way.
This working method is referred to as making a space. There are now three loops on the right hand needle again, composed of the yarn twice around the needle nd one knitted stitch. On the following row the first arn around the needle is knitted and the 2nd yarn round the needle is purled, then the 3rd stitch is nitted, to complete the space.

Vorking basic filet net

his is worked entirely in spaces, plus one edge itch at the beginning of the row. The 3rd stitch of each space forms the bridging stitch between each space.

Working blocks and spaces

As each block requires four rows to complete it and a space only requires two rows, the pattern rows must be worked twice to give the necessary square shape to each block.
When a block changes to a space in a pattern, treat the three stitches of the block as a space, or when changing a space to a block, work the three stitches of the space as a block.

Filet lace insertion

This simple pattern can be used in many ways, either as center front panels on a fabric or knitted blouse, as

an insertion on a dainty slip or on household linens. It is worked over a total of five squares, each consisting of three stitches, plus three edge stitches at the beginning of the rows and two edge stitches at the end of the rows. Only two stitches are needed to balance the end of the rows, as the last stitch of the last space is taken into this edge. The chart given here does not show the edge stitches.
Cast on a total of 20 stitches to work the insertion.
1st row (RS) K3 edge sts, work 2 spaces, K3 sts for a block, work 2 spaces, K2 edge sts.
2nd and every alt row K to end, purling the 2nd yarn around needle of every space.
Rep 1st and 2nd rows once more to complete the center block.
5th row K3 edge sts, work 1 space, (K3 sts for a block, work 1 space) twice, K2 edge sts.
6th row As 2nd.
Rep 5th and 6th rows once more to complete the

blocks, then rep them twice more to complete another block.
13th row As 1st.

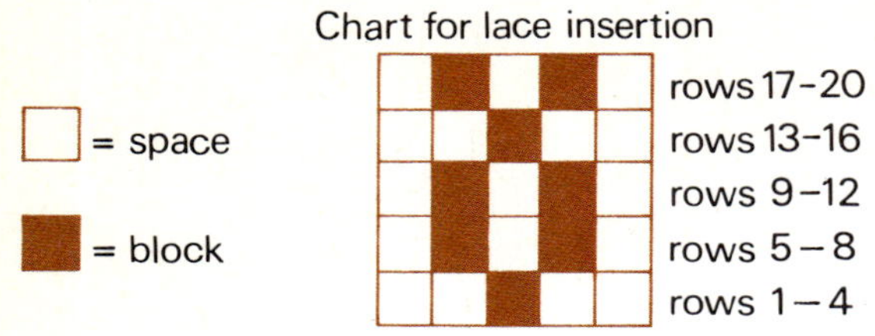

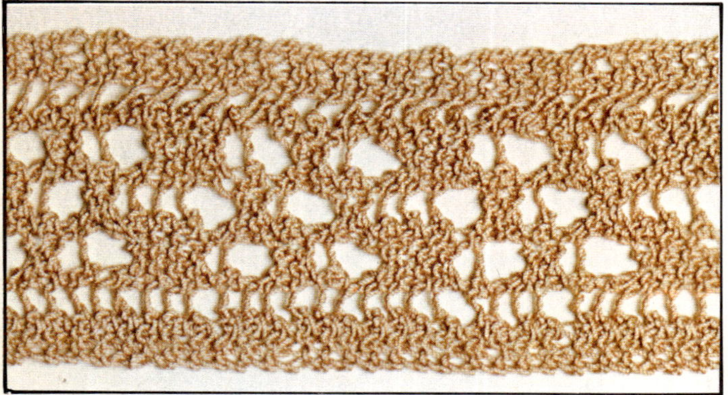

14th row As 2nd.
Rep 13th and 14th rows once more to complete the center block.
17th row As 5th.
18th row As 6th.
Rep 17th and 18th rows once more to complete the blocks.
These 20 rows form the pattern and are repeated for the required length of the insertion.

Filet lace edging
This pattern has a notched edge along one side and

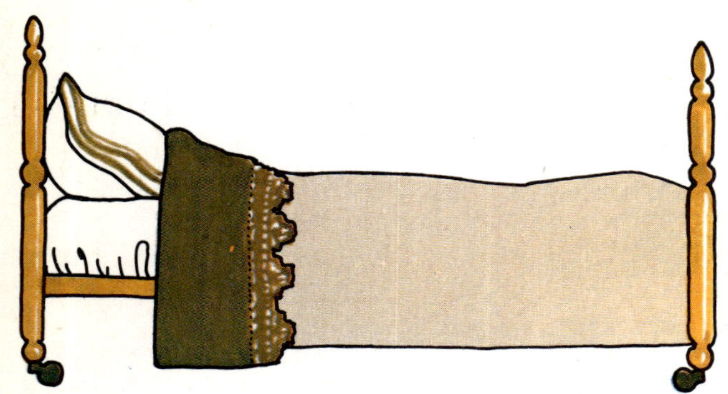

forms an ideal trimming for all types of household linens. The serrated edge is formed by casting on additional stitches two rows before they are taken into the pattern.
The pattern consists of three squares at the beginning, each comprising three stitches, plus one edge stitch at the beginning of the row only, the last edge stitch being formed by the last stitch of the last space. The chart given here does not show the edge stitch.

Cast on a total of 10 stitches to begin the edging.
1st row (RS) K1 edge st, work 1 space, K3 sts for a block, work 1 space.
2nd and every alt row K to end, purling the 2nd yarn around needle of every space.
3rd row As 1st, then turn and cast on 6 sts to form 2 extra spaces on the 5th row.
5th row K1 edge st, work 1 space, K3 sts for a block, work 3 spaces.
7th row As 5th, then turn and cast on 3 sts to form 1 extra space on the 9th row.
9th row K1 edge st, work 1 space, K3 sts for a block,

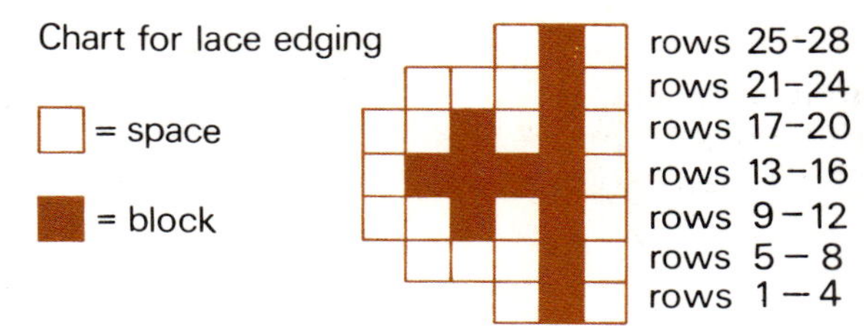

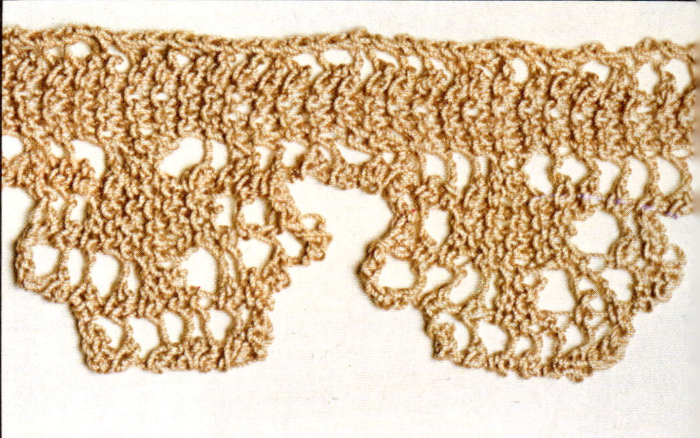

work 1 space, K3 sts for a block, work 2 spaces.
10th row As 2nd.
Rep 9th and 10th rows once more to complete blocks
13th row K1 edge st, work 1 space, K12 sts to form blocks, work 1 space.
14th row As 2nd.
Rep 13th and 14th rows once more to complet blocks.
17th row As 9th.
18th row As 2nd.
19th row As 17th.
20th row Bind off 3 sts to reduce one space, then wor as 2nd row to end.
21st row As 5th.
22nd row As 2nd.
23rd row As 21st.
24th row Bind off 6 sts to reduce 2 spaces, then wor as 2nd row to end.
25th row As 1st.
26th row As 2nd.
Rep 25th and 26th rows once more to complet block. These 28 rows form the pattern and a repeated for the desired length of the edging.